REFUELING
the PAST

**A History Of Service Stations
in Batavia, Geneva, and
St. Charles, Illinois**

ARCHIE BENTZ, JR

**Refueling The Past: A History of Service Stations In Batavia,
Geneva, and St. Charles, Illinois**
Published by Tri–City Gas
Crossville, TN

Publisher's Cataloging–in–Publication data

Names: Bentz, Archie, author.
Title: Refueling the past : a history of service stations in Batavia, Geneva, and St.
Charles, Illinois. / by Archie Bentz.
Description: First trade paperback original edition. | Crossville [Tennessee] : Tri–City
Gas, 2020. | Also published as an ebook. | Bibliography included.
Identifiers: ISBN 978-0-578-79623-9
Subjects: LCSH: Illinois–History, Local.
BISAC: ARCHITECTURE / History / Contemporary (1945–). | ARCHITECTURE /
Regional. | TRANSPORTATION / Automotive / History.
Classification: LCC F547.K2 | DDC 977.3–dc22

Cover and Interior design by Victoria Wolf, wolfdesignandmarketing.com
Cover Art Painting by Thomas Trausch of Trausch Fine Arts

QUANTITY PURCHASES: Museums, companies, professional groups, clubs, and
other organizations may qualify for special terms when ordering quantities of this
title. For information, email tricitygas@gmail.com.

My interest in old gas stations started in the attic of the circa 1928 McCornack service station where I started my tenure as a Texaco dealer in 1977.

Photographs courtesy Bentz Family and St. Charles History Museum

TABLE OF CONTENTS

PREFACE

Please join me in a sentimental journey to explore the history of the full–service gas station, once a fixture of every neighborhood in America. I started work in my father's Standard Oil service station at the age of eleven and witnessed his success in growing to the pinnacle of Standard Oil Company rankings in the Midwest. Bentz Bros. had expanded to five locations with the help of four brothers in the early 1960's. By 1977, I had opened my own business, Bentz Texaco, and in 1980 adding a second repair garage, Archie's Arcada Automotive. In my retirement I realized that my family had been involved in the industry from 1945 to 1999 and that I represented a multi-generational era of independent dealers. This book captures the essence of our local history and is universal in the application to your own neighborhood.

I reviewed over 250 years of newspapers, page by page, along with the R. L. Polk and Bell Telephone directories as I fell down the "rabbit–hole" of research. The Yellow Pages were great listings, but understand, not all businesses paid to participate and,

therefore, were not an all-inclusive resource for business listings.

The Polk Directory was like the Yellow Pages from the standpoint of listing all residents and most businesses, but it was a great cross reference for ownership especially when a business was listed in the owner's first name such as "Sam's Garage" with no reference to the surname. This also applied when the business would not include the any part of the owner(s) name, but instead it might be called "Batavia Garage" in the business listings which when cross referenced in the white pages of the directory, the ownership would be declared.

Newspapers offered advertisements for grand openings, seasonal sales, and weekly promotions. The more obscure sources in the papers were: building permits, articles on change of ownership, oil company announcements, armed robberies or burglaries, obituaries, and car accidents in the vicinity indicating who operated the tow truck. The newspapers also acknowledged community sponsorships such as: Little League, bowling teams, Soap Box Derby, Christmas and New Year best wishes, Memorial Day, 4th of July, Armistice Day, Kane County Fair, Knights of Columbus Corned Beef and Cabbage, Swedish Days, Boo-Boo Days, and Little Seven Conference high school games.

Tri-City High School Yearbooks were also resources with advertising sponsorships and Graduation Congratulations.

My father, Archie Bentz, had been employed with Clark's Pure Oil in 1945, then enlisted in 1946-47 for military motor pool training, followed by a return to Clark in the 1950's and tool and die work at Burgess Norton. He had participated in more than 20 business ventures starting in 1959, which, contrary to popular belief, were not just Bentz Bros service stations. More recently, since my father's passing, family members have come to me with additional information regarding his business history. In addition to my own memories, I am in possession of scrapbooks compiled by my mother, Anna Mary Bentz, of his business and mayoral accomplishments.

In 2016, I was working on the compilation of my father's business history when I was contacted by John Dillon from the City of Batavia, Illinois. John was seeking biographical information on former Batavia mayors, my father being one of them, having served as mayor from 1977-1981. Providing John with a condensed one-page personal biography of my father became quite a task. As I shared research with John it became very apparent that I also possessed knowledge of many Batavia businesses, especially automotive related, from the 1940's to 1990. I explained to John that my father had business ventures in Aurora, Batavia, and Geneva, some of which I shared through my employment and management, and then there were my own business experiences.

I have in my possession numerous publications, which will be referenced later, that have been authored by educated people who are experts in the evolution of the oil companies and service stations. While the publications present a good overview of the evolution of the automobile and supply of petroleum products, they lack the perspective of the local service station operator who could personally acknowledge their customer by name, model of car, and where they lived.

So, what started as a family biography soon morphed into my researching all gas stations, garages, and automobile dealerships in Batavia, Geneva, St. Charles and the surrounding area. This work is centered on the widespread adoption of the automobile and its impact on our Fox Valley environment in the late 19th and the 20th Century.

★

While it seemed that we had progressed to a gas station on every corner in every town, the architecture and cultural changes of those stations have been hidden under new facades for the replacement business. The mobility of the family automobile also spawned many roadside amenities such as cabins for rent, tourist courts, motels, diners. The words "drive-in" and "roadside" became common phrases in conjunction with food, movie, banking, dry cleaning, and vegetable stands. All were related establishments to a new highway network. Previously, many remote locations around the country were accessible only by rail. Now families began driving on vacation to the developing National Park system, or driving to visit extended family in faraway places. Americans were flaunting their new mobility and prosperity.

The development of the automobile had a great impact on our modern cultural history. There is no denying the importance of the advancements of the industrial age, but my focus will be the internal combustion engine as an essential element and a significant factor in the development of the automobile, the trucking industry and our overall cultural landscape. This will help the reader understand the historical evolution of our automotive based society and understand that current day hybrid electric cars are shockingly a repeat of the technology from the early 1900's.

The evolutionary changes in gasoline marketing the last half of the 20th century have brought to light that today's stations are in many ways a reintroduction of station types that existed before 1930. While the full-service station corresponded to the old-fashioned repair shop, the modern convenience store calls to mind the early gas station combined with the general store.

The following Pure Oil Company advertisement from the 1944 *Geneva Republican* captures the spirit of your neighbor's desire to serve you in his capacity as a gas station entrepreneur and is the viewpoint from which this book was written.

The copy from the 1944 advertisement is transcribed on the next page to make reading easier.

THAT FELLOW ON THE CORNER

Perhaps you have always thought of American Free Enterprise in terms of such things as better motor cars, radios, or electric refrigerators.

But just look down on the corner for one of the best examples of Free Enterprise....We mean the Service Station, run by That Fellow on the Corner–with his heart, his ideals and his own money in his business. He is a free businessman.

Way back in your "Merry Oldsmobile" you chugged up to the drug or grocery store for a can of something that smelled like cleaning fluid and you poured this fuel into the gas tank by hand.

Blacksmiths went out and garages came in. The automobile came to stay. Free Enterprise went to work.

"Filling Stations" with self-measuring gas pumps sprang up at convenient locations. As traffic increased, pumps were moved back from the curb and drive-in facilities were provided.

Competition started and American Free Enterprise shifted into high.

Station A put in a Free Air Hose...
Station B added a rest room...
Then Station A installed a grease pit...

and Station C stole a march on both of them by announcing facilities to charge your battery and check your plugs!

Facilities for tire inspection and repair were added. Stocks came to include spark plugs, battery cables, radiator hose, light bulbs and fan belts as well as tires, batteries, and all kinds of accessories.

Free Enterprise marches on!

Before long, you could make your Service Station wait more pleasant with a cool "Coke" or a candy bar.

Whatever brand of gasoline and oil he sold; his brand of courtesy set a new pace for American business.

We even had jokes about all the Services a Service Station offered–but the American motorist admitted it was easier and safer to see through a clean windshield...to run with a full radiator...to tour with a good road map.

Because there was no lid on Free Choice and no ceiling on Free Enterprise the gasoline pump at the curb became the Service Station on the Corner.

And isn't it lucky we have 'That Fellow on the Corner', ready and equipped to save and service that car of yours that can't be replaced these days of war?

Spring Bumper-To-Bumper Change Over Service

One kind of service that has made the Pure Oil dealer's brand of Free Enterprise so popular is his Bumper-to-Bumper Change-Over service. It's thorough car-saving care at 40 to 50 vital points in your car.

He is making appointments now for this service which is more important than ever this third spring of war.

Cars need it more in '44
"Be sure with Pure"
The Pure Oil Company, Chicago, U.S.A

ACKNOWLEDGMENTS

To quote one of my high school teachers, Marilyn Robinson, who has numerous publications to her credit, *"The style in which I've listed sources for each chapter breaks the rules of every stylebook. However, because so many newspaper accounts were used, to make a footnote or a complete citation for each one, pages would have to be sprinkled with little numbers like specks of dust, or there would have to be even more source pages."* I have chosen to use this same formatting. In some cases, quotes are exact, and others are paraphrased or extracted for clarity.

The same issue would hold true to referencing the newspapers, yearbooks, Polk and Yellow Page Directories I used while crafting this book. I have done my best to credit my sources. Photographs utilized are individually acknowledged.

Realizing that I and many of my contemporaries have shared a wealth of knowledge about the Fox Valley's Tri–Cities gas stations and auto repair facilities, I set out to preserve the names, locations, and, in some cases, residual architecture still hiding in plain sight.

To that point in 2016, having compiled about 40 pages from memory, I ventured back from retirement in Tennessee to the Fox Valley and started research with the help of Chris Winter of the Batavia Depot Museum and George Scheetz, Director of the Batavia Public Library. I was pointed in the direction of R. L. Polk City Directories and local telephone directories from decades past. On a second trip, I was assisted by Jennifer Putzier, Director of the Depot Museum, utilizing a Sanborn Insurance directory to convert the old Batavia addresses to post 1948 numbers. I have joked more than once about "falling down the rabbit hole" while being consumed with this research.

On February 13, 2018 Jessica Strube and Terry Emma of the Geneva History Museum hosted a 'Brown Bag' symposium on the topic of gas stations. Over lunch each of the Tri City museums made brief presentations on the gas stations in their respective communities. The room was packed with interested citizens. Jessica has since provided her comprehensive research on garages and service stations in Geneva. From there she and I utilized a combination of our individual research results which are reflected in the Geneva chapter of this book. So often the histories of Batavia, Geneva and St. Charles intertwined as entrepreneurs often started businesses in one or more of these cities. It was wonderful to see all three museums come together to share their history. Jessica was quite pleased with the results of this symposium and looked forward to doing more collaborations on different topics with the St. Charles History Museum and the Batavia Depot Museum.

Another factor in triggering further research was the 90th anniversary of my former Texaco station, now the location of the St. Charles History Museum. The anniversary was commemorated with displays and a special visit from a McCornack family member, Patricia McCornack Clarrissimeaux. The event featured Patricia as the key speaker focusing on the history of the McCornack family and businesses. A collaboration between the then Executive Director Alison Costanzo, all of the museum staff and Patricia, resulted in a more complete understanding of the evolution of all McCornack Oil Company facilities and the family connections.

Additionally, the following resources were utilized and are referenced:

- *The Gas Station in America* by John A. Jakle & Keith A. Sculle
- *The American Gas Station,* by Michael Karl Witzel
- *Pump and Circumstance–Glory Days of the Gas Station,* by John Margolies
- *Fill'er Up,* by Daniel I. Vieyra

While the Margolies and Witzel publications are a good pictorial resource for gas stations, pumps and associated products, I felt *The Gas Station in America* was the best resource to understanding the evolution of gasoline retailing from its infancy. This book refers to the ultimate expansion of not only the petroleum industry, but the various impacts to domestic architecture in shaping our neighborhoods and the interstate highways. The book also touches upon the associated development of travel–related roadside motels, fast food restaurants, and targeted tourist destinations advertised on roadside billboards.

An antique dealer in Elburn, Illinois had about a dozen clippings from Batavia in the 1940's, some of which advertised Clarence Carlson's Texaco at 51 South Batavia Avenue. This intrigued me, so I made the purchase. In 1964, my father bought a Standard Oil location at 27 North Batavia Avenue from Clarence "Clancy" Carlson, but research confirmed this Carlson advertisement was for a Walter Clarence Carlson, two decades earlier. Is it possible that this could be the same Carlson or perhaps a relative? To further complicate matters, the ad was for an address that no longer existed. The following ad is from my personal collection, and I will make reference to this ad and others for a correlation to current locations.

Courtesy Bentz collection of *Batavia Herald* advertisements

A special thank you to Dan Ryan, partner in Thompson Auto Supply, for his ongoing support in my endeavor. His continued presence in the Fox Valley facilitated conversations with surviving service station owners, operators, and employees. Dan also suggested and implemented two roundtable discussions, for which the attendance list quickly outgrew his conference room, causing us to move to the Batavia Public Library. We invited many contemporaries and interested parties to share their knowledge, experiences, and old photographs. It was a receptive forum for dealers who were former competitors in the market, along with local historians offering additions, corrections and photos. There was much welcomed input both during and after the meetings.

I am also grateful to the following persons:

- My wife, Linda, for her everlasting patience in editing and support.
- My son, Travis, for his encouragement and tech savvy support.
- My daughter, Nicole, for her enthusiasm.

- Frank "Randy" Ledbetter for his Batavia contributions.
- Connie (Bentz) Deal, my sister who still lives in the Fox Valley and worked at Bentz Bros, IV Kings and the State Bank of Geneva, for helping with local contacts.
- Paul & Bonnie (Bentz) Stratton, my sister and her husband, both former employees of Bentz Bros, for family archives.
- David Pietryla, copy editor extraordinaire, for providing additional editing support and advice at the early stages of this manuscript.

ROUNDTABLE PARTICIPANTS & OTHER CONTRIBUTORS AND THEIR AFFILIATIONS

- Dan Ryan–Thompson Auto Supply, Bumper to Bumper
- Wayland Wilson–Way's Standard R.I.P.
- Ronn Pittman–Pittman Phillips 66, Bentz Bros, and automotive historian
- Lee Singer–Duke & Lee's
- Joe Jakubaitis–Reber & Foley, Bentz Texaco
- Bill Dreymiller–Abe & Doc's,
- John Fortman–Lou's Jeep
- Rick Eckblade–Bentz Bros Pure & Bentz Bros Standard R.I.P.
- Pete Hansford–Bentz Bros Mobil & automotive historian
- Mike, Jill, and Troy Feece–Feece Oil
- Dave Coppert–Chuck Fitzsimmons Standard
- Joe Parrillo–Parrillo Shell
- John Clark–Avenue Chevrolet
- Bob White–Batavia Township, Bentz Bros Standard, Flaherty's Standard
- Bill Ryan–Thompson Auto Supply
- Bob Sinclair–Thompson Auto Supply
- Bill Schwab–West Side Boat House
- Mike Hill–Automotive Historian
- Dave Peeples–Batavia Historian
- Melvin and Tom Peterson–Wasco Blacksmith Shop
- Bart Needham–Needham's Blacksmith Shop
- Kee Moore–Bentz Bros and Eby Brown
- Rick Myers–Myer's Garage and Bentz Bros.
- Patricia McCornack Clarrissimeaux–McCornack Family Archives
- Don Rasmussen–Rasmussen Oil descendant and St. Charles historian
- Merle Korlaske–Fox River Tire
- Dave Stevens–Reber & Foley, Gorecki ARCO, Stevens Auto Repair

ORGANIZATIONS IN KEY ROLES OF SUPPORT

- George Scheetz–Director, Batavia Public Library
- Chris Winter–Curator, Batavia Depot Museum
- Jennifer Putzier–Director, Batavia Depot Museum
- Amber Foster–Curator of Batavia Depot Museum
- Alison Costanzo–Director, St. Charles History Museum
- Diana Brown–Board President, St. Charles History Museum
- Amanda Helfers–St. Charles History Museum
- St. Charles Library
- Jessica Strube–Curator, Geneva History Museum
- Terry Emma–Director, Geneva History Museum
- Geneva Library
- Laura Chaplin–Lawrence J. Martin Heritage Center, Elburn Library
- Sugar Grove Historical Society
- Sammi Maier King–Daily Herald

PUBLICATIONS UTILIZED IN MY RESEARCH

- *R. L. Polk & Co. City Directories*
- *Illinois Bell Telephone Directory*
- R. H. Donnelly & Co. Publishers of *Illinois Telephone Directories*
- *Sanborn Insurance Maps–Library of Congress*
- *John Gustafson's Historic Batavia*–John Gustafson, Marilyn Robinson, Jeffery D. Schielke–1996, 1980, 1998
- *Batavia Historian*–Batavia History Society and Batavia Public Library
- *Batavia High School Yearbook Archives*–Batavia Public Library
- *Batavia Places and The People Who Called Them Home*–Marilyn Robinson–1996
- *Geneva Illinois, A History of Its Times and Places*–Published by The Geneva Public Library 1977–Julia M. Ehresmann, editor
- *Reflections of St. Charles*–Ruth Seen Pearson–1976
- *"Bet–A–Million"–The Story of John W. Gates,* authored by Lloyd Wendt and Herman Kogan and first published in 1948.
- *The Sidewalks of Elburn*–Marilyn Robinson–Village of Elburn–2005
- *Wasco Illinois: A History*–Adam D. Gibbons–2018
- *Petroleum History Chart*–Professor Bruce Railsback, Department of Geology, of the University of Georgia, Athens
- *The American Gas Station* by Michael Karl Witzel–1992
- *The Gas Station in America* by John A. Jakle & Keith A. Sculle–1994

- *Pump and Circumstance–Glory Days of the Gas Station,* by John Margolies–1993
- *Fill'er Up*–Daniel I. Vieyra–1979
- *The First Drive–In Service Station–American Oil & Gas Historical Society*
- *"We're in The Movies"*–1941 John B. Rogers Film Production
- *Google Earth/Maps*
- *Batavia Herald* and *Batavia Republican*
- *Kane County Chronicle*
- *Geneva Republican*
- *St. Charles Chronicle*
- *Elburn Chronicle*
- *Prairie Farmer Directory of Kane County*
- *C.R. Childs Picture Postcards*
- *Chicago Tribune/HudsonJet.net*
- *Wikipedia*
- www.lincolnhighwayassoc.org
- The Studebaker Museum, Southbend, Indiana
- The Auburn, Cord, Duesenberg Automobile Museum, Auburn, Indiana
- Cloquet Chamber of Commerce, Cloquet, Minnesota
- Buffalo Transportation Pierce Arrow Museum in Buffalo, New York

ONE

Introduction to Early "Gasolene" Distribution

The following quote from the *Batavia Herald* for the year 1909: *"Railroads killed 196 persons in Chicago for the first nine months of the year, street–cars 106, teams and wagons 48, and automobiles only 10."*

The American Gas Station, by Michael Karl Witzel provides a history of the early adventures of traveling by motor car in the late 1800's. The book also discussed the lack of refueling outposts for the infrequent "oddity" of the horseless carriage at that time. "Gasolene" as it was called, was the waste product of refining oil for the more valuable commodity of kerosene, used to illuminate our lives prior to the light bulb. Most oil companies that we know of today evolved from one of three sources: companies sourcing crude oil from which to refine kerosene, companies sourcing natural gas and 'accidently' discovering crude oil and becoming by default an oil producer, and finally, companies that evolved from trades, splits, acquisitions, and other means determined in corporate board rooms most of which we see the results in Professor Railsback's chart in Fig. 3.6

While my early goal of this manuscript was to record and save for posterity the local history of gas stations in Batavia, Geneva, and St. Charles, IL there have been many detours along the way. For example: historically almost all early automobile dealers either started as a blacksmith, livery stable, general store or gas station and thus became a vital part of the evolution of gas stations, not only in our area, but all across the country.

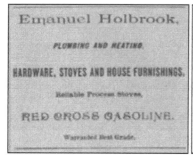  

Our earliest gasoline purveyors in the Fox Valley date back to 1891 with two hardware stores: M.M. Kinne and Emanuel Holbrook. The use of gasoline at this time was to fuel the "modern" cookstove in the home, hence the advertisement of "deodorized" to reduce the unpleasant smell. The Holbrook store, dating back to 1855, is recognized as the first hardware store in Kane County. FIGURE 1.1–1.3 *Batavia Library Yearbook* archives 1891–Vox Alumni and 1916–Bee Aitch Ess

Holbrook's tenure from 1891–95 was one of many in the succession of hardware store owners in a business ownership transgressing pre–Civil War to that of the Art Swanson hardware family, closing after 154 years. FIGURE 1.4 Courtesy Batavia Historical Society

Early refueling took place by dispensing "gasolene" from cans, barrels and other bulk containers, sometimes filtered through a chamois–lined funnel. The early automobiles, often referred to as "horseless carriages," were open cabs, sometimes equipped with a canvas cover, but certainly uncomfortable and unreliable in severe weather conditions. Many autos were stored in the barn over the winter; thus, the supply of "gasolene" was a seasonal venture. Eventually the enclosed sedan enhanced passenger comfort, enabling year–round use. This new use enabled the growing need to fuel these "new–fangled contraptions." As a result, a network of gas stations and garages sprang up across the nation.

Credit for the first gas pump goes to Sulvanus F. Bowser, of Fort Wayne, Indiana, which was an adapted version of his well water pump in 1905. The following "Correct–O–Meter" advertisement depicts the evolution from can and funnel to a modern, measured gas pump manufactured by the Correct Measure Company.

FIGURE 1.5 *Courtesy "Fill'er Up"*

Kerosene to be supplied by Delno Oil, predecessor to McCornack Oil Co.
FIGURE 1.6 January 17, 1902 *St. Charles Chronicle.*

Blacksmith shop with early Gasolene hand pumps. FIGURE 1.7 Photo from *Wikipedia*.

Due to the importance of blacksmiths, who possessed the skill set to make early automobile repairs, they became early purveyors of gasoline and motor oils. I have included in the Appendix a list of Tri–City blacksmiths as gleaned from the newspapers and Polk Directories. Due to limited historical data, many early blacksmiths and liveries existed beyond this listing and the years, as noted, are not totally inclusive of their tenure. The list is limited to early blacksmiths and does not include many modern–day farriers.

Carl Newton More, nephew to Don Carlos Newton, shown in his 1913 Stutz Bearcat on South Batavia Avenue in the area of Foster Garage and Pomp & Peterson Blacksmith Shop, with a livery out of camera range to the right. An era of transition from horse and buggy to the automobile. FIGURE 1.8 Courtesy Batavia Historical Society.

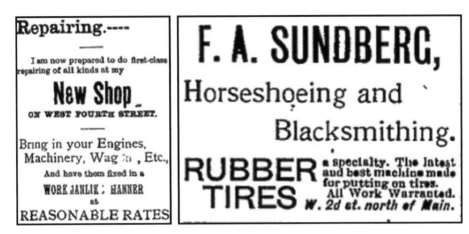

Advertisements depicting the evolution from horses to automobiles. FIGURE 1.9 & 1.10
Courtesy 1892 & 1903 *St. Charles Chronicle*

REPAIRING THE AUTOMOBILE

Repairs to automobiles were initially made by blacksmiths, then machinists and only later by mechanics and now today's technicians. Since the beginning, the history of auto mechanics has followed the history of the automobile from its earliest days to its current technological advancements. In the 1940's through the 1960's, entire generations of boys grew up tinkering with their cars in what became a rite of passage of sorts. Then, as automobiles became more complex the need for trained mechanics grew and now as technology continues to advance, skilled technicians are still in demand.

An abridged side note found on the subject of early automobiles in the *Batavian Historian* demonstrates need for mechanics early on.

"In September of 1900, according to the *Batavia Herald*, A.D. Mallory was the first auto owner in Batavia. He bought a double seater model and ran it from Detroit to his home here. Other early auto owners were Dr. A. A. Fitts, E.C. "Ned" Brown, L.A. Parre and Thomas Snow."

"Batavia's first horseless carriage was made right here by Edwin K. Meredith. He was an inventor, and was Superintendent of the Batavia Light and Water Plant, preceding L.A. Parre. He entered his homemade car in the first auto race to be held in America, November of 1895, the course running between Chicago and Milwaukee. Mr. Parre said 'The car started for the Chicago race alright, but soon overheated and never reached its destination.'

In the beginning, automobile ownership was basically limited to the wealthy, so they often employed chauffeur/mechanics as servants who would drive and maintain their vehicles. Early Sanborn insurance maps also reveal that most affluent automobile owners had gasoline storage tanks incorporated into their garages, which were formerly liveries. But as automobiles became more affordable and popular, where did those owners get their vehicles fixed?

There were general stores and other merchants ready to supply gasoline, oil, tires, tubes, and even the automobile, but as merchants, most still lacked the ability to service those vehicles after the sale. Blacksmiths were at the ready to straighten that bent axle or fabricate a new engine mount, but there was a need for those who took the time to educate themselves on the internal combustion engine with magnetos and ignition systems, the working gears of the transmission, the various systems used for stopping/braking the vehicle, and even the electrical systems. One famous example was Walter P. Chrysler, who as a young man working as a railroad builder of steam locomotives, was so taken by the new invention of automobiles that he bought one solely for the purpose of disassembly just to explore what made it tick. He then reassembled the auto and disassembled it again to make his own improvements. He became the inventor of the Chrysler automobile.

Early on, there were no "factory technicians" staffed in "factory dealerships" waiting to service vehicles on the long highways. With over 200 early varieties of automobiles, many with complex and diverse power plants, repairs were a challenge. Vehicles were not limited to just gasoline engines with one cylinder or more, they also included wood or coal–fired steam engines and electric motors. 100 years ago, there were even examples of hybrids with a combination of internal combustion engines and electric motors.

One example of the *Automotive Renaissance Men* who led the way in automotive repair was my uncle, LeRoy "Bruce" Myers. Born in 1918 in the Sugar Grove–Big Rock, Illinois area, he had the advantage of a high school education in an era where rural young men quit school to work the farm. As a youngster he built a tractor for his father's farm from junk and scrapyard parts. He also possessed a talent for music and had his own dance band that resulted in a scholarship offer to further his education. He declined as WWII loomed and he was increasingly needed on the farm. He then worked at Durabilt on Jericho Road in Aurora and learned the tool and die profession while supplying our troops with things like foot lockers and ammunition cans. While engaged at the family farm and Durabilt, he started another business on the farm: Myers' Garage. His skills were utilized by neighbors from far and wide. He possessed intuitive skills enhanced by his tool and die training. On a visit to that farm, you can still see the concrete block building that by the late 1930's was equipped with a full machine shop, engine hoists, and even an in–ground hydraulic lift–something many company gas stations of that era did not possess.

Bruce was known to have one of the fastest cars in the county: a Chevy six–cylinder, enhanced with a concoction of transmission and differential gearing that could outrun the normally faster Ford V–8. When WWII gas rationing was implemented, he devised the modifications to make his 1941 Chevy six–cylinder run on just three cylinders at highway speeds; thus, saving gas. Then he further modified that gasoline engine to run on diesel. Later he made the sand–casting mold for a new cylinder head that would further modify the same engine to run on propane. Had he taken the opportunity to receive a formal education, there is little doubt this man could have been a top engineer in the automotive industry.

> "At the General Motors Motorama for 1954, Pontiac debuted it's all new Bonneville Special, a concept car envisioned by head designer Harley J. Earl. The concept was equipped with the "Special"–8, a high output 268–cubic–inch (4.39 L) engine that was painted bright red and detailed in chrome."

Two years prior to this momentous occasion, in Pontiac's effort to realize more power from the 268 engines, the company made modifications that were problematic, especially to a very vocal customer at the Pontiac dealership in Aurora. Customers in general complained about a lack of power at highway speeds and the Pontiac mechanics were at their wits end with troubleshooting multiple running issues. Pontiac then sent a couple of top engineers to Aurora who spent two frustrating days working with their mechanics to no avail when one of the local boys suggested they take a trip to Sugar Grove and visit with a well–known farmer/engineer/troubleshooter, Bruce Myers.

My father, Archie Bentz, returned from his military motor pool training and was working with his brother–in–law Bruce at Myers' Garage, when the 'suits' from Pontiac pulled up and explained their problem. Bruce and Archie listened to the engine, checked for engine misses the old–fashioned way (by pulling spark plug wires one at a time), ran the engine at a higher rpm while partially restricting the air intake to the carburetor, and at the same time listened to the inner workings of the engine using a ball peen hammer as a stethoscope. One end of the hammer was held against the running engine while you put your head inside the compartment to place an ear against the other end of the hammer.

When the engine was shut down, Bruce turned to Archie and said, "are you thinking what I'm thinking?" and Archie responded, "valve springs." They had determined that the valve springs were not strong enough to facilitate the open and close function fast enough to keep up with higher rpms. This issue is now called 'valve float' when the valves are not closing to allow full compression.

They asked the Pontiac men if they would allow them to fix it and the engineers just stood there with their mouths open. Archie started pulling the head off the motor while Bruce rummaged around his spare parts and came up with used tractor valve springs which he shortened to fit in his machine shop. In a matter of an hour the car drove down the road at full power. These farmers had diagnosed and repaired Detroit's problem in less than two hours!

When it comes to Bruce Myers, I cannot over emphasize the word intuitive. As a kid hanging around on the farm, I witnessed examples of his handiwork: power steering modifications on a tractor from the 1930's, and sheet metal shields added in the exhaust manifold area to bring warm air to the carburetor making a cold engine run smoother–a feature introduced 20 years later in Detroit. He machined replacement parts for cars, trucks, motorcycles, and all types of farm equipment and usually made them better than the original. As an adult, I better understand an uncle who had an early technical influence on my father. Archie went to Burgess–Norton in Geneva to gain further training as a machinist in the tool and die department.

I relate this story with the understanding that these scenarios took place across the country by those who took up the role of auto repair. Bruce Myers did not invent the automobile but he, and many men like him, kept them running and improvised improvements.

The 2019 remains of Myers' Garage built in the 1930's still stand at the corner of Scott and Dugan Roads in the Sugar Grove/Big Rock area. There was a fully equipped machine shop in the left portion of the building. Overhead garage doors had been invented in Knoxville, TN in 1921 and this building possessed two that were large enough to accommodate the biggest grain trucks and farm equipment of the day. In addition to the machine shop, the building was equipped with an in–ground hydraulic lift which was accessed from the door on the left. This was an era when most under–car repairs were still being performed from in–ground pits.To emphasize the age of this structure, the outhouse was located out back. As far back as can I remember, there was never any signage indicating the repair shop; the locals knew where to go. Since the time of this photo, the roof has collapsed. FIGURE 1.11 Courtesy Connie Bentz Deal.

TWO

EVOLUTION OF SERVICE STATIONS

Initially, refueling of automobiles took place at local pharmacies where Ligroin, a hydrocarbon petroleum–based cleaning solvent, was available as fuel. The stories quoted below demonstrate the beginnings of the early filling station and discuss the first purpose–built facilities.

Source: *Wikipedia* "Karl Benz, (very distant relative to the author), is generally credited with the invention of the first automobile with the creation of the 'Benz Patent Motorwagen' in 1885. The automobile was entirely designed to generate its own power, not simply a motorized stage coach or horse carriage which is why Benz was granted his patent in 1886 and regarded as its inventor.

Benz Patent Motorwagen. FIGURE 2.1 Sourced on *Wikipedia*

"In the first long distance automobile trip, Bertha Benz, supposedly without the knowledge of her husband, on the morning of 5 August 1888, took this vehicle on a 104 km (65 mi) trip from Mannheim to Pforzheim to visit her mother, taking her sons Eugen and Richard with her. In addition to having to locate pharmacies on the way to fuel up, she repaired various technical and mechanical problems and invented brake lining. After some longer downhill slopes, she ordered a shoemaker to nail leather on the brake blocks. Bertha Benz and sons finally arrived at nightfall, announcing the achievement to Karl by telegram. Thus, it could be argued that Bertha Benz invented the first brake linings and turned the local pharmacy in Wiesloch, Germany into the first 'Filling Station 'with the procurement of Ligroin, a petroleum based Naptha solvent which acted as the fuel of the Benz automobile."

An excerpt from the book *The First Drive-In Service Station--American Oil & Gas Historical Society:*

"Although Standard Oil will claim a Seattle, Washington, station of 1907, and others argue about one in St Louis two years earlier, most agree that when Good Gulf Gasoline went on sale, Gulf Refining Company opened America's first true drive-in service station."

"The motoring milestone took place at the corner of Baum Boulevard and St Clair Street in downtown Pittsburgh, Pennsylvania, on December 1, 1913. Unlike earlier curbside gasoline filling stations, an architect purposefully designed the pagoda-style brick facility, offered free air & water, crankcase service, with tire and tube installation. 'This distinction has been claimed for other stations in Los Angeles, Dallas, St Louis and elsewhere,' notes a Gulf corporate historian. The evidence indicates that these were simply sidewalk pumps and the honor of the first drive-in is that of Gulf and Pittsburgh. The Gulf station included a manager and four attendants standing by. The original service station's brightly lighted marquee provided shelter from bad weather for motorists."

Gulf Refining Company's decision to open the first service station (left) along Baum Boulevard in Pittsburgh, Pennsylvania, was no accident. By 1913 the boulevard had become known as "automobile row" because of the high number of automobile dealerships. FIGURE 2.2 Photo courtesy of the Library of Congress and Gulf Oil.

Given the debate as to when the first purpose-built gas station was constructed in the U.S., I felt it germane to the subject of the development of gas stations in the Fox Valley. The September 1, 1924 edition of *Petroleum News*, a national publication, acknowledged a new purpose-built service station in Elgin, IL. The article by R.A.M. "Andy" Anderson, touted the modern steam-heated gasoline service station newly built on the NW corner of State and Highland by Herman Bunge. The research of McCornack descendant Patricia McCornack Clarrissimeaux revealed that this location at 24 State St, Elgin was built by her grandfather, Charles McCornack in June of 1923 and the "ornate red brick building" was leased for operation to Bunge. The new facility boasted numerous air stands, water pumps, and available lubrication with 8 gasoline pumps under cover featuring Sinclair gasoline. At this time, it is important to acknowledge that Charles McCornack, a significant early independent gasoline, oil, and kerosene supplier, was not only familiar in the St. Charles market, but also the Elgin market as the Elgin Oil Co, along with Aurora Oil Co and DeKalb Oil Co.

1920 was the year McCornack built his first retail gas station in St. Charles with 5 pumps under cover at the corner of Third Street and West Main, yet to be followed by his grand "Super Service Station" facility on East Main in 1928 which is currently the St. Charles History Museum.

The oldest gas stations in the Tri-Cities, defined as: constructed to drive in for the primary purpose of selling gas, with repairs as the secondary endeavor were:

- **St. Charles: 1920–McCornack Oil:** Red Hat gasoline, East Main & 3rd Street
- **Geneva: 1922–Blue Ribbon Filling Station–Diamond Gasoline:** E.D. Jones, 728 W State–SE corner 8th and State. Opened, April 28, just months before the Standard Oil at State & 1st street. Standard lets bids for construction in March and opened in June under Roger Micholson and Lawrence Freeman as assistant. Freeman later became manager of Blue Ribbon.
- **Batavia: 1924–Frank Seavey Standard Oil,** Batavia Avenue and Main Street

It would only stand to reason that one should construct either a garage or service station at a location that would be visible and convenient to the passing motor traffic. In the beginning, most of the early motorists did not venture more than 10 miles from home because most of their daily needs were met within that area. Travel was also limited by the unreliability of early autos and their components. The lack of passable roads would also inhibit traveling to distant locations.

The author's 1946 Chevy parked by an early portable filling station at the Rock County Thresheree grounds in Wisconsin. The building was built on skids and could be moved from one location to another, testing the market until the most productive location was proven for more permanent construction. This is one of the few remaining pre–fab construction filling station sheds. FIGURE 2.3–Photo courtesy Bentz family.

One of my Batavia High School teachers, Marilyn Robinson, authored multiple books and many historical articles based on our local history. The article about the Lincoln Highway from *The Batavia Historian, Volume 43, No. 2* is available online and it is from that writing I gleaned some insights as to the development of the first national highway and how it passed through the Fox Valley and impacted our communities and the resulting service station development.

The Lincoln Highway Association held its first meeting on July 1, 1913 and brought forth a concept originated by Carl Fisher of the Prest-O-Lite Company, (the man who invented the early acetylene gas headlamp for cars), that a national highway should stretch coast-to-coast and be jointly financed by federal, state, and community funds. Illinois had established a state highway department with $1.2 million for its 1/3 contribution and along with Congressional approval of federal funds it seemed that a highway from Times Square in New York could eventually reach the Golden Gate Bridge in San Francisco.

In 1914, Mooseheart, *'The Child City'* between Batavia and North Aurora, was chosen to inaugurate this new era of road building in Kane County, primarily because they volunteered to pay for the road in front of their property. The conditions were that the State of Illinois would furnish the necessary equipment and Mooseheart would furnish the labor and materials.

First Day's Work

The Lincoln Highway Construction Project in front of Mooseheart.
FIGURE 2.4 Courtesy Marilyn Robinson & Batavia Historical Society

Mooseheart committed $12,000 to the project and recruited volunteers from local Moose Lodges. On April 15, 1914 over 1,000 citizens and officials gathered with much pomp and circumstance and included Illinois Governor Dunne digging the ceremonial first shovel before the real work began. About 200 workers and 40 teams of horses, using wagons, graders, pick and shovel; moved dirt, rock, and clay while providing a sub–grade comprised of 130 cubic yards over the three–quarter mile surface in one day. *"Crew foremen from the tri–cities included John Van Burton and James Kinney of Batavia; A. L. Carlisle and J. A. Fauntleroy of Geneva; and Bert Norris and F. E. Glenn of St. Charles. Norton VanSicklen of St. Charles was overseer of all the work."*

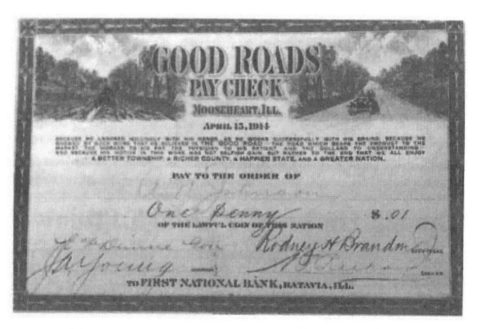

The day was so special that Batavia factories, the post office and schools closed so everyone could visit "Good Road Day." Everyone who worked on the road received a membership into the "Hod Carriers and Common Laborers Union" and a memento check for one penny signed by Gov. Dunne and drawn on the First National Bank of Batavia.
FIGURE 2.5 Courtesy Batavia Historical Society.

In the days that followed, Mooseheart's construction crews, using state equipment, poured the 15–foot wide cement slab that was to form the first ever concrete highway in Illinois. *'The original roadway that stretched across Illinois went from Chicago Heights through Joliet, Aurora, North Aurora, Mooseheart, Batavia, Geneva, DeKalb, and on to Fulton on the Mississippi River.'* The underground passageway to the opposite side of the road was later blasted through solid rock in 1935. The original Lincoln Highway heading west from Geneva is what we now know as Keslinger Road.

In 1919, an army convoy left Washington D. C. on its way to San Francisco via the Lincoln Highway on the U.S. Army's first ever inter–coastal trip to check the feasibility of moving men and materials via roadway, versus railroad. The seventy–nine–vehicle convoy did stop in Batavia while traversing the country in sixty–two days. One of the 295 men in the convoy was Capt. Dwight D. Eisenhower who later, while serving as the commander of allied troops in WW II, had the opportunity to observe and travel Germany's new superhighways we now know as the Autobahn. 37 years later, as President of the United States, he signed *The Federal–Aid Highway Act of 1956* initiating the interstate highway system that we use today.

The simple answer as to why early road construction is included in the history of service stations is: location, location, location. By mid–century it will seem that every prime corner across the country will have a service station competing for the passing motorist. You will see this pattern throughout the Tri–Cities and the Geneva chapter. The impact of changing the Lincoln Highway route will be seen and felt more than once in the Fox Valley.

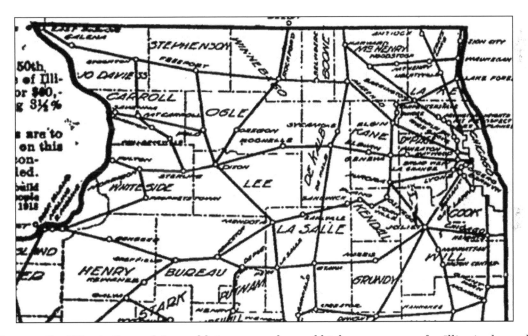

In 1917 the Illinois General Assembly's proposed paved highway program for Illinois showed only one westward highway from the Fox Valley area. That one highway was the Lincoln Highway which was already under construction and had received some federal money. Routes 64 & 30 were not yet proposed. The north–south highway was the East Elgin Road (Route 25). FIGURE 2.6 Courtesy *Elburn Herald*.

Free Truck Relief Service

and Other Great Benefits of the

Chicago Motor Club

Arranged for Members in this Vicinity

By 1921, 27,000 motorists have joined the CMC to ensure that their flat tire and towing charges were covered. Later referred to as A.A.A. Chicago Motor Club.
FIGURE 2.7 Courtesy *Batavia Herald*

Most Americans sought out and evaluated their local service station based on the individual merits for ease of convenience, trustworthy repairs, and dependable products. Their loyalty was to the people operating the business, with a secondary loyalty to the brand as something recognizable when they traveled. The oil companies recognized this loyalty and sought to provide a network of dependable dealers that could be consistently relied upon all across the country. To that point, the corporate identity was eventually developed with trademarks on names, logos, color combinations, architectural style, slogans, mascots and so on.

Standardized architecture design offered a familiar sight when traveling away from home, reinforced by the attendants in familiar uniforms that bestowed an air of legitimacy and authority for the personnel.

While the major oil companies concentrated on the lucrative urban markets, the expansive rural markets would require a different approach, which was left to either independents or licensed jobber/distributors. The Fox Valley was considered a rural market with less volume, so local distributors built and operated gas stations while also supplying area gas stations, which were independent of the oil companies. As the industry evolved, for the average consumer there would be no readily apparent means to distinguish if the gasoline station was company or wholesale/jobber supplied. There were even more jobbers in neighboring Aurora and Elgin ready to move into the Tri–City market. An example of this from the 1970's is Bentz Texaco being supplied directly by the company while Stan & Morgan's Texaco, just a few blocks away, was supplied by a wholesale/jobber with a local bulk plant.

In the early 1900's we had a number of jobbers representing either the major oil companies or some of the smaller independents. For a list of Tri-City jobbers please see Chapter 14.

While my emphasis will be focused on the service station marketing, it is still vital to have a basic understanding of the evolution of the other segments. The early history of the growth of the oil industry was segmented into production, transportation, refining, and marketing of the final product.

The Gas Station in America, authored by John A. Jakle and Keith A. Sculle, has been a great resource in referencing the early history and evolution of gas stations with regard to what they called "place-product-packaging," which I will loosely define as an identified territory, product differentiation, all packaged in recognizable image defined by color, shape, and slogans. Most of us over the age of 60 can recall and repeat the slogans of widely advertised brands when prompted with a few opening words? "You ask more from Standard..."; "See the U.S.A. in..."; "Trust your car..."; "Put a tiger..."; "As you travel..."; "Be Sure with...". *(Answers:* "and you get it"; "your Chevrolet"; "to the man who wears the Star"; "in your tank"; "ask us"; "Pure".)

Jakle and Sculle give you a very extensive understanding of the evolution of "Roadside of America" associated not only with regards to gas station architectural design but also with how this cultural icon influenced motel, fast-food and shopping centers for every community in this country.

> *"The preservation of roadside America needs not only to be promoted, but its promotion understood as a process of environmental management."*

During WWII the need for gas and oil to fuel the nation and our Allies took priority as our Allies used 7 billion barrels of oil during the course of the war with the United States supplying 85 percent of the total. For domestic consumption, gasoline was pooled and delivered from bulk plants to the nearest gasoline stations regardless of brand or company associations. Due to rationing, gas sales dropped to approximately 70% of 1941 levels which caused many bulk plants and over 25% of all gasoline stations to close and the number of registered motor vehicles to drop by about 4 million

The United States emerged from World War II with returning soldiers, new families, and a pent-up demand for every consumer product, including automobiles and gasoline. By 1955 motor registrations had soared to over 60 million and demand for petroleum product increased dramatically. The automobile came to epitomize the American conspicuous consumption, with the size of the auto increasing and powered by even larger gas–guzzling engines. Eisenhower's vision of a European–style interstate road system came about through the realization of Federal Aid Highway Act of 1956 which funded a national system of interstates and intercity express roads. The trust drew revenue from federal taxes on fuel, tires, and tubes. It was a temporary tax, in theory. Another "temporary tax" that never went away was the Illinois Toll Road fees that were supposed to "go away" once the initial funding of the Chicago area expressway system was in place.

The expanded oil production of the 1950's resulted in product surplus and subsequent "gas wars" with most of the large petroleum corporations expanding their territories based on market research of place–product–packaging. Several foreign corporations, such as Belgium's *Petrofina*, France's *Total*, and Britain's *BP*, joined the Dutch *Shell Oil* in the prosperous American market.

The 1950's was also a period of expansion of oil fields all over the world. While crude oil production in Mexico, Venezuela, and the Middle East had existed since World War I, one new consortium formed that involved Standard Oil of New Jersey, Atlantic, Gulf and Socony, together with Anglo–Persian (BP), Royal Dutch/Shell, and a French company to jointly invest in the ownership of the Turkish Petroleum Company (later the Iraq Petroleum Company). Standard Oil of California joined with the Texas Company to form Caltex as investors in Saudi Arabian crude and the American Independent Oil Company invested in Kuwait. The number of companies with 1945 oil concessions was eleven. That expanded to twenty–eight companies by 1953. It is only with hindsight that we can see how the United Stated influenced the development of the oil industry in many other countries. The irony is that the development of the oil industry in the Middle East, funded by foreign corporations including the United States, later became "nationalized" by the host countries in a takeover and the foreigners were required to leave their assets behind

The 1960's saw the continuing lure of the automobile and motor vehicle registration grew by another 31 million. During the '60s, one oil company executive's observation was *"Crude that stayed in the ground earned no money. Idle plant capacity cost money. Companies that moved more gasoline and increased their market share made more money. The chimera of the incremental barrel seemed the marketer's rule."*

By the 1970's motor vehicle registration had increased another 49 million and on October 17, 1973, the Organization of Arab Petroleum Exporting Countries (OAPEC) authorized an embargo of oil shipments to the United States in retaliation for America's military support of Israel. The next day, the Organization of Petroleum Exporting Countries (OPEC) imposed a 70 percent increase from $3.01 to $5.12 per barrel of crude oil. By the end of the year, the barrel price had risen to $11.65 and by the end of the decade prices had been as high as $40.

OPEC's action was quickly followed by rampant inflation, high interest rates, recession, unemployment, unfavorable trade balances, and federal budget deficits. In part, this could be blamed on our own petroleum industries with record high profits resulting from inflated prices with reduced supply. As the OPEC price rise intensified, new domestic production was brought on Alaska's North Slope, but not enough to stem the epidemic of oil company mergers and acquisitions.

Most corporations withdrew from marginal markets cancelling contracts with both jobbers and dealers. This all greatly impacted wholesale jobbers, vastly reducing their number, and surreptitiously eliminated future competition for the oil company. For example: Standard Oil of Indiana's total of 3,793 jobbers in 1972 had been reduced to 1,963 by 1983. In the 1980's, the move by the oil companies to reduce their dealer-controlled locations began with the advent of self–service. By 1980, a move within ARCO had transformed 91 percent to self–serve. By 1990, the reorientation showed Phillips 66 at 88 percent self–service, and Citgo and Shell at 86 percent while the industry average stood at 83 percent. Between 1975 and 1982, Shell Oil divested itself of 3,300 dealer stations, while constructing 182 new company run outlets designed for high volume.

The 1990's revealed the top twenty refiners accounted for 79 percent of total production, with eight of those firms having descended from various Standard Oil companies accounting for 43 percent of the total. As measured by assets, Royal Dutch/Shell and Exxon were the world's fourth and fifth largest industrial firms in 1991, followed by General Motors, Ford, and General Electric. This was before the mergers of Exxon/Mobil and Chevron/Texaco.

THREE

EARLY HISTORY OF STANDARD OIL

Entire libraries could be dedicated to the history of John D. Rockefeller's Standard Oil. Rockefeller came to market with his kerosene as *the* product that provided the most consistent grade of kerosene and set the "Standard" for the industry. Early on, his company came to control refining and transportation and eventually, through aggressive and sometime hostile acquisitions, came into control of a large part of the industry often referred to as a Trust or Monopoly. By some estimates he controlled some 85% of the industry. Apart from control of the oil, Standard would collude with the railroads for favorable transportation rates for themselves while competitors would either be handcuffed with higher shipping rates or even denied transport.

President Theodore Roosevelt was backed by the popular "trust-busters" leading to the 1911 decision to break up Standard Oil. The company was divided into 34 separate companies as a result of the Sherman Anti-Trust Act. Each of these separate companies were assigned territories and the right to use the Standard Oil name in that specific area. Today, many are surprised to learn that Sinclair, Mobil, Conoco and Atlantic Refining were indeed offshoots of the original Standard Oil. In the 1890's for its Chinese trademark and brand, Standard Oil adopted the name *Mei Foo* (Chinese: which translates to Mobil).

The actual net effect of the break-up resulted in making Rockefeller wealthier. It wasn't long before each of these companies would seek to expand beyond their assigned territory, which was permitted as long as they adhered to the law and not use the Standard Oil name outside of their territory. Decades later, the former Standard Oil companies remain pre-eminent in their original trade territories–areas the Supreme Court approved for their respective trade name use. Per Jakle and Sculle, this opened up the market to an even broader spectrum of new brand names and trademarks. Just one example of this was SOHIO, Standard Oil of Ohio, developing the name plate of "Boron" for the purpose of invading Michigan, Kentucky, and Pennsylvania. Standard Oil of California would use their "Chevron" moniker in the same way to compete in other markets.

From *Wikipedia*, (Redirected from Standard Oil Trust):

> "The successor companies from Standard Oil's breakup form the core of today's US oil industry. (Several of these companies were considered among the Seven Sisters who dominated the industry worldwide for much of the 20th century.) They include:
>
> - **Standard Oil of New Jersey (SONJ)**–or Esso (S.O.), or Jersey Standard– merged with Humble Oil to form Exxon, now part of ExxonMobil. Standard Trust companies Carter Oil, Imperial Oil (Canada), and Standard of Louisiana were kept as part of Standard Oil of New Jersey after the breakup.
> - **Standard Oil of New York**–or Socony, merged with Vacuum– renamed Mobil, now part of ExxonMobil.
> - **Standard Oil of California**–or Socal–renamed Chevron, became ChevronTexaco, but returned to Chevron.
> - **Standard Oil of Indiana–or Stanolind, renamed Amoco (American** *Oil Co.)–now part of BP.*

Standard's Atlantic and the independent company Richfield merged to form Atlantic Richfield Company or ARCO, subsequently became part of BP, later sold to Tesoro, now part of Marathon Petroleum and in the process of being partially rebranded as Marathon or Speedway depending on each station ownership. Atlantic operations were spun off and bought by Sunoco.

- **Continental Oil Company**–or Conoco–later merged with Phillips Petroleum Company to form ConocoPhillips, downstream & midstream operations since spun off to form Phillips 66.
- **Standard Oil of Kentucky**–or Kyso–was acquired by Standard Oil of California, currently Chevron.
- **The Standard Oil Company (Ohio)**–or Sohio–the original Standard Oil corporate entity, acquired by BP in 1987.
- **The Ohio Oil Co.**–or The Ohio–marketed gasoline under the Marathon name. The company›s upstream operations are now Marathon Oil while the downstream operations is now known as Marathon Petroleum, and was often a rival with the in–state Standard spinoff, Sohio.
- *Other Standard Oil spin–offs* [which resulted in elimination of pre–1911 companies]:
  - **Standard Oil of Iowa–pre–1911–bought out by Chevron.**
  - **Standard Oil of Minnesota–pre–1911–bought out by Amoco.**
  - **Standard Oil of Illinois–pre–1911–bought out by Amoco.**
  - **Standard Oil of Kansas–refining only, eventually bought out by Amoco.**
  - **Standard Oil of Missouri–pre–1911–dissolved.**
  - **Standard Oil of Louisiana–originally owned by Standard Oil of New Jersey (now by Exxon).**
  - **Standard Oil of Brazil–originally owned by Standard Oil of New Jersey (now by Exxon)."**

SOCONY, Standard Oil Company of New York, competed in markets like Minnesota as White Eagle with no reference to the Standard moniker. SOCONY primarily conducted business as the Socony–Vaccum moniker, which evolved to Socony–Mobil and then Mobil. It also conducted business as Magnolia, White Eagle, Wadhams, and Lubrite. The Mobiloil Gargoyle was replaced with the Pegasus which had evolved from the branding used by SOCONY in South Africa and it became the now familiar Mobil Oil Pegasus trademark.

FIGURE 3.1 & 3.2 From author's collection

The ESSO name came on the scene in 1923 with Standard Oil of New Jersey, and it was developed from the common moniker of S.O. pronounced as ESSO. Color, shape, and texture all played important roles in developing the identity for a product that could be recognized all across the country. The ENCO name was based on "World's Largest ENergy COmpany".

Phillips 66 borrowed the "catchy" number that rolled over your tongue from the federal highway and then even adopted the highway marker shape of Route 66. The blue Pure Oil gear shape logo, the Cities Service green shamrock shape, the Union 76 play on the "Spirit of 76 with Minute Man Service," the Athenian runner Pheidippides as the early logo for Marathon known to be "Best in the Long Run" are just some of the examples of integrating colors, shapes, logos, and theme to differentiate your product. Battles were fought in the courts for trademark rights that would simplify the customers recognition from down the road in picking into which service station they would pull.

As mentioned earlier, the small oil companies and wholesalers/jobbers are referred to as the "Independents" which predominately developed in the rural markets. These independents were not supplied by the major companies, who placed their emphasis in the urban markets with a higher density of automobiles. The Red Hat brand had been introduced by the National Petroleum Marketers Association for independent retailer use, but then later came the Standard Oil court challenge claiming the name infringed on its Red Crown trademark. Locally, we know that independent McCornack Oil had developed brand recognition of the Red Hat brand throughout the Fox Valley and it is purely my speculation that the loss of using that brand name may have fueled McCornack's need to sign on with Texaco.

A key element to the antitrust breakup of 1911, was that the oil industry overall was told that they had to promote a competitive retail market. The previous model had been with the company owning the oil fields, refining, transportation, wholesale distribution, and retail distribution. It was felt that this "cradle-to-grave" ownership and the control over every step of the way did not promote fair and competitive pricing to the ultimate consumer. Thus, it was declared that the oil companies would relinquish the competitive control of the retail market and distribute gas and oil at the retail level through either locally-owned stations or company-built stations that would be rented to dealers who, in theory, would be free to operate independently of the company's influence on the final price charged to the consumer. The separation of wholesale from retail was defined as the "divorcement" process within the industry. Since most working-class folks normally could not finance the land and construction of their own gas station, this would open the gates for many "Mom 'n Pop" opportunities to lease company stations and start business for themselves in order to achieve "The Great American Dream".

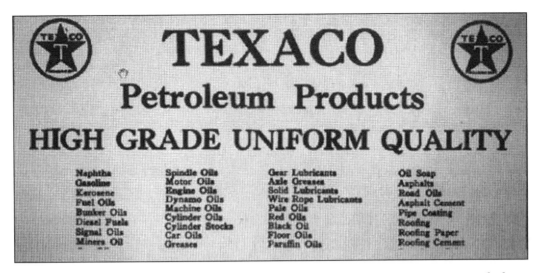

The list of products derived from petroleum was just starting and went on to include fertilizers, beauty aids and the yet to be discovered world of plastics.
FIGURE 3.3 Courtesy *St. Charles Chronicle*.

During the Great Depression era of the 1930's, the automobile manufacturers, previously numbering over 100, now declined to a much lower number, eventually settling around the "Big Three" of GM, Ford, and Chrysler as the dominant groups. At the same time, the petroleum industry had many more competitors and around twenty large oil companies accounted for three–quarters of the nation's refinery capacity. Eight of the former Standard Oil companies accounted for 40 percent while only four of those were responsible for an aggregate share of 35 percent. The companies soon learned the demographics of each market and targeted their choices of urban over rural markets, leaving the rural markets for jobber–based distribution and the farmer based "cooperative" movement. Lower priced gasoline was supplied to farmers through the Illinois Farm Supply Company, which by 1939 had expanded to serving 64 farmer affiliated co–ops in 102 counties. This was based on two bulk terminals, one on the Illinois River near Peoria, and the other on the Ohio River near Shawneetown.

The Depression caused fewer registered automobiles, which of course meant less gasoline and oil consumption. At the same time, more oil fields were discovered across the world. With the glut of product, independent private brands thrived in undercutting the majors through no–frills merchandising and selling gasoline for pennies less, back when pennies were significant. With the adoption of the National Industrial Recovery Act during the Roosevelt administration, the larger companies began to set prices through its "code of fair competition" temporarily easing cutthroat competition. Indictments were brought about by the Department of Justice in 1936, charging the oil companies with price fixing. The charges were upheld, and the disapproved coordination of setting prices was terminated.

Congress debated legislation to improve the position of the nation's dealers and jobbers which would bring about further dismemberment of "big oil." Divorcement proposals would be introduced repeatedly, and unsuccessfully, over the following half-century. Unfortunately for many dealers like myself, the pendulum swung in the wrong direction in 1981 when Congress chose to deregulate the oil industry and reverse many of the Sherman Anti-Trust laws.

This is just the tip of the iceberg in understanding how the oil industry evolved and operated through the 20th Century. To show how it applied to the Fox Valley, I for one, thought when OK-Oklahoma opened stations in both Geneva and Batavia, that the company was another off-brand competitor when it was indeed another Standard Oil company competing in our market. These two stations later were converted to ENCO, a more readily apparent Standard Oil company.

Predecessor to Sky Chief was Texaco with Ethyl additive.
FIGURE 3.4 & 3.5 Sourced on *Wikipedia*

How many remember referring to premium gasoline as Ethyl? The gasoline additive derived to improve performance and life of your engine was the collaborative effort of Standard Oil and General Motors. All the major oil companies became dependent on the much-desired additive, tetraethyl, to meet customer demands until the patents expired and individual company premium products evolved. Texaco introduced "Sky Chief" gasoline in 1938, a premium fuel developed from the ground up as a high-octane gasoline rather than just an ethylized regular product. In 1954, the company added the detergent additive Petrox to its "Sky Chief" gasoline. For decades people would still say "fill 'er up with ethyl."

The Jakle and Sculle book is a great resource to understand how companies like Diamond X company evolved to D-X and Atlantic merged with Richfield becoming Atlantic-Richfield Company which evolved to ARCO. This small paragraph cannot begin to help with your overall comprehension of the 260 page *The Gas Station in*

America published in 1994. I purchased a copy on Amazon and would encourage any history buff to do so.

FEBRUARY 5, 1937 *GENEVA REPUBLICAN*

"It is estimated that 6,000,000 workers--one out of every seven employed in the United States--owes his job directly or indirectly to the automobile industry... how vital a part motor manufacture plays in many of these fields. For example, 10% of all cotton raised in the south; 22% of all steel manufactured, 28% of nickel; 35% of lead and even 72% of all plate glass manufacture go into automobiles. Railroad car loadings total 3,500,000 in hauling raw materials, parts, etc., for automobiles, of which since 1930 more than 40% have been manufactured by General Motors. Of course, railroads also haul finished cars."

The next chart, FIGURE 3.6 has the simplest, yet most comprehensive chart that I have seen displaying the evolution of the petroleum history from 1860 to 2002. The chart was developed by Professor Bruce Railsback, Department of Geology, of the University of Georgia, Athens. He has provided a copy for us to view in this document. You will gain some insight of how names like Texaco, Amoco, Marathon, Valvoline, Total, and Mobil were used for products long before their producing companies revised the company name to be the same as the product.

An example of this is in the 1928 photograph of my service station in St. Charles, FIGURE 9.7, where there is a pedestal sign in front of the independent McCornack service station. That sign advertises *Mobiloil* with the old Gargoyle logo, and that oil was sold as a quality product to independent service stations. The SOCONY Company, Standard Oil Company Of New York, distributor of *Mobiloil,* was primarily an oil and lubricant arm of Standard Oil prior to the breakup. The products evolved from *Mobiloil* and *Mobilgas* were eventually dropped in favor of calling all of SOCONY the new name, Mobil, and even then, the *Mobilgas* name remained until sometime in the 1950's.

You can also view this online and enlarge the document for easier reading at: http://www.gly.uga.edu/railsback/PGSG/818PetroleumHistory6.pdf

FIGURE 3.6 *Courtesy Professor Bruce Railsback*

Continuous Oil Refining Co. founded 1866   First Valvoline Products 1868   Company became Valvoline 1902

Freedom Oil Works founded 1879   Purchase of Valvoline 1944   Merger with Ashland 1950

Swiss Drilling Co. founded in   Swiss Oil Co. founded   Ashland Refining   Swiss merged into   Merger of Ashland with Scurlock and
Oklahoma 1910; dissolved 1916   in Kentucky 1918   founded by Swiss Oil 1924   Ashland 1936   acquisition of Permian Corp. 1991   Ashland*

Cumberland Pipeline Co. Divested 1911   Bought by Ashland 1931

Anglo-Persian Oil Co founded 1909   Became Anglo-Iranian in 1935   Became British Petrol'm 1954   UK gov't stock sold 1987 BP

Standard Oil of Ohio incorporated 1870   Standard of Ohio   Sohio   Unowned stock bought by BP 1987

Warden, Frew &Co. Est. 1860 Merged to form Atlantic Petrol'm 1866   Bought by Standard Oil 1874   Divested 1911   Arco

Richfield Oil Co. organized 1911   Merged with Atlantic 1966 to form Arco

Sinclair Oil Co. organized 1916   Acquired by Arco 1969

Merger 1998 formed BP Amoco

1999

American Oil Co. organized 1922 50% interest bought by Pan Am 1923

Controlling interest in Pan-American Petroleum by Standard of Indiana 1925

John D. Rockefeller entered
the refinery business in
Cleveland 1863; Standard
Oil of Ohio founded 1870 by
Rockefeller et al.; its trust
over Standard companies
dissolved 1892 by Ohio
Supreme Court. Trust was
held by Standard of New
Jersey until 1911, when
dissolved into 33 companies
by order of U.S. Supreme
Court under the Sherman
Antitrust Act of 1890.

Standard Oil of Indiana Incorporated 1889   Stanolind   American   Became Amoco 1985   Amoco

Standard Oil of Nebraska bought by Standard of Indiana 1939

Humble Oil Founded 1917 >50% interest acquired by SONJ 1919

Carter Oil Co. founded 1877   60% bought by Standard 1894

Standard Oil of New Jersey founded 1882   Esso   Enco   Became Exxon in 1972   Exxon

Anglo-American Oil Co. founded 1887 Divested 1911 Bought by Jersey Std 1930

Exxon-Mobil

Standard Oil of Kentucky   Bought by Socal 1961

Pacific Coast Oil Co. incorporated   Became Standard   Divested in   Socal   Chevron Oil Co formed by   Chevron
in Standard Oil Trust 1879   of California 1906   1911 as Socal   Standard of California 1953

Standard Oil of Iowa incorporated 1885   Bought by Socal 1906

Gulf incorporated 1907 from Mellon holdings   Bought by Standard of CA (Chevron) 1984

Merger 1998

Magnolia Petroleum's first refinery 1902   >50% interest bought by Standard of NY 1918-20   Became part of Socony Mobil 1959

Vacuum Oil incorporated in NY 1866   Standard of New York (Socony) formed 1882   Socony-Vacuum became Socony Mobil 1955
Bought by Standard Oil 1879   Socony & Vacuum Merged to Socony-Vacuum 1931   Socony Mobil became Mobil Oil 1966

Merger 2001 to form ChevronTexaco

Ohio Oil Company   Bought by   Divested by Standard   Marathon completely   Ohio Oil renamed   Marathon bought by US   Marathon*
founded 1887   Standard Oil 1889   Oil in 1911   acquired by Ohio Oil 1936   Marathon in 1962   Steel (later USX) 1981

Continental Oil Co. founded 1875   Acquired by Standard 1884   Divested by Standard 1911   Conoco   Bought by DuPont 1981   Divested by DuPont '96 Conoco

South Penn Oil Co. incorporated in Standard Oil Trust 1889   Divestiture of South Penn, American Transit, South-West   Merger
Pennsylvania Piplines, & Eureka Pipeline Companies 1911   1963   Pennzoil

Purchase of Pennsylvania Company by American Transit (Standard Trust Member) 1881

ConocoPhillips

"Total", "Texaco", "Amoco", "Marathon",
"Valvoline", and "Mobil" were names used for
products long before their producing
companies took those names.

Contract between Standard of California   Purchase of 50%   Casoc became Arab   Shares bought by   Ownership transferred   Saudi
and Saudi gov't 1933; California Arabian   of Casoc by   American Oil Co.   Standard of NJ and   to Saudi gov't in   Aramco*
Standard Oil Co. (Casoc) formed   Texaco 1936   (Aramco) 1944   Socony 1948   1970s & 1980s

The Texas Company incorporated 1902   Acquisition of California Petroleum 1928   Texaco   Texaco*

Pacific Western Oil Corp incorporated 1928   Became Getty 1956   Bought by Texaco 1984

Skelly incorporated 1919   Bought by Getty 1957

Tidwater Pipe Co.   Tidewater Oil organized by   Tidewater & Associated   Bought by Getty 1957
founded 1878   Tidewater Pipe 1888   merged 1926

to form

Merger 1998

Merger 2002   Purchased 2002

Local Oil City lumber concern begins   "Quaker State" brand marketed by   Aquisition of brand name by Eastern Refining   19 companies merged into Quaker
leasing land days after Drake's discovery   Phinney Bros. Oil Co. 1913   Co, which became Quaker State Oil Co. 1924   State Oil Refining Co. 1931   Quaker State

This chart does not show the
many national oil companies
(e.g., Petroleos de Venezuela
SA) that are entirely state-owned.

Phillips brothers' first well 1905   Phillips Petroleum founded 1917   Phillips   Phillips

General American Oil Co. founded 1936 in Dallas   Bought by Phillips ca. 1982

Union of California narrowly avoided a takeover by Union of Delaware, a Royal Dutch/Shell subsidiary, in 1921-1922.
Hardison, Stewart, & Co. founded in California 1883   HS&C and others merged into Union Oil Co. of California 1890   Became Unocal 1983   Unocal

Pure Oil Co. organized 1895   Pure bought by Union 1965

Amerada Hess founded ca. 1922   Amerada Hess

A Genealogy

Occidental founded in California 1920   Acquired Placid Oil 1994   Oxy

Cities Service organized 1926   Cities Service bought by Occidental 1982**

of

Sun Oil incorporated 1889   Sun in US became Oryx 1988   Sun/Oryx

the Oil Industry

1939 Discovery in Aquitaine spurred formation of   Successors of ERAP formed   Merger with
la Régie Autonome des Pétroles (ERAP)   Elf 1967, later Elf Aquitaine   Elf   TotalFina ~1999

TotalFinaElf

LBRailsback
Dept. of Geology, U. of Georgia
12/1996; rev. 4/2002.

Compagnie Financière Belge des Pétroles (Petrofina) founded 1920 in Antwerp   Fina   Merger with Total ~1998   TotalFina

Compagnie Francaise des Petroles (CFP) founded 1924   CFP became Total CFP 1985, which became Total 1991
The TotalFinaElf merger created the world's fourth-largest oil company.

"Shell Shop"   Royal Dutch   1st Shell   Shell Transport   1st Shell-Royal Dutch   Shell bought Roxana   Merger of Shell of California,   Shell Union   Remainder of U.S.   Shell*
opened in   founded   oil tanker   Co. organized   collaboration in Asiatic   & 5 small Oklahoma   Union of Delaware, and   became Shell   Shell bought by Royal
London 1833   1890   1892   1897   Petroleum 1903   companies 1912   Roxana into Shell Union 1922 Oil Co. 1959   Dutch/Shell in 1985

*Shell, Texaco, and Saudi Aramco merged much of their U.S. refining and marketing in 1998. Marathon and Ashland did likewise as of 1/1/1998.
**When Cities Service was bought by Occidental, the Citgo refining and retail component was sold to Southland Corporation, owner of 7-Eleven stores.
Southland sold half of Citgo to Petroleos de Venezuela SA (PDVSA, the Venezuelan national oil company) in 1987 and the second half to PDVSA in 1990.

FOUR

ARCHITECTURAL
EVOLUTION

We have already touched on the subject of early gasoline distribution, branding, and trademarks, so now let us explore the evolving influence of gas and automobiles on the architecture of America. While the gas station is the most widespread type of commercial building nationally, it is the most ignored and hidden building in our local landscape. Here is a rudimentary document from the Jakle and Sculle book that spoke to that evolution:

While the majority of stations would not qualify as architecturally significant to the art historian it is important that we capture the historical trend of the most numerous buildings in our hometowns. The first style is a "curb side," which is usually defined as having a pump added in front of an existing business. Then there were sheds with curbside pumps. Oftentimes these were unattractive, poorly constructed, barely held–together shacks with a couple of hastily–installed gas pumps. Next came the more familiar house–like structure to architecturally compliment the town; a house with a canopy over the pumps, then a house with bays added. The "Oblong Box" structure covered with porcelain is the design that Baby Boomers most likely remember the most.

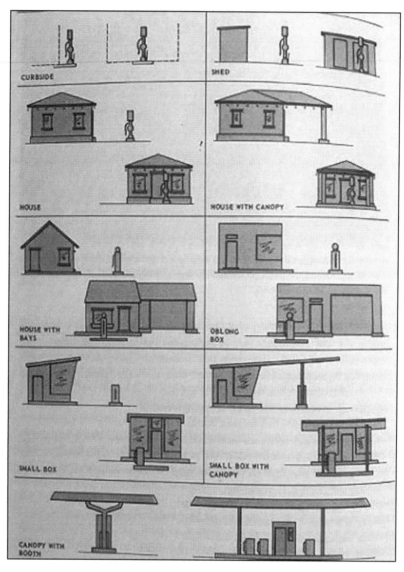

1910–1990, Gas station types identified in an illustration from National Petroleum News.
FIGURE 4.1 Courtesy *"The Gas Station in America."*

The "Small Box" was typical of the Clark brand of gas station. In Illinois we saw limited use of the "Booth" style due to the resistance to self–serve legislation. Since this illustration ended in 1990, the free–standing canopy around a convenience store should be added. We have experienced all these architectural styles in the evolving Tri–Cities, and I will point out some examples as we move on our journey from Batavia, to Geneva and St. Charles, and I will reference this illustration repeatedly. The most architecturally significant locations in the Fox Valley would be the cottage style of the Pure Oil on the west side of Geneva; the Tudor style of the McCornack Oil gas stations; and the art deco style of the former Baker Hotel Garage and Texaco filling station.

As mentioned earlier, corporate identity through "place–product–packaging" was key to differentiating any company's perceived image to the consumer. The physical shape and color of the building became a key factor with the consumer recognizing their favorite brand from down the road and anticipating the upcoming turn. Some examples that I grew up with were the Texaco oblong box, with white porcelain panels, green stripes, and red stars bordering green lettering; and the Standard Oil oblong box which shared the popular white porcelain panels but sported red stripes and blue lettering. Standard further distinguished itself with the shape of the oval and torch sign, while Texaco displayed the "banjo" shaped sign with a circle on top of a pole. Cities Service with the shamrock shape, the blue gear shape of Pure, and the yellow "Shell." The common denominator of many stations was this type of metal frame building sporting white porcelain panels and a basic floor plan, typified by the 1938 Texaco plans shown below.

Standardized architectural design offered a familiar sight when traveling away from home and was reinforced by attendants in familiar uniforms that bestowed an air of legitimacy and authority for the personnel. We will also visit novel architecture designed to intrigue and temp the driver to pull over for a fill–up.

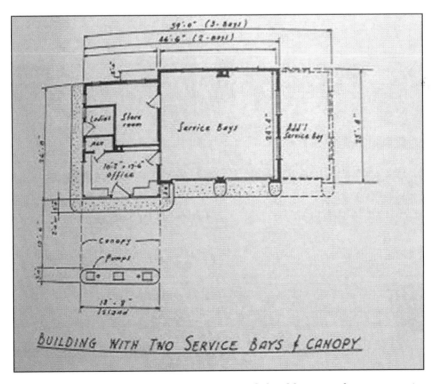

1938 Texaco Type 'C' plans, front canopy and third bay are shown as options.
FIGURE 4.2 Photo courtesy "Gas Stations of America" and Texaco. 1962 Texaco Dealer Training video, 25 minutes, full color: https://www.youtube.com/watch?v=saj7KNZux08

This video is a fundamental 'service–with–a–smile' training that goes on and on. Just as the customer views his new car as more than just a convenience, he has come to expect his local station to be more than just a building with pumps to dispense gasoline.

Front Elevation of Oblong Box design used throughout the industry. FIGURE 4.3 Photo Courtesy of H. Wayne Price & "Gas Stations of America."

The evolution of Mobilgas design from 1950's with the profile of the Pegasus. FIGURE 4.4 Photo sourced from *Wikipedia*.

1972 modern Mobil lighting and circular pumps and by 1985 they revived the Pegasus again.
FIGURE 4.5 Photo sourced from *Wikipedia*.

Windmill Shell Oil–Chan's Place Holland, MI–the upper floor was living quarters.
FIGURE 4.6 Photo sourced from *Wikipedia*.

While the architectural style of our Fox Valley stations generally reflected our conservative, homey lifestyle, there were other national examples of gas stations that definitely bordered on outrageous designs to attract motorists from the high–speed transcontinental highways like Route 66 and the Lincoln Highway. It is unknown how many stations were designed nationally to mimic windmills, airplanes, and lighthouses. This style of architecture is referred to as *Mimetic Design* on the plaque associated with the airplane in FIGURE 4.9.

While this windmill motif would be a novelty to some, we already had a real windmill at Fabyan's Estate/Forest Preserve. FIGURE 4.7 Photo sourced from *Wikipedia*

Currently used as a barbershop in Knoxville, TN. FIGURE 4.8 Post card photo.

The author recently posed with the Airplane Filling Station in 2019. The historic plaque reads: "In 1931 to tap the market newly created by the evolution of transportation and mobility of Americans, brothers Henry and Elmer Nickle of Powell, Tennessee, opened a gasoline filling station in the unusual shape of an airplane. The airplane is one of Tennessee's finest examples of mimetic design, a novelty type architecture, which takes the form of buildings that resemble the products sold there or some other novel design to attract drive–by customers. The Airplane Filling Station was placed on the National Register of Historic Places in 2004." FIGURE 4.9 Author's photo.

July 1940. "Cabins imitating the Indian teepee for tourists along highway south of Bardstown, Kentucky. (Wigwam Village #2, Cave City)." FIGURE 4.10 Photo sourced from *Wikipedia*

The Teapot Dome Service Station was originally located on Hwy. 410 between Zillah and Granger, WA. was handcrafted by Jack Ainsworth in 1922. He was inspired by the Harding Administration Teapot Dome Scandal where the federally owned naval oil reserves were surreptitiously leased to private entrepreneurs for personal exploitation. FIGURE 4.11 Photo sourced from *Wikipedia*.

World War II Bomber, Milwaukee, WI. FIGURE 4.12 Photo sourced from *Wikipedia*.

Can there be any doubt to the brand of gasoline dispensed here?
FIGURE 4.13 Photo sourced from *Wikipedia*.

Sinclair in the image of 'Dino' in Binghamton, New York.
FIGURE 4.14 Photo sourced from *Wikipedia*.

Kramer's Café, Browning, MT. You know the family could not just pass by the Wigwam!
FIGURE 4.15 Post card photo.

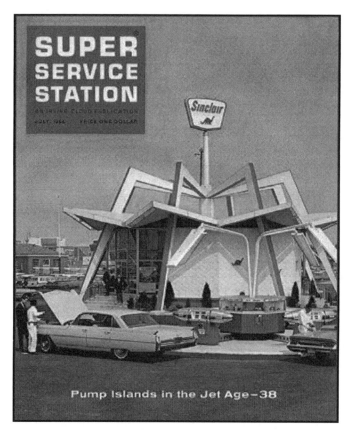

1964 Jet Age Service Station of the Future! (I remember when this edition came out.)
FIGURE 4.16 Source *Super Service Station* publication.

This is just a small sampling of the many architectural designs utilized in the dispensing of gasoline and services. If you desire to further investigate this subject, I do recommend *"Fill'er Up" An Architectural History of America's Gas Stations, by Daniel I. Vieyra.*

"Despite the many changes in gasoline marketing the last half of the century, there have been no new gasoline distribution methods. In fact, today's stations are in many ways a reintroduction of station types that existed before 1930. While the full-service station which corresponded to the old-fashioned repair shop; the modern convenience store calls to mind the early bulk station combined with the general store that sold gasoline."–Daniel I. Vieyra

The following is my attempt to preserve historical Tri-City information to the best of my knowledge. The dealer-based network that represented the oil industry has been eliminated, replaced by large corporations seeking larger profits. I feel a kinship to remember as many of the dealers and their families who serviced vehicles in the Fox Valley. While many of the older and architecturally significant locations were still in operation when I was a young man and there are still examples of recognizable former service stations and garages, most have been remodeled in such a way to disguise the previous function of the building.

Regarding our local history, you will see many photographs of our architectural evolution that have not been published before this.

FIVE

BATAVIA EAST SIDE

Batavia Historian–August 1947 "the city council passed an ordinance changing the house numbering system to the modern block system of 00–99, 100–199, 200–299, etc. The river and Wilson Street were designated the dividing lines east to west, north to south. Until now, buildings were numbered in consecutive order, disregarding cross streets and blocks." Please keep an open mind when attempting to correlate an older location to a present–day facility; the numbering system for addresses has changed and does not necessarily reflect a current address. Batavia addresses will be listed using post–1948 addresses followed by the **pre–1948 address in (parenthesis).** Note that I have attempted to list each location with the **oldest proprietors first** and the current addresses.

9 NORTH RIVER STREET

- **1924–28: River Street Garage**–Fred J. Briggs
- **1928: Stephano Bros. Texaco Filling Station**–Walter J. Stephano Ph 1304
- **1932: Werbeckas Coal Co**–Joseph Werbeckas, listed as gas station

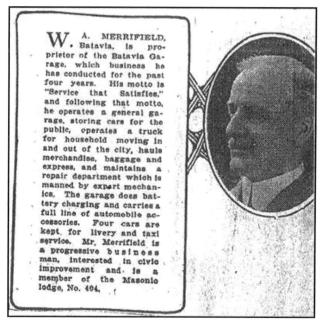

Aurora Beacon News Nov 30,1919 'Progressive Men and Women of Batavia'.
FIGURE 5.1 Courtesy Batavia Historical Society.

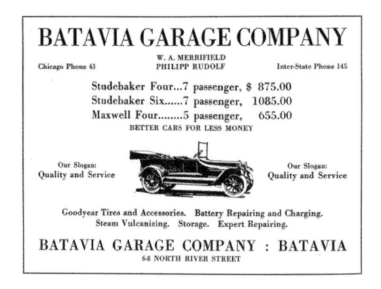

FIGURE 5.2 Courtesy 1916 Bee Aitch Ess yearbook

6-8 NORTH RIVER STREET

- **1914–31: Batavia Garage Co**–Willis A. Merrifield, early partner, Philipp
  Rudolf–1916 Sanborn Fire Insurance map reveals 540–gallon gasoline tank.
  Batavia Garage advertisement: Apr 1916 Studebaker Four, 7 passengers
  $875.00; Studebaker Six, 7 passengers $1085.00; Maxwell Four, 5 passengers $ 655.00–All with Goodyear Tires & Accessories.

- **1932: Batavia Garage**–Frank A. Weisbrock prop.
- **1932–33: Lies Chevrolet Sales**–Alois M. Lies, previously on Main Street.
- **1939: Batavia Tire & Battery Service**–Harry Sutton owner, Lee Wallis store manager.
- **1940: Batavia Tire & Battery Service**–G.W. Price

320 NORTH RIVER STREET (108 N)

- **1943: Harry Hobbdawson**–home based garage

525 N RIVER

- **1979: Jerry's Service Center**– Gerald T. Litney (from Jerry's ENCO)

M. J. OPPERMAN, has just opened a garage at 25 State street, which has been in operation for the past three months. He has lived in Batavia for 20 years, and is one of the oldest auto repair men in Batavia. He is a first class machinist, and capable of putting a machine into first class shape. His long experience in the auto repair business, makes his services much sought and his newly opened place of business is starting out with every indication of ultimate success.

Aurora Beacon News Nov 30,1919 'Progressive Men and Women of Batavia'.
FIGURE 5.3 Photo Courtesy Batavia Historical Society

115 STATE STREET (25)

Directly behind Wenberg Smithy on the corner of River & State

- **1919: M.J. Opperman Garage**–machinist. Prior to this Max was a partner in Korte & Opperman garage on the Avenue. In 1920, Max Opperman is operating the garage at 315 (125) Main Street.
- **1949: Thomas & Schwickert**–Implement dealers address 102 N. River, Ph 3086
- **1950's–60's: Thomas–Carlson Farm Implement**–Gordon W. Thomas & Verner Carlson
- **1979: Dewell & Dewell Garage**–Edward Dewell

(120) SOUTH RIVER STREET (RT. 25)

- **1933: Joe's Place**–Joe Werbeckas–Gas, Oil, Coal & Beer per Arnold Benson

559 SOUTH RIVER STREET

- **1975–80: Staton Bros Garage**–David & Noel Staton

590 SOUTH RIVER STREET

- **1983: America Auto Repair**–Michael Gardner (race car driver)

860 SOUTH RIVER STREET

- **1980: Valley Corvette**–David Hansen

Kinne & Jeffery Store, (28 East Wilson)–Curbside Pump.
FIGURE 5.4 Photo Courtesy Batavia Historical Society.

104 EAST WILSON STREET (28 E)

- **1874–1977: M.M. Kinne/Kinne & Jeffery Store**–Issac B. Kinne & John W. Jeffery.
In 1912, the store was the agency for the **Overland** automobile and sold a total
of six automobiles. The early sales of gasoline from 1891 have progressed from
cans. A Sanborn map from 1916 details 500–gallon fuel storage tank under front
sidewalk, an example of a curb–side location, *(refer to Curbside Pump Figure 4.1)*
As of mid–century the store was identified as **Schielke's Store**.

Aurora Beacon News November 30, 1919 'Progressive Men and Women of Batavia'.
FIGURE 5.5 Photo Courtesy Batavia Historical Society.

108 EAST WILSON STREET (30)

- **1919–1924: Spencer "Dri-Kure" Vulcanizing Shop**–William C. Spencer (later sold to Funk about 1924–25 who moved business to Batavia Avenue)

Early Photos of McCornack Service Station, 122 East Wilson Street. FIGURE 5.6 Photo Courtesy McCornack Family & St. Charles History Museum. McCornack Service Station, Batavia: Initially an independent gas dealer featuring Red Hat, Aviation, and Globe brand gasolines (later becoming in Texaco in 1934). There are Globe curb signs touting the independent high-grade gasoline with the Ethyl brand additive with the gas pump standing out as the white pump on the left. Also refer to House w/Bay–figure 4.1

122 East Wilson (side view).
FIGURE 5.7 Photo Courtesy McCornack Family & St. Charles History Museum

Later in this book you will learn more about McCornack and the St. Charles locations that preceded the Batavia location. One could assume that Geneva architect, Frank Gray was the designer of this McCornack service station, as this location succeeded the corporate headquarters in St. Charles for which he was the architect. All of the architectural elements are repeated from St. Charles with only one exception: the window muntins in St. Charles were diamond shape while these are rectangular. Note that even the clock is repeated in the gable end.

EXPLANATION OF THE SIGNAGE IN PHOTO 5.7:

The pole sign reads: McCornack Oil Co./Gas/Rest Rooms (note the sidewalk to the Ladies Rest Room in back of building). The sign partially blocked by the pole reads "Motor Oil" and is in the trademark "tombstone" design of Quaker State. The pedestal oval sign is the trademarked Gargoyle Mobiloil sign made by SOCONY and later branded as Mobil Oil. This type of branding is prior to the McCornack's Texaco affiliation and when combined with the style of electric gas pumps with "clock face dials," it would place the photograph date somewhere between 1930–32. This is the second McCornack facility built with an indoor service bay. The City of Batavia Survey for construction was dated September 1, 1930.

122 EAST WILSON STREET (42 E)

SW corners Washington and East Wilson

- **1930: McCornack Texaco Grand Opening**–Dec 1930
- **1932–40: McCornack Texaco**–James A. Daniels, manager. Ph 1213, Gearraed Spittael attendant.

Bob's Texaco opening July 1940. FIGURE 5.8 Photo Courtesy *Batavia Herald*

FIGURES 5.9 & 5.10 Courtesy Bentz collection of *Batavia Herald* advertisements

- **1940–41: Bob's Texaco**–Robert McGary, (formerly at Main Street Garage) Assisted by Mervin "Bus" Pye.

Alan Case announces opening in September 5, 1941.
FIGURE 5.11 Courtesy Bentz collection of *Batavia Herald* advertisements

- **1941–60: Allen Case Texaco**–Allen had worked at the McCornack St. Charles west side station since 1932.
- **1960–61: Bob's Texaco Service**–Robert McGary?
- **1962–65: Pete's Texaco**–Donald "Pete" Peterson

McCornack sold to Texaco Oil Co. January 1, 1963 but this location did not have sufficient volume to be desirable to them. I am making an assumption that Pete purchased the property and was supplied by the Texaco bulk plant.

After Pete left for new Citgo station on Main street, the property was sold, building razed, and was replaced with a 7/11 convenience store, now Batavia Smoke & Liquor.

206 EAST WILSON STREET (54 E)

John had been in business with Reber & Foley in St. Charles and now
he was letting old customers know where he was doing business.
FIGURE 5.12 & 5.13 Courtesy *St. Charles Chronicle* & *Batavia Herald.*

John "Tires" Rothecker. FIGURE 5.14 Courtesy *BHS Echo Yearbook.*

Rothecker Standard Service, built on the former site of the Crane home, with Crane Funeral Home in background.. FIGURE 5.15 Courtesy *BHS Echo Yearbook.*

- **1950–57: John's Standard Service**–John Rothecker, came from St. Charles Reber & Foley partnership in 1949.
- **1958–69: Rothecker's Standard**–John "Tires" Rothecker, succeeded by his son, Jon E. Rothecker, Jr.
- **1969–1976: Rothecker's Standard**–Jon E. Rothecker, who later relocated to Judd's location on Washington and then started Auto Parts Store in Geneva.
- **1976–86: Stewart's Standard**–Gene Stewart, also operated in North Aurora. Ray Clayton was a partner in 1978.

- **1987–88: Fox River Amoco**–Tom Porch, formerly at old Pure Oil building.
- **1988–91: Chip's Amoco Service**–Chip Zies 879–5166
- **2017: Marathon** building was sold and razed, vacant today.

Paul Young, Chip Zies & Manny Navarro c. 1987.
FIGURE 5.16 Photo Courtesy Batavia Historical Society.

Batavia Coal Yard and Oil Station, circa 1928-30.
FIGURE 5.17 Courtesy Batavia Historical Society.

336 EAST WILSON STREET (112 E)

(SW corners East Wilson & Prairie)

- **1911–1920: Lloyd D. Wood**–purveyor of Fuel, Poultry and Dairy Feed
- **1925: Dan F. Zwilling Service Station**–Ph 1499
- **1928–32: B C Y Oil Station**–Daniel F. Zwilling Ph 1499 **B**atavia **C**oal **Y**ard
- **1932–37: Batavia Coal Yard and Oil Station**–H. M. Dailey, David Anderson manager in 1936.

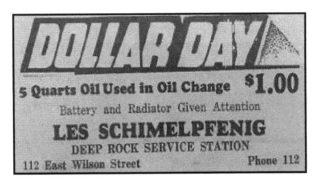

FIGURES 5.18 Courtesy Bentz collection of *Batavia Herald* advertisements

- **1940: Les' Deep Rock Service Station** #2–LeRoy Feece, agent for Deep Rock, Les Schimelphenig, Manager, Ph 1112
- **July 1940: Les' D–X**–Les Schimelphenig
- **1941: D–X Service Station**–Paul "Sinky" Hendrickson, formerly with O.T. Benson and went on to manage Deep Rock, 24 North Batavia Avenue.
- **1942: Red's D–X**–Charles "Red" Cleland, manager, Bob Hubbs attendant.
- **1943–46: D–X Service Station**–David P. Anderson, manager.
- **1947: Mac's D–X**–Thomas H. & Charles O. McDonald
- **1947: Wally's Standard Service**–Ph 3793
- **1950–54: Bob's Standard Service**–Robert C. Johnson
- **1954–62: Bob & Pete's Standard**–Bob Johnson & Lee 'Pete' Satterwaite
- **1964–69: Bob's Standard**– Bob Johnson
- **1971–72: Bob's Union 76**–Bob Johnson
- **1973–74: Elkins Union 76**–Keith Elkins, Jerry Mahan–manager
- **1979–80: Marathon**–Frank and Tom Knight
- **1984: Marathon**–Gregory S. White
- **1997: White Hen Pantry Mall**

Pure Oil Service Station at Wilson and Prairie St. FIGURE 5.19 Courtesy Bentz family.

Pure Oil's English Cottage architectural style of the 1930's will be discussed later in Chapter 8. This is an example of a 'modern' approach utilizing this 'Oblong Box' variant in built in 1946.

403 EAST WILSON STREET (125 E)

(NE corners East Wilson & Prairie)

- **1928: Geneva Oil Co**–Wm. C. Jeske, manager.
- **1932: Purol Gas Station**–Wm. C. Jeske
- **1936–37: Valley Pure Oil Station**–William C. Jeske
- **1940–49: Jeske Pure Oil**– Bill Jeske (Wm. C. Jeske)

As was the case with many small businesses, sometimes the family would visit the gas station just to see Dad during the day. Dorothy and Elizabeth Beronich with mother at Pure Oil. FIGURE 5.20 Courtesy Beronich family.

- **1952–54: Paul's Pure Oil**–Paul Beronich, former mechanic at Norm's
- **1955: Fred's Pure Oil**–Fred M. Spuhler

- **1955–58: Fred and Lou's Pure Oil**–Fred M. and Lou F. Spuhler

FIGURES 5.21 & 5.22 Courtesy *Batavia Herald*

- **May 1959–60: Bentz Bros. Pure Oil**–Archie Bentz & Bernie Bentz, Ph 3495. Their early employees as remembered by Rick Eckblade: Rudy Van Overmieren, Donny McDonald, Chuck Von Hoff, and Ronn Pittman.

  Bentz Bros. opened this station and made a large enough impact in town that it came to the attention of Standard Oil. By October of the same year, Bentz Bros. had also signed a contract with Standard Oil for the operation of the 144 South Batavia Avenue location. They finished out the one–year lease with Pure Oil and continued on with Standard Oil, eventually becoming the number one dealership in all of the Standard Oil of Indiana territory.

  By 1967, when I was a student at Northern Illinois University, I had fuel pump problems in DeKalb and pulled into the Standard on the Lincoln Highway. When the proprietor was filling out the repair order, he of course asked my name. When I told him "Archie Bentz" he as much as called me a liar and said, "Come on kid, give me your real name!" He further explained that he had gone through the Standard Oil dealer training and had heard so many examples of, "Archie Bentz did it this way," that there was no way the kid standing in front of him was that guy. Having been known as Butch in Batavia, I now had to call myself Archie Bentz, Jr.

Christmas 1959, two Bentz Bros. service stations in Batavia, and although there is no mention of being in business with conflicting oil companies, S&H Green Stamps were given at both locations! FIGURE 5.23 Courtesy *Batavia Herald*.

Paulson Pure Oil. FIGURE 5.24 Courtesy Ture Paulson family.

- **1961–66: Paulson Pure Oil**–Ture Paulson, former mechanic with Leuer's Chrysler Garage in the 1930's Elburn, his own garage in Big Rock, Larson Phillip's 66 in St. Charles, and then with Rothecker Standard. Ture's son, William, is with him in the business. Rod Kielion was attendant while in high school.
- **1968–69: Batavia Pure Oil**–Walter E. Becker
- **1970–72: Walker's Union 76**–Cloyd Walker
- **1973: Fred's Union 76**–Fred Payne
- **1973–74: Elkins Union 76 Towing**–Keith Elkins (also across the street)
- **1977: Walt's Union 76**–Walter Joyce Ph 879–8812
- **1979: Lindgren Automotive**–Steve Lindgren, no gas, Foreign Car Service
- **Year unknown: St. Charles Radiator**
- **1985–87: Tom Porch Auto Repair**–Tom's father, Dave, & grandfather, David had operated a Standard Oil service station in 1949 at Somonauk, IL while living in Batavia.
- **1987–93: Steve's Repair**–Steve Pederson, went to St. Charles Car-X.
- **1997: Novak's Used Cars:** Don Novak, retired from Fox River Tire
- **2004–present: Park & Son's Auto Repair**–Kilo Park

EAST WILSON 1 E OF C&NW

- **1890–30: John Peterson Auto Livery**–Horse Livery evolved to Auto Livery, former address Batavia Avenue and First St.
- **1930: E.S. Carlstedt**–1932 moved to 115 North Washington

483 EAST WILSON (143 E)

In the vicinity of lumber yard and RR tracks

- **1936–47: Wells Service Station**–Vaughn Wells, Pete Konen manager, address listed as RR#1, Box 143
- **1954: Bowron Motor Service** at 466 East Wilson

Early Feldott Barn–Dealership FIGURE 5.25 Courtesy Batavia Historical Society

EAST WILSON & DELIA ST (165E)

NE & SE corners

- **1896–1960's: Feldott's**–C.H. Feldott–early automobiles, agricultural implements, pumps, and windmills, later relocated further east on Wilson, moving outside of city limits in 1949 with Theresa and Mary Feldott at the helm with Carl Lies as general manager. This 15,000 sq. ft. facility was a pre–cursor to the later *Farm & Fleet* style of merchandising.

855 EAST WILSON

- **1989: Larson's Auto Repair**–Dennis L. Larson
- **833 East Wilson**–had a history as general store w/gas pump at rear entrance.
- **1949–66: Erv's Drive–In Liquor Store**–Ervin J. Sanetra
- **1966–70's: Big Lee's Tavern**–LeRoy Wiesse

1495 EAST WILSON

NE corner with Kirk road

- Current Speedway Truck & Auto Center

503 NORTH VAN BUREN (173 N)

- **1928–48: William R. Miller Garage**–home–based garage faced Church St.

338 WEBSTER STREET

SW corner of Prairie Street–building still stands today.

- **1924–27: Lundeen Bros Hudson–Essex**–Emil and Frank Lundeen, Ph 1571, operated in conjunction with their Geneva locations. While they were based in Geneva and the locations there were identified, the ads below clearly indicate a Batavia location even though I could find no record of them there. It was through a process of elimination that I have placed them at this address. They were the authorized representatives for the Tri–Cities, Elburn and West Chicago. One of the Lundeen brothers, probably Emil, had been in business with Carl More in 1915, selling the Cole automobile in Batavia. You can follow a more extensive history of the Lundeen Bros in the Geneva Chapter.

FIGURE 5.26 Courtesy July 3, 1925 *Geneva Republican.*
FIGURE 5.27 Courtesy *Batavia Herald.*

- **1928–30: Lundeen's Studebaker**–a second venture with a Geneva location on West State Street operated as the base, and again the Batavia branch had no known address.

FIGURE 5.28 Courtesy *Batavia Herald*

- **1949–53: Norm's Garage**–Norman & Ray Anderson moved from West Wilson, repaired and sold GMC trucks, Ph BAtavia 3796. Paul Beronich worked for Norm 1948–1951, then opened Paul's Pure Oil on Wilson in 1952.

Paul Beronich's GMC truck parked at Norm's Garage, note gas pump behind truck.
FIGURE 5.29 Courtesy Beronich family.

115 NORTH WASHINGTON AVENUE

- **1932–33: Carlstedt Motor Service**–Eskil Carlstedt

414 STATE STREET

- **1956: Deep Rock Service Station**–William C. Jeske

1025 NORTH WASHINGTON AVENUE

- **1976: Norm's Auto Repair**–Norm Hawbecker
- **1985–86: Nick's Auto Repair**–Nicholas A. Bruscato

1109 NORTH WASHINGTON AVENUE (1000 N)

- **1932–40: Batavia City Limits Gas Station**–North Washington Avenue at North City Limits–William J. Bustard
- **1940–47: Hansford Bros Gas Station & Motor Sales–Phillips 66**–Ben S. & George D. Hansford built new station after WWII. Ben went on to start Hansford Chevrolet, Huntley, IL
- **1948: Pittman's Phillips 66**–Paul Pittman Ph 3460 5772
- **1949: Eddie's Phillips 66**–1000 North Washington–Ed Baum & Paul Pittman
- **1950–54: Paul's Phillips 66**–Paul Pittman & son, Ronn Pittman
- **1950: Jim's Service**–James T. Walsh Jr. (shop area in rear)
- **1952: Marty Stern Body Shop**–operated out of back of building, Ph BA 3460

- **1954: Snape & Son's**–Feb 1954 Ph 3493
- **1955: Central Radiator**–Ken Peifer, later moved to 1 E State St, Geneva

Grand Opening & Chamois Cloth promotion, "soak in water and clean your windows streak–free." A nostalgic gift from Earl Judd to the author when Earl retired in 1980.
FIGURE 5.30 & 5.31 Courtesy *Batavia Herald* & Bentz family.

- **1956–80: Judd's Texaco**–Ph TR9–7620 Earl L. Judd later joined by his son, Neil Judd. Earl's career dates to 1938 with his venture as a Cities Service station on north Bennett street in Geneva. In 1942, Earl went to California to work in WWII Douglas aircraft plants. Returning in January 1946, he took a position with Avenue Chevrolet in Batavia. He had also been service manager at Wheaton Ford, Aurora Motor Sales (Ford) then in 1953–56, Fanning Chevrolet in Geneva, and then this Texaco station in Batavia.
- **1980–82: Rothecker's**–Jon E. Rothecker
- **Year unknown: Batavia Transmission**
- **2016–present: Karl's Auto Repair**

200 EAST FABYAN PARKWAY, & ROUTE 25

- **1960's–75: Dog 'n Suds**–Ray & Geraldine Morrison, later at Twin Elms.
- **1976–1987: Pride**–Thomas Hughes with sons, Tony and Mike. Started the Pride brand at Warrenville in 1965, sold 9 locations to Phillips 66 in 1986.
- **1991: Phillips 66**–Jennifer Fitzgerald
- **Year unknown: Shell**

710 EAST FABYAN PARKWAY

- **Current: 7/11–Mobil**

"FILLING STATION BLUES"

submitted by Lyle Miller to the
Geneva Republican February 27, 1931

This one comes for water
That one comes for air,
This one wants directions,
I'm no millionaire.
That one wants the rest room,
This one wants a stamp,
That one seeks a pleasant
Spot where he can camp.
All the local idlers
Decorate my stools.
All the local grafters
Utilize my tools.
Many cars go speeding
O'er the road like glass–
Maybe someday one
Will drive in for gas.

SIX

BATAVIA WEST SIDE

373 SHUMWAY/ISLAND AVENUE
- **1964–2002: Chuck's Garage**–Charles E. Beckman Jr. was supplied **Cities Service** gas from Feece Oil, his location prior to this he was at L. R. Johnson on Rt. 25 1957–1964.
- **2002:** Sold to his son, Dennis Beckman.

WEST WILSON (51 W WILSON)
- **1928: John Peterson Livery/Garage**–Ph 1571.
- **1936: Petty & Rimkus Garage**–Noble I. Petty & Anton Rimkus.

147 WEST WILSON & NORTH WATER
(59 W. Wilson)
- **1924–27: Tom Joyce Garage**–Ph 1402 Joyce became the Ford dealer on Batavia Avenue and my grandparents rented a portion of his home on

Washington. In 1920, he was a **Nash** and **Marmon** dealer on north second street in St. Charles.

- **1940–41: Anderson Motors–Plymouth/Desoto–**George Anderson & Harry Paver–Livery barn between old RR station and pond.
- **1948: Norm's Garage–**Norman Anderson, moved to Webster & Prairie St.
- **1950–1966: Wally's Body Shop–**Walter Stephano Jr. Garage was destroyed by fire.

217 WEST WILSON (77 W. WILSON)

- **1924–25: Batavia Bicycle and Electric Shop–**Sold Motorcycles.
- **Current:** Olmsted's TV & Appliance.
- **Carlson Texaco 51 S address changed to 101 S Batavia Avenue about 1948**

FIGURE 6.1 Photo Courtesy Batavia Historical Society.

101 SOUTH BATAVIA AVENUE (51 S. BATAVIA AVE.)

House w/Canopy Style–Figure 4.1

- **1860's: Moore & Buck Store/Post Office–**Amos M. Moore postmaster
- **1929: Lally's Service Station–**Edmund Lally
- **1930–50: Carlson Texaco–**Walter Clarence Carlson, Ph 3480. In 1934 Walter married Hilma Frydendall.

FIGURES 6.2 & 6.3 Courtesy Bentz collection of *Batavia Herald* advertisements.

- **1950: Frydendall's Service**–Vern Frydendall, step–son, took over when Walter Clarence Carlson died January 17, 1950. Same staff; Bob & Vern Millett, Dale Winter & William Lundeen, the latter two were part–time. Gerald "Jerry" Jobe, mechanic, joined in October.

Lee Wallis Texaco. FIGURE 6.4 Photo Courtesy Batavia Historical Society.

- **1951–60: Lee's Texaco**–Lee Wallis Ph 3480/5440– employees: Frank Ledbetter, Laverne "Tootie" Millett, Jerry Jobe, Harold "Lindy" Lindgren, (Lindy later had Shell on Lake and Illinois in Aurora), Lee Hinkle, Ronnie Briggs. Wallis also acquired a second Texaco location in Geneva about 1952.

FIGURE 6.5 Courtesy May 1954 *Batavia Herald*.

FIGURE 6.6 Courtesy Bentz collection of *Batavia Herald* advertisements.

- **1961–63: Abe & Doc's Texaco**–John 'Abe' Lincoln and William 'Doc' Dreymiller purchased after Wallis died in 1960. Their spouses, Lois Lincoln &

Maxine Dreymiller were sisters. In 1964 they built the Phillips 66 across the street when George G. Guy & Son Filling Station w/Fred Larson Lunchroom was demolished.

- **1963–64: Hickernell's Texaco Service**–Lee and Frank Hickernell (Aurora residents)
- **1964–69: Pavlack Bros**–Carl & Art Pavlack, Wally Jeske employee. Carl had previously been Carl's Shell in Geneva. Carl later managed Goodyear store in Aurora.
- **1969–73: Wally's Texaco**–Wally Jeske
- **1973: Jim's Texaco**–James Moore 879–9643
- **1973–83: Batavia Texaco**–Albert C. McDonald
- **1984: Pour Richard's Liquor Store**–Richard "Dick" Ernzen. Currently being remodeled to a restaurant.

101 South Batavia Avenue, 1984 Remodeling underway for conversion to Pour Richards liquor store. FIGURE 6.7 Courtesy Ernzen family.

1916 post card A. E. & C. electric train station signage at the new high school on the corner.
Also, a local garage sign with hand pointing south to what would be Batavia's first garage,
previously Null Garage and now operated by Foster.
FIGURE 6.8 Courtesy C.R. Childs postcard

108–116 South Batavia Avenue (56–58–62) 1907 site of garage building, blacksmith shop and
a separate livery, which eventually merged into Abe & Doc's current location on east side of
street. The genealogy of these separate business sites becomes complicated
with overlaps, separations and combinations through the decades.
Refer to FIGURE 1.8 to see Carl More in his Stutz Bearcat in front of theses
storefronts. FIGURE 6.9 Courtesy Batavia Historical Society

108 SOUTH BATAVIA AVENUE (56)

- **1907–1909: Korte and Opperman Garage**–August Korte and Max J.
  Opperman were the earliest 'machinists' on record operating as an automotive garage in Batavia. The Batavia Depot Museum was able to find this

article in an April 1, 1909 edition of *Motor World:* "August Korte and Max J. Opperman have sold their garage and repair shop on South Batavia Avenue, Batavia, Ill, to J.A. Null & Son, who also conducts a business in Saybrook, Ill. Opperman will continue with the establishment as machinist."

Martin O. Nelson started a plumbing business in 1909 and this is a quote in the Batavia Historian from his son Bussy Nelson; "When my dad first started in (plumbing) business, automobiles had just come out, and he took Leo Opperman's father into partnership as an auto mechanic. There were only a couple of autos in town, however, so he didn't have much work, while my dad had most of the plumbing business in town. Finally, my dad got tired of splitting the profits with Opperman and disbanded the partnership." I am reaching a bit to assume this Opperman with no first name, is the same as the Opperman who partnered with Nelson, and was listed as "M.J. Opperman" on State Street in 1919, and then Max Opperman on Main Street in 1920–21.

- **1910: James A. Null Garage**–also a car dealer. Sold in November to Frank Anderson of Aurora and Roy Foster of Lee, IL with Foster in charge.

FIGURE 6.10 Courtesy *Prairie Farmer Directory of Kane County*

- **1911–1918: Foster Garage–Roy W. Foster, with Robert L. Guy** as a partner in 1914 selling **Oakland and Overland** automobiles. **Buick** dealer in 1917. Guy then joined the Army in November 1917. Sanborn Insurance map reveals a 420–gallon underground gas tank in 1916.

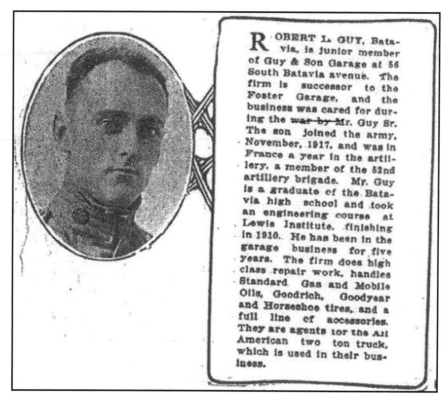

ROBERT L. GUY, Batavia, is junior member of Guy & Son Garage at 56 South Batavia avenue. The firm is successor to the Foster Garage, and the business was cared for during the ~~war by~~ Mr. Guy Sr. The son joined the army, November, 1917, and was in France a year in the artillery, a member of the 52nd artillery brigade. Mr. Guy is a graduate of the Batavia high school and took an engineering course at Lewis Institute, finishing in 1910. He has been in the garage business for five years. The firm does high class repair work, handles Standard Gas and Mobile Oils, Goodrich, Goodyear and Horseshoe tires, and a full line of accessories. They are agents for the All American two ton truck, which is used in their business.

Aurora Beacon News Nov 30,1919 'Progressive Men and Women of Batavia'.
FIGURE 6.11 Courtesy Batavia Historical Society.

- **1917–31: (56–58 S. Batavia Ave.)–Guy's Garage–Sinclair,** later **Standard Gas–**George & Robert L. Guy, also known as Guy & Son Garage. Ph 1409. Even though there was already a 420–gallon gas tank at their current location, the business was doing so well that in 1920, they decided to expand by building a new filling station next door and operating an **Oldsmobile** dealership in their current location. They then purchased their garage building from their landlord as well as the adjacent blacksmith and livery buildings. In 1928, George died and then in 1931, Robert succumbed to injuries from being crushed between two trucks. After their deaths, the garage building was split from the filling station making two separate businesses.

Paving of the Lincoln Highway. "Authorized Buick Dealer" sign now hangs from former blacksmith shop and curbside gas pump is visible in front of Guy & Son Garage sign.
FIGURE 6.12 June 10, 1923 photo Courtesy Batavia Historical Society.

This 1918 photo of Guy's Garage was supplied to the Herald by William Davis in 1952, a week prior to this 108 (56) S. Batavia Ave. building being razed.
FIGURE 6.13 Courtesy 1954 *Batavia Herald*.

- **1932–35: (56) Jack's Garage Plymouth & DeSoto**–L.E. "Jack" Frost, Ph 1409 He also acquired **Buick** some time, probably when Scoop Clark dropped the line during the Depression.
- **1936–37: (56) Johnsen Motor Sales Buick & Pontiac**–Raymond Johnsen
- **1938: (56) Anderson Motor Sales–Plymouth–DeSoto**–George M. Anderson & Harry W. Paver Ph 1926
- **1939: (56) Peterson Motor Sales**

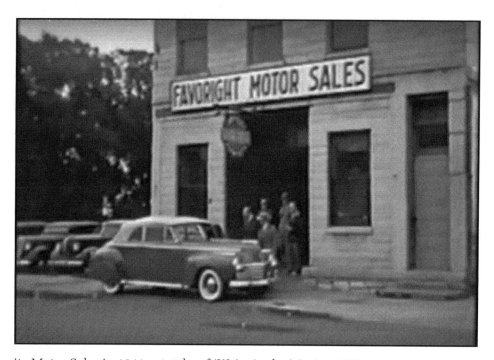

Favorite Motor Sales in 1941 out–take of 'We're in the Movies.' FIGURE 6.14 Courtesy 'We're in the Movies.' Favoright Motor Sales was shown in the 1941 Batavia film "We're in the Movies" a John B. Roger film production. Many Batavia landmarks are shown along with O.T. Benson's Phillips 66 next door to the south, and Maurie's Standard Oil Service. This 1941 film is available for viewing in 5 segments on YouTube.

- **1939–42: (56) Favoright Motor Sales–Chrysler/Plymouth** Laurence T. Favoright
- **1943–49: (56) Leonard Cash Garage**–Lenny later went to work for Clark Bros Pure Oil in Geneva and stayed there for decades.

108 SOUTH BATAVIA AVENUE (FORMERLY 56 S. BATAVIA AVE.)

- **1950–52: Batavia Motor Sales**–Walter G. Braken used cars.
- **1952–53: Aurora Motor Sales–Ford, Batavia Branch**–Ph 5397, Al Cory–Sales. The Batavia City Council granted the original permit for this business and notified the business that the permit was expired October 1952.

They were ordered to vacate and demolish the building. In August 1953, the company was purchased by Owen Kane.

The caption attached to this 1952 demolition photo states that the oil company (Phillips 66) was in negotiations for this property. Those negotiations must have failed, because the car dealership later operates on the vacated lot. In 1955, Ted Larson the Phillips 66 dealer, moves from the outdated station next door to a new location in St. Charles.
FIGURE 6.15 Courtesy 1952 *Batavia Herald*.

Aurora Motor Sales operating on the former site of the building.
FIGURE 6.16 Courtesy December 1952 *Batavia Herald*.

- **October 1953: Kane Ford–Batavia Branch–**Owen Kane, owner, with Tom Joyce and Bill Weber in sales.

Larson's Phillips 66 & Batavia Coffee Shop c. 1953 These are the former sites of the smithy on the left and the livery on the right. FIGURE 6.17 Photo Courtesy Batavia Historical Society.

114 SOUTH BATAVIA AVENUE (58, LEFT SIDE OF BUILDING)

- **1883–97: Gustaf Peterson Blacksmith–**moved to 14 South Jackson
- **1908–17: Pomp & Peterson Blacksmith Shop–**Pomp moved to Island Avenue across from the theatre building.
- **1920–31: Guy & Son–**built this filling station when they acquired the livery property to the south of their garage building.
- **1932–44: Benson's Phillips 66–**Oscar T. (O.T.) Benson, assisted by Paul "Sinky" Hendrickson. Ph 1812. In August, 1944 O.T. became Batavia Police Officer, and Paul eventually opened the Popcorn Stand.
- **1944–48: Larson's Phillips 66–**Ted & Dick Larson–Ph 3484, this location had a single outside hydraulic lift for repairs.
- **1949–55: Larson's Phillips 66–**Ted Larson, Ph BAtavia 3484 moved to a new Phillips 66 location with 2 repair bays on East Main street in St. Charles.

116 SOUTH BATAVIA AVENUE (62, RIGHT SIDE OF BUILDING)

- **1900–15: (62 S.) Artlip & Gilikson's Livery**
- **1916–17: (62 S.) Wheeler & Sons Avenue Livery**
- **1930: (62 S.) Batavia Sandwich Shop–**J.V. Anderson
- **1933: (62 S.) Batavia Café–**Steve Demakes & Steve Panos *"located on the Lincoln Highway with the convenience of filling station next door"*.

- **1939–42: (62 S.) Batavia Coffee Shop**–Alex Fillis, September 4, 1942 announcement: Closed weekdays for duration of war.
- **1956: (62 S.) Bergeson–Milke Men's Clothing**–probably in the diner location
- **1956–58: Carnation Motor Sales**–Clarence Augsburg
- **1964: building demolished and new facility for Abe & Doc's was built.**

FIGURES 6.18 & 6.19 Courtesy Bentz collection of *Batavia Herald* advertisements

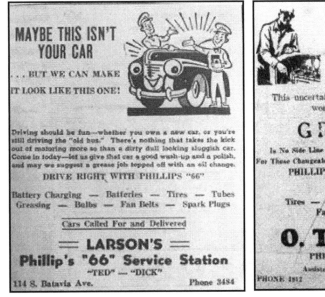

FIGURES 6.20 & 6.21 Courtesy Bentz collection of *Batavia Herald* advertisements

Abe & Doc's, Batavia's first modern pump canopy. There had been a canopy on the old Texaco. FIGURE 6.22 Photo Courtesy Batavia Historical Society.

108-116 SOUTH BATAVIA AVENUE (58, 60, 62)

- **1964–1988: Abe & Doc's Phillips 66**–Abe Lincoln & Doc Dreymiller
- **1964–82: Abe & Doc's Phillips 66–Abe Lincoln and Doc Dreymiller**
- **1982–November 2020:** Abe & Doc's Goodyear–Mark Lincoln and Bill Dreymiller cease selling **Phillips 66** and **SUNOCO** gas in 1988. Dean Ekstrom, son of Farmer Ekstrom, was a mechanic here before setting up shop in Wisconsin. Mark and Bill just retired with the sale of the property to a tire store chain.

William 'Doc' Dreymiller and John 'Abe' Lincoln circa 1963

From left to right, Lois (Abe's wife), Bill (Doc's son), Mark (Abe and Lois' son), and Jason Eads (worked here since '98). We recently lost John "Abe" Lincoln February 9. 2020 and Maxine Dreymiller at the age of 100 years in 2020.
FIGURE 6.23 & 6.24 Courtesy at Abe & Doc's Service.

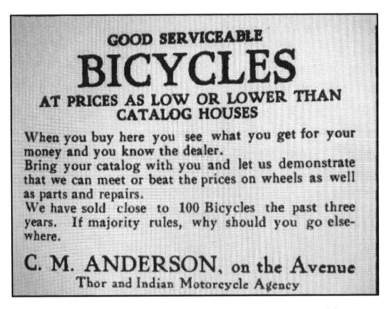

FIGURE 6.25 1915 advertisement *Batavia Herald*

(71) SOUTH BATAVIA AVENUE

West side of street

- **1910–1916: Carl Anderson Motorcycle Shop and Tire Vulcanizing–**Fire destroyed business. He then built garage on Main Street and eventually went to work for Tri–City Garage in Geneva. Other advertisements in 1913, tout the **Thor** and **Indian** motorcycles, with the **Thor** being manufactured in Aurora. Later the Pierson Grocery on the north side of the alley.

130 SOUTH BATAVIA AVENUE (68 S)

On the East side of the street

- **1875: H. H. Williams Greenhouse**
- **1913: Henry Wenberg Home:** burned down Feb 1, 1913
- **1905–26: Ethel Alexander Millinery** (one house south of Wenberg) Ethyl Alexander later operated Millinery shop on Geneva's Third street, closing June 30, 1952.
- **1928–31: Funk's Service Station (Shell)–**William H. Funk–Ph 1528, see second location listed below.
- **1931: Lord Filling Station–**F.S. Lord Ph 1423
- **1932: TYDOL Filling Station–**Spencer Omick
- **1935–36: Omick's Sinclair–**Spencer Omick
- **1936–40: Omick & Omick Conoco–**McCrea 'Mac" & son, Spencer
- **1940–44: Omick's Sinclair Service Station–**Spencer Omick

Free road maps represented some of the earliest forms for promoting brand loyalty. When a motorist would open the glove compartment, one of the first things to greet them would be the familiar company name and logo to remind them of the brand represented by their trusted mechanic at home. The other subtle messages on the outside of the map would include light engine repair with oil and lubricating services, where available, wherever the branded sign was displayed. Rand McNally promotional slogan to the dealers was to, "Put Your Sign Post in His Pocket," so the customer would carry your company logo with them everywhere.

137 SOUTH BATAVIA AVENUE (79 S)

On the West side of the street, one building south of old Revere House Hotel.

- **1925–28: Funk's Tire Shop–**Ph 1598, William H. Funk, had purchased William Spencer's vulcanizing business and moved it here from 30 E Wilson. Sold tire vulcanizing services, Shell gas & oil, utilizing a curbside pump.

Funk's Shell Road Map "Both sides of Lincoln Highway in Batavia."
FIGURE 6.26 Courtesy of the Walter Pierson Family

144 SOUTH BATAVIA AVENUE

(70 S) Batavia's oldest purpose–built gas station
- **1917: Batavia Greenhouse Company**
- **1924–25: Geise Oil & Gas**–Standard built in 1924–Frank Seavey, manager
- **1928–29: Standard Oil Co.**–Weldon Hopkins
- **1932–38: Stan's Standard Service** (76 S. Batavia Ave.)–Stanley S. Heeg

Maurie's Standard in 1941 out–take of 'We're in the Movies.'
FIGURE 6.27 Courtesy 'We're in the Movies.'

- **1939–43: Maurie's Standard**–Maurie Johnson, and employee Don J. Anderson, both left for WWII. Don was later reported 'Missing in Action'.
- **1944: Ford's Standard Service**–Stanley Ford

FIGURE 6.28 *Courtesy Batavia Herald*

- **1944: Fadness & Miller Standard Service**
- **1945: Mac's Standard Service**–T.W. McDonald Sr, T.W. Jr, & Charles McDonald Ph 3464.
- **1946–49: Maurie's Standard**–Maurie Johnson was back from serving in WWII.

144 S. Batavia Ave.–Flaherty's Standard with 1953 construction started behind current building. FIGURE 6.29 Courtesy Batavia Historical Society.

- **1950–58: Flaherty's Standard–**Bill Flaherty, Ph 1468, with the station being rebuilt in 1953. Jack Glenn and Gene Glasco, mechanics; Bob White and brother, Paul White, were high school attendants and brothers to White Bros Trucking, Joe and Chuck, in Wasco.

  Note the architectural style of the tile–roof. The original yellow brick building is consistent with that used by Standard. The one–bay enclosure is a separate addition to the site. The third phase, in 1953, is evident with the steel framework behind the building that is the new construction underway for the two–bay white porcelain Standard Oil that Flaherty, and then Bentz Bros. would later occupy. There would still be room between the Standard and the new A&P building next door to accommodate an outside electric drive–on hoist. The GMC truck in the background could be the one acquired by Bentz Bros. as a service truck since it was customary to purchase all of the previous owner's inventory and equipment with the truck passing from Flaherty to Bentz.

Segment of a full page 1955 advertisement announcing Batavia's most modern service station is now available 24–hours every day. FIGURE 6.30 Courtesy May 1955 *Batavia Herald*.

Bill Jr, Bill Flaherty, Paul White, George...
FIGURE 6.31 Courtesy *BHS Echo Yearbook*

FIGURE 6.32 Courtesy April 1959 *Batavia Herald*

- **1958–59: Ron's Standard–**Ron Schietlin, Ph 5427, first of 5 different locations for Ron over his career.

When Archie and Bernard chose to go into business as Bentz Bros. Pure Oil in Batavia in 1959, they did such a good job at that low–traffic location that their competitor, Standard Oil, took notice. In a matter of months, Bentz Bros. entered into a Standard Oil contract for the location on the Lincoln Highway, 144 South Batavia Avenue. How many of you remember the promos of the 50's and 60's? "A free steak knife with every fill–up (over 8 gallons please)", or how about place settings of real china, and then there was the introduction of the Sperry and Hutchinson trading stamps...S&H Green Stamps. Bentz Bros. biggest promotion of all was a 1964 Amphicar which we as a family drove down the Batavia Boat Club ramp, through the river and onto Duck Island! Customers received one free entry to win the boat/car with every fill–up of 8 gallons or more. FIGURE 6.33 *Courtesy October 29, 1959 Batavia Herald.*

- **October 1959–67: Bentz Bros. Standard**–Archie Bentz and Bernard Bentz, TR9–5427. Mechanic, Ben Chesley, was a former partner in Ben & Lou's in Geneva. This station was the beginning of Bentz Bros. expansion into multiple locations. In 1967 when it came time to re–build a new Standard Oil station for Bentz Bros. at their 27 North Batavia Avenue location, the company required Bentz to surrender their lease at this station. Standard then sold this property with a 99–year condition that Archie Bentz could never own the property in order to limit his future competition from this location with any other brand of oil company.

FIGURE 6.34 Photo from Author's collection

Glass globe pump toppers in the shape of crowns that were used by Standard Oil. Those globes would come in various colors; Blue was for an Economy sub–regular, Red for Regular, and solid White for Premium 1941–56, then Gold was Premium 1956–61. Grey was Diesel 1956–61, Orange for Aviation, and Green for Naphtha White Gas. In 1962 Standard instructed their dealers to remove the globes because they no longer reflected a modern image. Archie removed the globes and stored them by an outside tire rack and someone threw used tires on top of the fragile glass. Those globes are worth $500–1,000 each to collectors today.

In photo 6.35 longtime memorable employees, Roy Hadley and Stan Dunn, had just finished with a truck load of Atlas tires. Back then, tires were wrapped in paper to maintain a fresh rubber product and to protect the vulnerable whitewalls from scuffs. Note the 1956 Buick Bentz Bros. Courtesy Car, loaned to customers while their car was serviced, and one of the yet to be broken glass pump toppers to the left, behind the Buick.

Hadley undoubtedly went to the Coke machine right after this picture. He would always challenge others to the Coke geography game. Every bottle would have the City/ State of the bottler stamped into the bottom of glass bottle. Your geography lesson started with determining whose bottle was from the furthest distance. . .that person paid for the 10 cent Cokes. Sometimes disputes would be settled using the free "As You Travel, Ask Us" roadmaps.

Bentz Bros. Standard. Roy Hadley and Stan Dunn unloading a delivery of tires.
FIGURE 6.35 Photo courtesy Bentz family.

I returned home from school one day to find our 2-car garage at home stacked to the rafters with a similar load of tires and was told it would be my job to sort and stack them by size and product line: AMOCO 120, Plycron, Bucron, GripSafe and snow tires. A 1963 newspaper ad touted, "1542 Atlas tires in stock; Batteries $8.95 & up; Tune-up $5.50 including points, condenser, spark plugs, and labor...8 cyl $2 more." Another ad, promoted, "Over $40,000 in tires on sale."

This is a photo is out of a Standard Oil Training Packet where Bentz Bros. were featured as an example of how Bentz made it very apparent they were in business to sell TBA (Tires, Batteries, and Accessories). FIGURE 6.36 Courtesy Bentz family.

3 Bentz brothers and a nephew. Bernard Bentz, Archie Bentz, Jerry Mason, Thryselius and John Bentz. FIGURE 6.37 Photo courtesy Bentz family.

Another memory of mine is that on the south side of the building there were two underground tanks that were outfitted with hand pumps. One was for kerosene and the other was naphtha, more commonly known as white gas. White gas was still used for lawnmowers and outboard engines. I would remove the lid, hang the handle of the can on the spigot and pump the can full for 12 cents. FIGURE 6.38 Photo courtesy Bentz family.

FIGURE 6.39 Courtesy Bentz family archives

A HISTORY OF BENTZ BROS.

The Bentz Bros. name started with Pure Oil then moved to a career with Standard Oil starting at the 144 S. Batavia Ave. location which became the nucleus for their rapid expansion. Bentz Bros. grew their name into the largest Standard Oil operation in Illinois, Indiana, and Wisconsin. This included the following 5 Standard Oil locations in the 1960's:

- **144 South Batavia Avenue, Batavia**
- **Illinois and Lake Street (Rt. 31), Aurora:** managed by Bernie Bentz
- **Corner Broadway (Rt. 25) and Illinois, Aurora**: owner/manager, John Bentz
- **East Galena and Oak Street, Aurora**
- **27 North Batavia Avenue, corner of Houston Street, Batavia**

In addition to the Bentz Bros. Standard Oil stations, Bentz Bros. also operated at least four other locations for Standard Oil Company, two in Aurora and two in Geneva, on four different occasions. The premise was that when a station closed, Bentz would operate the station until a new dealer was found, thus keeping the existing customer base accustomed to frequenting that business.

Bentz Bros. East Galena and Oak Street, Aurora, the largest Standard of Indiana Facility at the time. Note the new 1961 Bentz Bros. truck just purchased at Avenue Chevrolet.
FIGURE 6.40 Photo courtesy Bentz family.

East Galena and Oak Street, Aurora: 3–bay service station and full–service car wash. The Grand Opening was celebrated with over $5,000 in gifts and prizes along with a TV spot on the WGN nightly news with Fehey Flynn and P.J. Hoff, the weatherman. At this time five Bentz brothers were involved. Archie, Bernard, John, Fred, and Wallace.

I was twelve years old and worked as the 'towel–boy' on busy weekends when the car wash facility would turn out about 1,000 cars. My duties were washing and drying towels for the personnel detailing of the washed car. At a rate of over 100 cars per hour, keeping pace was quite a task with about 8 fresh towels needed for every vehicle.

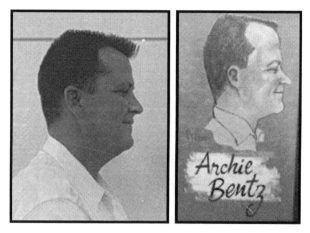

Polaroid photograph P.J. Hoff used as model for his chalk drawing presented to Archie as a memento of his night on the WGN News Hour. FIGURES 6.41 & 6.42 Courtesy Bentz family.

Family members who worked for Archie and Bernard at Bentz Bros.: John Bentz, Wallace Bentz, Fred Bentz, Clifford Mason, Robert Lee Mason, Dale Mason, Jerry Mason, John Bentz, Jr, Richard Myers, Brian Myers, Bill 'Butch' Clever, Bob White, Lois (Clever) White, Wayne Robbins, Archie 'Butch' Bentz, Jr, Gary Elwood, Bonnie (Bentz) Stratton, Paul Stratton, Connie (Bentz)Deal.

Longtime and/or memorable full–time employees: Ben Chesley, Glen "Farmer" Ekstrom, Bernie Kratsch, Stan Dunn, Rick Eckblade, Phil Weimer, Roy Hadley, Pete Whitt, Dewey "Mick" Wyatt, Dick Hughes, Quinion Rhodes, Bob and Jim Benson, Emil Punter, Chris and Rod McCleary, Steve Spears, Emil Smith...and numerous other Batavians as part–time employees. I apologize if anyone was omitted.

Aurora Beacon News–1961 Grand Opening East Galena at Oak St, Aurora.
FIGURE 6.43 Photo courtesy Bentz family.

Check out all of those new high–tech electric gadgets! The most advanced gadgets of the era would be COLOR TV and the Polaroid camera. The Bobo clowns were the plastic punching bags that would bounce back when punched because the bottoms were weighted.

Miss American Oil posing while Grand Opening flowers are delivered.
FIGURE 6.44 Courtesy Bentz Family archives.

To keep things in perspective, remember that $5,000 in door prizes would have equated to about two automobiles in 1961. Our children cannot relate to when we thought an electric toaster was a big deal. I can remember with extreme prejudice that some stranger was going to receive a brand–new boy's bicycle while I had an old used clunker.

A&P next to Bentz Bros. Standard on South Batavia Avenue.
FIGURE 6.45 Courtesy Batavia Historical Society

The Bentz Bros. legacy also included:
- **Bentz Bros. Car Wash, 618 South First Street, Geneva**
- **Bentz Bros. Studebaker, 315 Main Street, Batavia**
- **Bentz Bros. Garage, Houston Street, Batavia** (located behind the Standard Oil station)–Ben Chesley, chief mechanic and Glen 'Farmer' Ekstrom.

The IV Kings Restaurant and Cocktail Lounge in the former A&P.
FIGURE 6.46 Courtesy *BHS Echo Yearbook*.

- **1969–72 The IV Kings** restaurant with Archie & Bernard Bentz in partnership with Denny Piron and Bill Tosaw. Later, Bob White bought out Bernard's share and supervised the cocktail lounge. Archie oversaw the dining aspect of the restaurant.
- **1973–85:** Bernard and Wallace Bentz formed another partnership in **Bentz Bros. Amoco** in Seffner, Florida.
- **1977–1981: City of Batavia Mayor**–retired, Archie served the community as mayor with no potential conflict of active business interests.
- **1991–96:** Archie and Bernard Bentz owned and operated **Bentz Bros. Pronto,** Mountain Home, Arkansas.

South Batavia Avenue circa 1965, Bentz Bros. Standard in foreground, the Phillips 66 past the A&P on the right, would be the new Abe & Doc's and the Texaco on the left is Pavlack Bros. FIGURES 6.47 Courtesy Batavia Historical Society.

In 1961, Archie & Bernie purchased the old Moose Hall, the tall building on the right, to aid the lodge with funding for building the new Batavia Moose Lodge by Lincoln Inn. The $25k purchase price was less of a business investment and more of a philanthropic gesture to help fund the construction. This was later sold to Bader Publishing.

In 1962, Bentz saw the potential and wanted to replicate his Aurora Car Wash success in Batavia. At the same time, as a local businessman, Archie was invited to the Grand Openings of both the Holiday Inn and Hilton Inns on Route 31 in North Aurora. Inspired by meeting Conrad Hilton in person, Archie's new concept was to offer the Tri–Cities area a full-service car wash combined with a new Shell Oil contract, and a Holiday Inn at the location of the Osborne farm on the NE corner of Main Street and Randall Road. At that time the only overnight facilities, were mom–pop motels or outdated downtown hotels in the Tri–Cities, neither of which were available in Batavia. In 1963 Ed McArdle's Pheasant Run was just starting as a dinner/theatre with some rooms. That year also saw the expansion of Bentz Bros. into a Studebaker dealership which I cover when we are on Main Street.

On the subject of Randall Road, one needs to remember that in 1956 Randall Road did not exist as a complete north–south throughfare and some sections of were gravel road. To that point, the section between Rt. 64 and Alt. 30 (Rt. 38) passing by the Fox Valley Livestock Center (Kane County Fairgrounds) was called "Cut–Off Road".

By 1961, the rural north–south county road was a paved 65–mph two–lane county highway designed as the high-speed by-pass stretching the length of the Fox River Valley. To this point in time, the only development along this highway was in St. Charles.

In 1962, Archie Bentz had secured a contract to purchase the NE corner of Main Street and Randall Road, the site of June Osborne's horse farm outside Batavia. He also had in hand, contracts to construct a Holiday Inn and Shell Service Station with a full-service car wash.

While the property was outside the Batavia city limits, it fell within the 1½ mile radius area for which the city planners had control of future development and they denied that proposed commercial expansion on Randall Road. This was the beginning of decades-long battles between two distinct political groups: one in favor of residential homes on a 65-mph arterial highway in an effort to keep the residential "hometown feel;" while the opposing group believed that the planned growth of the community must include retail and commercial development since the downtown area was landlocked around a single bridge and the Fabyan Parkway bridge had yet to be constructed.

This prevailing opposition to development served as the impetus for Archie to seek the position of Mayor of the City of Batavia, not for personal gain, but to promote development outside of the downtown area. This would mean zoning Randall Road for retail on the west side and expanding the Kirk Road Industrial Park and future retail development on the east side.

A retired Archie Bentz was elected to the office of Mayor in 1977 and it was through his efforts that both Randall and Kirk Roads have been developed. The former service station operator was the visionary who possessed the business acumen and foresight to secure a healthy tax base on which to build his community.

1960 Aurora Beacon News 2-page ad sponsored by Standard for dealers from Batavia, Aurora, & Montgomery. FIGURE 6.48 Photo courtesy Bentz family.

I have included this copy of an ad from the summer of 1960 where the Standard Oil Company sponsored a 2-page tire sale advertisement including most of the dealers from Batavia south to Montgomery. I was eleven years old and can still relate to the names of Standard dealers often mentioned by my father. Bud Goding is at the top left of the ad. My father, Archie Bentz of Bentz Bros. is directly below Goding. Under the heading Paul's is Paul Rudiger with a location at Lake Street and Downer. He and his son, Bill, later bought out the Galena and Oak Bentz Bros. Car Wash location. The Probst Bros. were relatives by marriage to the Clever/Bentz family. Clarence 'Clancy' Carlson operated at 27 North Batavia Avenue and John Rothecker on East Wilson in Batavia. The Konen Bros., Erv and Rich, were on East New York Street. As I mention later in my Geneva history, Erv Konen later operated on East State Street, Geneva. Eddie Richardson is the name torn in the upper right corner.

There was an article in the Aurora Beacon News on April 13, 2018 about the closing of Goding's Marathon service station at 1150 Prairie Street in Aurora. One of the few remaining full-service gas stations in town that still worked on cars, the business was started in 1956 by the late George "Bud" Goding, whose son Mike took over the business more than three decades ago in 1987.

During the writing of this manuscript, Bill Rudiger of Paul & Bill's Car Wash retired and sold their location on East Galena and Oak where they had been in business since purchasing from Bentz Bros. in 1962.

144 SOUTH BATAVIA AVENUE, CONTINUTED

- **1968: Southland Corp (7-Eleven)**–no gasoline.
- **1973: Batavia Bank**–razed multiple businesses to construct their new facility. Along with this building they demolished the former Four Kings Restaurant (previously the A&P), Moose (previously the Knights of Pythias), Seneca Heat Treating, and the *Batavia Herald* Building.
- **Year Unknown: Chase Bank** acquired the building and is currently closed with the advent of on-line banking replacing live tellers.

BATAVIA LOCATIONS CONTINUED: 325 ELM STREET (135)

- **1925–36: Elm Garage**–Arthur H. Anderson
- **1925:** Arthur and brother, J. Edward Anderson (later Batavia Mayor), had a REO automobile agency in Aurora and opened a branch in Geneva. *Wikipedia*: "Ransom E. Olds was an entrepreneur who founded multiple companies in the automobile industry. In 1897 Olds founded Oldsmobile. In 1905 Olds left Oldsmobile and established a new company, REO Motor Car Company, in Lansing, Michigan." Since he could no longer use his name to

identify his automobiles, he used his initials.

- **1936–40: Anderson Garage** Arthur "Smash" Anderson, also a car salesman in Geneva and St. Charles, then in Real Estate and Insurance. Not to be confused with his son, Glen, who carried on the tradition with the family nickname "Smash".

SOUTH BATAVIA AVENUE & CARLISLE ROAD

- **1928–36: Carlisle Barbeque Stand and Gas Station–**Dewey Carlisle. Dewey was well known and appreciated for running a "soup kitchen" out of his station during the depression. Frank Mittman, attendant, Ph Batavia 1958.

315 Main Street (115–127 Main), the right side of building was the showroom.
FIGURE 6.49 Author's current photograph.

315 MAIN STREET (115–127 MAIN)

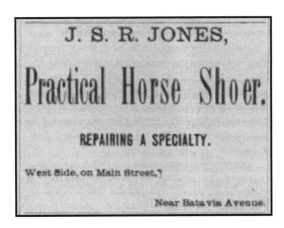

FIGURE 6.50 1894 Vox Alumni– Batavia High School yearbook

- **1894: J. S. R. Jones Blacksmith** on Main Street near Batavia Avenue.
- **1916–17: Blacksmith Shop**–Phils Hawley. A 1916 Sanborn map showed the 115 address as a garage next to the alley and 125 as a print shop with an open lot between. The garage had no gas tanks and an eight–car capacity at this time. Frank P. Smith credited Hawley with building *"the first tall bicycle in the city, it had wooden wheels like a buggy wheel."*

Jennifer Putzier, Director of the Batavia Depot Museum, found the obscure article in the Aurora Beacon News Nov. 30, 1919 titled *Progressive Men and Women of Batavia* to which I have made earlier references on Merrifield, Spencer, Opperman, Guy and now, Anderson. I want to point out that without this one article, all of our joint research would have missed the Opperman location on the east side of town. Until now, we had no record of C.M. Anderson at this location after the fire that burned down the Carl Anderson Motorcycle Shop on the Avenue in 1916.

The article calls out the address as 123 which was an empty lot per the Sanborn map reference above; so, I would conclude from this that Anderson was responsible for the construction of the building we still see today.

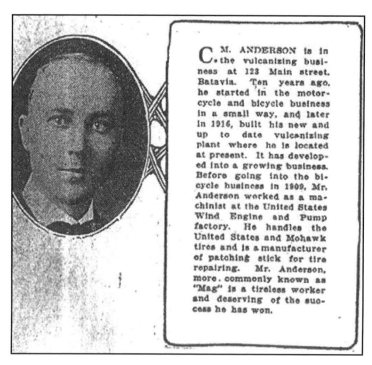

Aurora Beacon News November 30, 1919 'Progressive Men and Women of Batavia.'
FIGURE 6.51 Courtesy Batavia Historical Society.

Over the next half Century, this location was home to at least 9 dealer-ships selling no less than 23 brands of automobiles. While the garage faced

Main, the rear of the building, site of a former livery, offered a second business location in the same building.

FIGURE 6.52 1918 *Prairie Farmer Directory* for Kane County

- **1917–19: Anderson Vulcanizing–**C.M. 'Mag' Anderson (advertised as Main Street Garage in 1917 yearbook)
- **1919: Tri–City Broom Factory–**probably in the rear of building.
- **1920–21: Main Street Garage–**Max Opperman bought out Anderson.

     The Depot Museum discovered another *Motor World* article dated Nov. 28, 1921, "Garage owners are warned to be on the lookout for a swindler who pretends to be in quest of a good, paying business and who has a habit of tendering worthless checks in payment...Such an individual obtained $100 from a St. Charles, Ill. proprietor...The same man purchased the garage of Max Opperman of Batavia."

- **1922–23: Main Street Garage–**Richard Bergeson & Robert McGary. Bob later went to east side Texaco.
- **1924–28: Batavia Electric Station–**William Spencer & Willis Krause, probably in the rear of building.
- **1924–27: Lundeen Bros Hudson–Essex–**Possibly at this location, but I listed it at the Webster St address along with their **Studebaker** venture,
- **Year Unknown: Batavia Motor Co–**Ph 3010
- **1928–29: Lies Chevrolet Sales (125 Main)–**Alois M. Lies. Later re–opened on N River St.
- **1930–35: Main Garage (123 Main)** January 1, 1930–Scoop Clark & George Nelson, former employees of Tom Joyce Ford. They initially sold **Hudson/Essex** which was later dropped in favor of **Pontiac/Buick** in 1932. Then in 1935 they became **Chevrolet** when moving to Batavia Avenue. The following quote is Don Clark talking about his father, Scoop, in the *Batavia Historian,* "A young man by the name of Leo Opperman came to Dad and said he had done all of the monkey business he wanted and had been to California. He had worked for Dad previously at the Ford Dealership (Tom Joyce Ford) so

Dad hired him in late 1930 or 1931." Leo worked for Scoop for about 50 years as shop foreman.

- **1933: Spencer Main Street Garage, (123 Main)–**John Stenman, in rear of building.
- **1935–36: Tom Joyce Motors–Ford,** Ph 1402 Previously on the Avenue, rumors about town were that Joyce supplied the fast Ford V–8 for bootleggers and saw a rapid downturn in business with the repeal of prohibition. . . I repeat, rumors. In 1934 he had a brief stint as a **Chrysler** dealer in the Warber building in Geneva.
- **1936–39: Brandow & Watt Ford–**the date is from the memory of Lloyd Kautz with the purchase of his 1936 Ford Delivery Truck for $676 in 1936. *Source: Batavia History Museum*
- **1940–41: Main Street Motors–Ford, Mercury, Lincoln/Zephyr–**Stewart Cooper Ph 3011 Cooper was also the Ford dealer in Geneva.
- **1947–61: Batavia Pattern Works–**John Ahlgren & son, John Wilbur Ahlgren. They owned the building and leased the front to the various car dealers while operating the pattern works in the rear portion. The family continued ownership of the building for decades.
- **1950: Stern's Auto Body–**Marty Stern, Ph 3096
- **1952–56: Del Manning Inc.–Chrysler Plymouth new & used cars,** Del 'Manny' & Grace Manning, Al Cory salesman. Ph 3700

Looking west on Main, Chrysler–Plymouth signage of Del Manning.
FIGURE 6.53 Courtesy *Batavia Herald* 1954.

1954 interior views of 315 Main that I later became familiar with as a Studebaker dealership.
FIGURES 6.54, 6.55 & 6.56 Courtesy *Batavia Herald* 1954.

A separate car lot fronted Batavia Avenue on the land that was the former site of Revere House. The sign was replaced with the one on the right. Later a new building on the former car lot was home to The Clothes Tree, Dr. Frank Nelson D.D.S. and the Benson, Mair, & Gosselin law firm. FIGURE 6.57 & 6.58 *Courtesy Batavia Herald.*

- **1957–62: Batavia Motor Sales–Chrysler Plymouth–Nash–Buick** Feb.1957– Orville W. & Lorraine Rosengren. In 1958 they added **INCA** *"Simca Aronde 4 door sedan, 40 mpg and 80 mph"* and **Triumph,** and then **Jaguar** by 1961. They later moved the dealership to Aurora.
- **1962–1994: Ryan Body Shop–**Dee Ryan leased the Pattern Works portion of the building from the Ahlgren family for over 3 decades.

FEATURED AT AGENCY — The new Bentz Brothers Studebaker Sales will feature this unique sliding roof Wagonaire station wagon by Studebaker, with all new 1964 styling. Basic roof design is carried in '64 models, but the sweeping front fender, hood and grilline lines add length and balance to the triple purpose utility vehicle. The new Batavia car agency will be located at 315 Main Street, and expects to open in one week.

Both the 1963 and 1964 Studebaker Wagonaire models featured a sliding roof converting the rear passenger area to cargo hauling. The tailgate was also equipped with a feature now utilized in many modern trucks; a fold–down step.
FIGURE 7.59 1963 *Batavia Herald* Courtesy Bentz family archives.

- **1963–64: 315 Main Street, Bentz Bros Studebaker**, Ph 879–5079. Bentz Bros. had leased the building in April in anticipation of their new Studebaker dealership, which was started October 1, 1963. The head mechanic, Ben Chesley, was a former partner in Ben & Lou's Jeep in Geneva. Phil Weimer was the salesman, and 14–year–old Archie Jr. was the part–time lot boy, responsible for detailing new and used cars.

  A popular Studebaker motor oil additive, sold as *Scientifically Treated Petroleum– "STP"*, was sold at all Bentz locations. One of the primary reasons for becoming a Studebaker Dealer, was the advanced engineering of the product lines in 1963–64, the Avanti, Gran Turismo Hawk, and re–designed Cruiser, Daytona, and Commander. Sporting a new cockpit–style padded wrap–around dash, many comfort features, a 289–cu–in Packard engineering inspired engine backed by a 3–speed automatic transmission, and available factory disc brakes That type of brake would not become available as a Corvette option for another 2 years, and Ford and GM transmissions still remained 2–speed for years to come. Another option offered by Studebaker was the R2 Paxton Super–Charger which could propel the Avanti R2 to a new land speed record of 159.2 mph for factory production. There were 72 new U.S. Auto Club records set by the entire line of Studebakers, including 132 mph for the R2 Super Lark/Daytona and 140 mph for the R2 Super Hawk.

  Then a good investment went bad when Studebaker ceased production in the U.S. after a UAW strike had sapped its financial reserves. It was rumored that the "Big 3" were threatened by the new Studebaker and that they influenced the strike in early 1963. Studebaker ceased operations on December 20, 1963 and after just 80 days in the dealership, Bentz Bros. Studebaker was no more. After Studebaker, the Bentz Bros. Garage stayed in operation facilitating major repairs that could not be performed in the smaller

2–bay station on the Avenue. In 1964, this operation was moved to 27 North Batavia Avenue behind the former Carlson Standard Oil building.

L–R: interior of Hawk, Daytona convertible, Gran Turismo Hawk.
FIGURE 6.60 Courtesy Bentz family archives.

The last Bentz Bros. Studebaker advertisement in January 1964.
FIGURE 6.61 Courtesy Bentz family archives.

This newspaper advertisement was the last for Bentz Bros. Studebaker in January 1964. People were skittish about buying Studebakers once the plant closed and existing inventory was sold for less than cost. Bernard Bentz offered his used 1962 Pontiac Bonneville for sale, (bottom of the list), and stated that between the last Studebaker, a Gran Turismo Hawk, and the Pontiac, whichever sold first, he would keep the remaining car. The two–year–old Pontiac sold for $500 more than the new Studebaker Hawk. The Hawk was sold to Arlene Bentz, Bernard's wife, as verified by the Studebaker Museum in 2016, FIGURE 6.60; along with a sedan sold to Ben Chesley's son, Alan. Below is my father's handwriting on the sales registration punch cards which now reside in the Studebaker Museum.

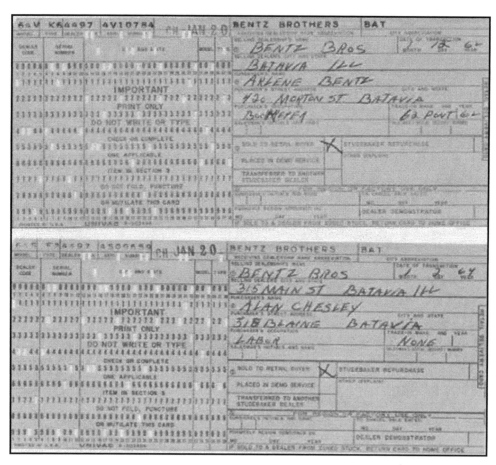

Studebaker punch card: Sales Registrations.
FIGURE 6.62 Photo courtesy Studebaker Museum.

- **1970's: Swanson Hardware Garden Shop**–The garage was later used as a lawn and garden facility with John Deere lawnmowers on display in the former Studebaker showroom in the right side of the building.

709 MAIN STREET

- **1989–2018: Ollie's Garage–**Ollie Beckman, Chuck Beckman's brother, now operated by Ollie's son Dave Beckman.

729 FIRST STREET

- **1985–98: Pete's Auto Repair–**Don "Pete" Peterson moved here after the CITGO on Main Street. Farmer Ekstrom made the move here with Pete.
- **Current: Village Auto Body**

FIGURE 6.63 1968 Yellow Page advertisement

750 MAIN STREET

- **1964–85 Pete's CITGO:** Don "Pete" Peterson moved here from east side Texaco when Feece Oil built a new station on their Main St warehouse property in the 1960's.

  Glen "Farmer" Ekstrom worked for Pete after previous employment with Avenue Chevy, Bentz Bros. Garage, Ben Hansford Chevrolet, and Shipley Distributing. His 55 years of wrenching had started with Avenue in 1945.
- **1985–91: Batavia CITGO–**Jeff Jones, cousin to Archie Bentz, Jr
- **1993–94: Bill's Batavia CITGO–**Bill Butz

750 Main Street, *Closed Batavia Citgo now owned by Scott Pederson.*
FIGURE 6.64 *Current Google Earth.*

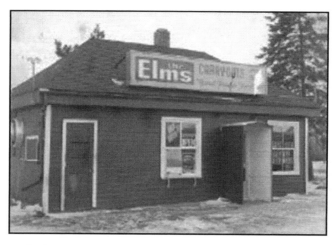

Former blacksmith shop and Twin Elms filling station converted to hamburger stand.
FIGURE 6.65 Courtesy Batavia Historical Society.

912 MAIN & WHIPPLE

- **1932–43: Twin Elms Service Station–**Alfred Thryselius, also a blacksmith & welder performing automotive repairs.
- **1943–56: Twin Elms Store & Gas–**Henry O. & Harriet (Maher) Carlson
- **1956–68: Twin Elms Restaurant–**Richie H. & Evelyn Benson
- **1968–1969: Twin Elms–**brothers Jeff, Mark, & Chris Voigt
- **1970–1975: Twin Elms–**Don Hable
- **1976–present: The Elms–**Raymond & Geraldine "Geri" Morrison. The Morrison's sold out the Dog 'n Suds on Route 25 to Tom Hughes for a Pride gas station about the same time Fabyan Parkway bridge was built. The Twin Elms building was changed to full restaurant venue sometime in the 1980's.

913 MAIN STREET

- **1950's–1960's: Weirich Salvage Yard–**Ray Weirich, a source of many local race cars and parts.

27 NORTH BATAVIA AVENUE

Former site of the James Derby home, later home to Bruce B. Paddock, then E.M. Oswalt.

Clarence Carlson Standard Service, 27 N Batavia Ave.
FIGURE 6.66 Courtesy *BHS Echo Yearbook*.

- **1953–64: Carlson's Standard–**Clarence "Clancy" Carlson Ph TR9–3100

October 1959, Carlson knew he had Bentz as competition with the same brand, so it was time for him to get aggressive with more advertising! FIGURE 6.67 Courtesy *Batavia Herald*.

- **1964–67: Bentz Bros. Standard–**Archie and Bernard Bentz bought out Carlson. They also purchased Carlson's 'fleet' of radio dispatched tow trucks (2) with a contract for towing disabled cars from the tollway.

I still remember the official call letters of the Motorola radio, "KBS–680, unit 24 calling base," which was always laughable as unit 24 was one of two trucks. The radio was very useful in cold weather when you were on the other side of town and could check in for any stranded motorists before heading back. We represented both Chicago A.A.A. Motor Club and AMOCO Motor Club which paid us about $3.00 for the service call to start your car or change a flat tire.

- **1964–68: Bentz Bros. Garage–**TR 9–5079. The garage was located behind the gas station facing Houston Street. Glen 'Farmer' Ekstrom from Avenue Chevrolet, joined mechanic Ben Chesley at this new location. In 1964, Bentz had acquired the State of Illinois Truck Testing Station from Avenue Chevrolet where Farmer had been the Illinois Certified Mechanic/Tester. In 1968, the garage business ended to make way for a new station building on this site; and the truck testing lane was moved to Bentz Bros. in Geneva. At this time, having worked with Bentz Bros. at three different locations since 1959, Chesley retired; and Farmer moved on to Hansford Chevrolet.
- **1968–71: Bentz Bros. Standard–**Archie & Bernard Bentz–Phone TR 9–3100 and they kept TR 9–5427 from the other location.

Bentz Bros. was in business at 144 S. and 27 N. Batavia Avenue with an overlap of the Studebaker Garage before relocating that operation to the building on Houston Street, behind the former Carlson Standard. FIGURE 6.68 1964 *Batavia Herald* Advertisement.

The proceeding ad was from the *Batavia Herald* newspaper. Take a moment and let those prices sink in! An 8–cylinder engine tune–up was $7.50 and that included both labor and parts. With 1,542 tires and hundreds of batteries in stock! The purchasing power of Bentz Bros. was to the point that other Standard Oil dealers would buy from Bentz at better prices than what their volume would allow them to purchase directly from Standard Oil.

New Bentz Bros. Standard constructed 1968. Note the phone booth in the foreground on the corner. The Standard Oil brass eagle on top of the cupola was often targeted by thieves. The previous building was a typical oblong white porcelain box, 2–bay station with additional pole shed garage behind it. The 1968 construction of this new 3–bay plus station located to the rear of the lot, resulted in the garage building being donated by Bentz and moved to the new high school to be used as the bus barn.
FIGURE 6.69 Photo courtesy Bentz family archives.

1968 Grand Opening–Bentz Bros.–One Year Free Gas! L–R: Archie Bentz, Pete Whitt, Pepper the Pony, kids unknown, Bernie Kratsch, and Archie Jr (Butch). Bernie Kratsch later went into business on Farnsworth Avenue in Aurora. There is that 1961 Chevy truck again in the background. FIGURE 6.70 & 6.71 Photos courtesy Bentz family archives.

Note that the gas island is designated as a *No Stamp Island* with a price posted which is lower than the other two islands. 1968 would be the stepping–off point with customer's understanding that the S&H green stamps were truly not free and that their cost was added to the overhead for the price paid for gasoline and repairs. I remember going to the S&H outlet to restock with stamps with a cost of over $500 for one roll for the dispenser. This island was later designated as the self–serve island.

- **1971–72: Batavia Standard**–Bentz sold on a one–year contract to Al Gaskil, a former Standard Oil Representative.
- **1972–73: Bentz Bros. Standard**–Archie regains control of the station when the above contract fails (Bernie had already relocated to Florida).
- **1973–77: Phil's Standard**–John P. 'Phil' Weimer, John Kerfoot, Fred Wasser, Emil Punter. Phil had worked for Bentz Bros. Studebaker as a salesman, purchasing the only Avanti sold there. Phil expanded to Geneva Car Wash and Montgomery Standard. Phil eventually relocated to Oregon, IL and had a successful operation of multiple Standard stations in the area.
- **1977–81: Emil's Standard**–Emil Punter had worked for Phil. He had Ronald Winter as a partner until 1980; Ralph Ledbetter managed a second location in Montgomery; and Jeff Jones, employee, was future owner of Batavia Citgo.
- **1981–2003: Batavia Amoco**–Stan Oke
- **2003: Batavia BP, January–June**–Stan Oke
- **2003–2010: Avenue CITGO**–Stan Oke

27 North Batavia Avenue is the last remaining Service Station in the Tri–Cities offering repairs and gasoline. FIGURE 6.72 Author's photograph.

- **2010–Present: Batavia Mobil**–Stan Oke, Mark Novak, Steve Oke, Alan Wolff, Chris Sainty, Raquel Ivie, Ed Celaya, and Bettye Hulsey.

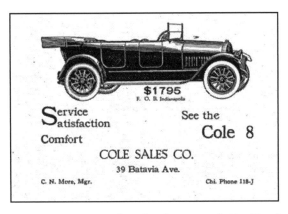

Advertisement from 1917 *Batavia High School Bee Aitch Ess Yearbook.* FIGURE 6.73.

Current Google Earth view from Batavia Avenue & Houston Street, the garage was built to facilitate. "Cole Automotive" behind Carl More's home. FIGURE 6.74.

113 NORTH BATAVIA AVENUE (39 N)

- **1915–17: Cole Automotive**–Carl N. More & Lundeen, possibly one of the brothers, Emil and Frank Lundeen, that opened Tri City Garage, Geneva in 1917. Later advertisements list only Carl More.

     There was an earlier photo of Carl Newton More and his Stutz Bearcat in FIGURE 1.9 and the following is an expansion on his passion for fast cars in the early 1900's. Carl was third generation Newton Wagon Works Batavia and had the means to pursue his passion which included this excursion as an automotive dealer for the Cole Motor Car Company. His home had a very substantial livery/garage that still stands on the alley behind his home from which he operated his Cole Automobile Sales. The Cole had one of the first V–8 engines, perfect for a young man seeking the thrill of speed. Mr. More lived in this same home until his death around 1980. This garage was not on the 1916 Sanborn map making it seem the garage had been constructed for the automobile

dealership and in the years to come, the loft supported his pigeon hobby. Today, the pigeon coup is still apparent over the former Cole Automotive garage at the rear of the home (Batavia Dairy buildings in the background).

Per Joe Burton in the Batavia Historian: "There were at least four Batavians who raised and raced pigeons. The four I definitely know raced were Sherman Anderson, John Van Burton, Carl More, and John Van Northwick, Jr. Each had his own loft and a flock of fifty or more birds. During the First World War, these owners as well as others all over the United States, gave homing pigeons to the Army which used them extensively to carry messages."

As the Cole Automobile Dealer in 1917, Carl has this promotional photo with the ladies posed in one of his automobiles that happens to be staged in front of the family homes. FIGURE 6.75 Courtesy Batavia Historical Society.

1917 Cole production included four different models all equipped with eight–cylinder V–type engines. 1) Model 860 seven passenger Touring Car $1,695.00 2) Model 861 four passenger Tuxedo Roadster $1,695.00 3) Model 862 seven passenger Toursedan $2,295.00 and 4) Model 863 four passenger Tourcoupe $2,295.00. 1916 was the first year that Joseph J. Cole used a Northway eight–cylinder V–type engine in one of his automobiles. This was about one year after Cadillac introduced its first Northway V–8 in an American automobile.

100–108 NORTH BATAVIA AVENUE

NE corner of Batavia Ave. & Houston St.
- **1968–77: Jerry's ENCO–**Gerald T. 'Jerry' Litney
- **1978: OK Oklahoma–**Lakeshore Petroleum–Gerald T. Litney
- **1978–82: Greg's Phillips 66–**Greg Cryer. Greg had been lead–mechanic

for the Sheriff's garage prior to this and later retired as Service Manager for Avenue Chevy after 28 years.

- **1983–1986: Quick–Fill–**Lakeshore Petroleum Convenience Store. Greg Cryer was the manager for the transition.
- **1987–89: White Hen Pantry/A–Plus Service, Road Ranger–**Deborah Julseth, Manager
- **1989: Phillips 66**
- **Current: Shell**

108 N. Batavia Ave., Current Shell Gas Station & former Avenue Chevrolet building on the right. FIGURE 6.76 2019 Google Earth view.

Smith Home, 24 N. Batavia Avenue, moved to North Jackson Street to make way for the construction of a new dealership/garage/gas station building.
FIGURE 6.77 Courtesy Batavia Historical Society.

24 NORTH BATAVIA AVENUE

SE corner of Batavia Ave. & Houston Street

- **1860s: Smith Home:** E.S. Smith, postmaster, father of Frank P. Smith. The home was moved to 231 North Jackson Street to make way for construction.
- **1925–34: Tom Joyce Ford Dealer–**Also a filling station, Tom Joyce Pres, William B. Joyce Treas, 'Scoop' Clark, service manager until 1930. Tom previously had been a **Nash and Marmon** dealer in St. Charles where he grew up.
- **1935–38: Main Garage–On the Avenue, Shell Gas, Chevrolet, Buick, & Pontiac,** William H. 'Scoop' Clark & George Nelson partners. Ph 1255. The depression brought on another partner/investor and in 1936 Carl Wright is listed as president and W.H. Clark sec/treas. They dropped Buick/Pontiac due to low sales during the depression.

    Batavia Historical Society: "A list of employees per Wendell Pitz, bookkeeper; "Leo Opperman, shop foreman; Bob Johnson, mechanic; Arnold Erickson, body man; Ernie Bartholomew, body man and mechanic; Bob Fowler, gas station; Carl Wright, salesman; and Walter McGary, salesman."

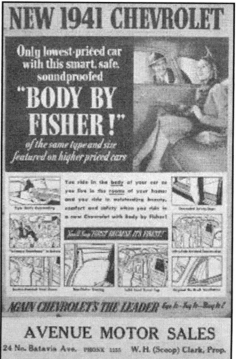

Late 1940 and early 1941, the country was recovering from the depression when Japan attacked Pearl Harbor December 7, 1941. All manufacturing turned to war production; civilian car manufacturing stopped on January 1, 1942 and no new automobiles could be purchased after February 22, 1942 and there were no more civilian motor vehicles until late 1945.FIGURES 6.78 & 6.79 Courtesy *Batavia Herald* archives.

With no new vehicles to sell, the emphasis shifted to maintenance to prolong the life of your car. Since civilians had to make five tires last the entire war, they had to conserve their trips and speed. People were encouraged to drive less; in fact, the primary purpose for nationwide gasoline rationing was to protect tires. May 4, 1942 a "Victory Speed" of 35 mph was instituted because tires wore half as quickly at 35 mph than at 60 mph. Slow and steady starts, stops, and turns were encouraged to reduce wear on tire treads. FIGURE 6.80 Courtesy *Batavia Herald* archives.

WIKIPEDIA ON THE OFFICE OF PRICE ADMINISTRATION DURING WORLD WAR II

"Tires were the first item to be rationed by the OPA, which ordered the temporary end of sales on 11 December 1941 while it created 7,500 unpaid, volunteer three–person tire ration boards around the country. By 5 January 1942 the boards were ready. Each received a monthly allotment of tires based on the number of local vehicle registrations and allocated them to applicants based on OPA rules. There was a shortage of rubber for tires since the Japanese quickly conquered the rubber–producing regions of Southeast Asia. Although synthetic rubber had been invented before the war, it had been unable to compete with natural rubber commercially, so the US did not have enough manufacturing capacity at the start of the war to make synthetic rubber. Throughout the war, rationing of gasoline was motivated by a desire to conserve rubber as much as by a desire to conserve gasoline."

"The War Production Board (WPB) ordered the temporary end of all civilian automobile sales on 1 January 1942, leaving dealers with one half million unsold cars. Ration boards grew in size as they began evaluating automobile sales in February (only certain professions, such as doctors and clergymen, qualified to purchase the remaining inventory of new automobiles). As of 1 April 1942, anyone wishing to purchase a new toothpaste tube, then made from metal, had to turn in an empty one." Now I understand why my parents had learned to brush their teeth with baking soda.

"To receive a gasoline ration card, a person had to certify a need for gasoline and ownership of no more than five tires. All tires in excess of five per driver were confiscated by the government, because of rubber shortages. An 'A' sticker on a car was the lowest priority of gasoline rationing and entitled the car owner to 3 to 4 US gallons of gasoline per week. 'B' stickers were issued to workers in the military industry, entitling their holder up to 8 US gallons of gasoline per week. 'C' stickers were granted to persons deemed very essential to the war effort, such as doctors. 'T' rations were made available for truckers. Lastly, 'X' stickers on cars entitled the holder to unlimited supplies and were the highest priority in the system. Clergy, police, firemen, and civil defense workers were in this category. A scandal erupted when 200 Congressmen received these 'X' stickers."

GENEVA REPUBLICAN JANUARY 30, 1942

"The gasoline service station operators and garages of Geneva, Batavia, and St. Charles are having meetings of the operators in these three towns to consider a plan to shorten the customary business hours to a maximum range of 7 a.m. to 7 p.m." (Remember over 25% of the stations were closing for lack of business.)

"...conservation of station operating equipment for longer life and... relief from long hours conserving the operating costs can be balanced with decrease volume of business."

"A government regulation put into law on Feb. 1,1943 prohibits all credit buying of gasoline by owners of private cars. It was expected that this action will prevent much bookkeeping by service stations and garages." There were stories before the rationing such as the fellow in St. Charles that "came to a filling station with a lawn roller that usually has water in it for ballast. He wanted the roller filled with gasoline. Another one is the fellow who brought a case of pop bottles to be filled with gas." "The hoarding of gasoline found stored in other than a 5–gallon, red painted cans, will be not less than $10.00 nor more than $50.00 for each day of the offense."

BATAVIA HERALD JANUARY 8, 1943 FRONT PAGE: "TIRE INSPECTION STATIONS"

"War Price and Rationing Board 6245.3 announces the appointment of Tire Inspection Stations under the Mileage Ration program, all appointments effective as of January 8, 1943".

"The tires of all trucks and buses must be inspected by January 15th and tires of all passenger cars by January 31st. Thereafter tires of trucks and buses must be inspected every two months or at the expiration of 5,000 miles of driving, whichever occurs first. Tires of cars for which a 'B' or 'C' books have issued must be inspected every two months and tires of cars with only an 'A' book must be inspected every four months."

"The stations for periodic inspections of passenger tires are: Avenue Motor Sales, Oscar T. Benson (Phillips 66) Service, Carlson's (Texaco) Service Station, Allan Case (Texaco), William C. Jeske (Pure) Service Station and Maurie's Standard."

"Stations for periodic inspection of truck and bus tires are Avenue Motor Sales and Maurie's Standard Service."

Here's 3,600 pounds of scrap rubber, ready for its part to beat the Axis powers. Rubber is being collected at all service stations in town and this photo was taken in front of the Deep Rock Station on North Batavia Avenue. Behind the pile of rubber are, left to right, Robert Koubenec, operator of a fleet of milk haul trucks (the source of the truck tires); Emil Lundeen, manager at the station; William H. "Scoop" Clark, proprietor of the Avenue Garage; and LeRoy Feece, Deep Rock distributor. The box in front contains rubber heels, a contribution from Joe O'Bolsky, the West Wilson street shoe repairman.
FIGURE 6.81 Courtesy 1942 *Batavia Herald* archives.

24 N. Batavia Ave., Avenue Chevy 1966, note the gas pump retained at the corner of the building and the older sign on the building. FIGURE 6.82 Photo courtesy of Batavia Historical Society and the Clark family—a complete article can be found in Batavia History, Oct 2000, Vol. 41, No. 4.

24 NORTH BATAVIA AVENUE

SE corner of Batavia Ave. & Houston St.), continued

- **1939–88: Avenue Motors–Chevrolet–**Scoop Clark, now sole owner, with son, Don joining the business in 1946. Donald W. Clark became sole owner with the passing of both his father, Scoop, and mother, Stella in 1975. Don's son, John W. Clark joined the firm in 1983. Glen 'Farmer' Ekstrom worked here from 1945–1965.

Early Sanborn maps show a separate gas station building in front of the dealership for greasing and oil changes along with three gas pumps:

- **1936–56: Deep Rock Service Station #1–**LeRoy H. Feece, agent; Ph 1911
- **1936–40:** William H. Krause, manager
- **1941:** Paul (Sinky) Hendrickson, manager, he went on to own Paul's Popcorn Stand on Wilson street.
- **1942:** Roy Phillips, manager
- **Sept. 1942–46:** Emil Lundeen, manager (former car dealer)
- **1947–49: Baumy's–**Ralph A. Baum, proprietor
- **1950–56** Allan Feece, manager, brother to LeRoy Feece. Allan left here to start his operate his own Shell station at 628 S First St in Geneva.

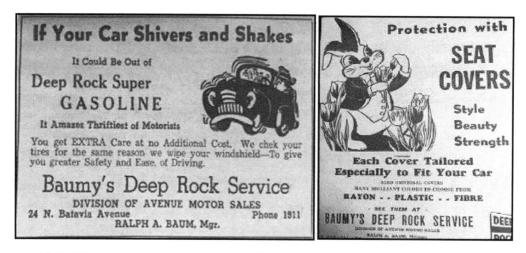

FIGURES 6.83 & 6.84 Courtesy Bentz collection of *Batavia Herald* advertisements

- **1956–58: Baumy's Deep Rock Service–Division of Avenue Motors–**Scoop Clark & Don Clark with Ralph Baum as Manager.

JFK on the campaign trail in downtown Batavia, Avenue Cities Service in the background.
FIGURE 6.85 Courtesy Hubbard family & Batavia Historical Society.

- **1958–64: Avenue Cities Service Station–**The Cities Service sign is visible over Kennedy's shoulder in this Hubbard home movie on October 25, 1960. Retail sales of gasoline ended there about 1964 but a pump was retained for company use.

1998 WEST MCKEE STREET

SE corners Randall Road and McKee Street
- **1988–2009: Avenue Chevrolet–**relocated to new facility at McKee Street & Randall Road until hard times fell on the mother–company, General Motors. The federal 'bail–out' funding was conditional on the elimination of what the government perceived as an over–population of dealerships. Avenue lost the Chevrolet franchise to this action in June of 2009.
- **2009–2011: Avenue Motor Sales–**Clark operated as an independent used car dealer while seeking other possible franchises, but this ended with the December 2011 closing of what had started as Main Garage in 1930 and encompassed four generations of operation over 82 years.

2074 MAIN STREET

SW corners West Main Street & Randall Road–Windmill Lakes 23–acre commercial center.

- • 1990: **Mobil Gas Station/Convenience Store/Car Wash**
- • 1990: **Landmark Car Wash**–full service, inside & out
- • 1990: **Jiffy Lube**

164 SOUTH RANDALL ROAD

Circle K Shell–*the very corner where Archie wanted a Shell station in 1962!*

200 NORTH RANDALL ROAD

NE corners Randall Rd. and McKee St.
- • 1993: **Amoco Gas Station/Convenience Store/Car Wash**
- • **Current: Pride of Batavia BP**

801 NORTH RANDALL ROAD

- • **Sam's Club/Walmart Gas**

Feece Oil Bulk Plant, corner of Houston and Water St. located directly behind Avenue Chevrolet. FIGURE 6.86 & 6.87 Photos courtesy Feece family.

35 NORTH WATER STREET

Originally home–based business at 174 Blaine Street
- • **1932–49: Deep Rock Oil Corp.** LeRoy H. Feece, agent with two retail service stations and a bulk plant under his supervision. He officed in the Avenue Chevrolet building along with operating the gas station at the same location. Early Sanborn maps indicate there was a smaller building with pumps located in front of Avenue Chevrolet. The building was eliminated, but the pumps remained until the early 1960's as seen in the above photo of JFK. Originally the pumps were Deep Rock, then Cities Service.

FIGURE 6.88 *Courtesy Batavia Herald. Offices located at 24 N. Batavia Avenue in the Avenue Chevrolet building*

- **1949–58: Feece Oil Co–Deep Rock–**LeRoy H. Feece, owner. To this point Roy had been an agent for the Deep Rock distributorship. Now he has made the big step of ownership in September of 1949.
- **1958–65: Feece Oil–Cities Service–**Dale, Roy's son, joins the company after graduating Batavia High School.
- **1964**: 750 Main Street warehouse location had the addition of a new retail Cities Service station.

Dale Feece about 1959–FIGURE 6.87 Courtesy *BHS Echo Yearbook*.

- **1965: Feece Oil Company–branded CITGO–**Roy passed in 1976 leaving Dale in charge.
- **1980: Feece Oil Company–**With Mayor Bentz's encouragement, Dale moved the bulk plant out of the downtown area to 1700 Hubbard Drive in Batavia's industrial park as both a bulk plant and retail sales.
- **2000: Feece Oil Company–**With Dale's untimely death, his wife Coleen, and children Mike, Troy, and Jill have managed the company since then.
- **2000–14: Feece Oil Company–branded Marathon**. Today Feece Oil Company operates as an independent with four bulk–facilities in Batavia, Minooka, Ottawa & Plano Illinois with retail convenience store locations in both Batavia and Minooka.

SEVEN

GENEVA WEST SIDE

In August 1912, it was announced that the Lincoln Highway, a new transcontinental route connecting New York to San Francisco, would pass through Geneva.

The highway would enter Geneva from the south on Batavia Avenue, northward up First Street to State Street, then head west to Kaneville and Keslinger roads. Geneva was soon to experience the resulting explosion of service stations along this route to accommodate travelers and tourists.

The *Geneva Republican* April 7, 1915 quotes Supervisor A.E. McIntosh when he builds his garage on First Street near State. "Geneva did not begin to have sufficient quarters to care for the automobiles which came here last summer. In the coming summer and fall the number of cars passing thru here over the Lincoln Highway and Trans–continental routes will make it necessary for the city to have good motor accommodations if the tourists are to find storage and supplies such as they will demand."

In 1915 the San Francisco Panama Expedition was expected to stimulate additional traffic in our portion of Illinois to the tune of 5,000 automobiles carrying 15,000 people spending money along the route.

1960's aerial of Robert's Drive–In (left) and Shell service station (right), First St. (Rt. 31) in foreground, looking North with railroad tracks at rear of properties.
FIGURE 7.1 Courtesy Geneva History Museum.

3RD STREET AND CHEEVER AVENUE

An intersection of three streets with different addresses over the years: 609 S. Batavia Avenue, 609 S. 3rd Street, & 325 Cheever Avenue

- **1949: Roberts Drive–In**–T.W. Roberts and wife, Audrey
- **1952–66: Roberts Drive–In**–John Albertson & Jack Iding.

"Home of the Big Bob" a double–stacker hamburger before the "Big Mac." FIGURE 7.2
Courtesy 1959 *Batavia Herald.*

Current view of Duke & Lee's with no gas pumps. FIGURE 7.3 Sourced on Google Earth.

- **1967–75 Duke & Lee's Phillips 66**–May 1, 1967 Duke and Lee Singer
- **1975–85: Duke & Lee's Service Corp.–Texaco**
- **1985–2006: Duke & Lee's Service Corp.–Phillips 66**
- **2006–2020: Duke & Lee's Service Corp**, Lee Singer had ceased gas sales.
- **2020:** proposed site of condominiums over first floor business space.

Duke and Lee Singer circa 1980. FIGURE 7.4 Courtesy Singer family.

Typical Shell Station Design from the 1940's, this is similar to the original at 628 S. 1st Street.
FIGURE 7.5 Sourced on *Wikipedia*

618-628 SOUTH 1ST STREET

1941 Grand Opening of Triangle Shell, 618–628 South 1st Street. FIGURE 7.6 Courtesy
Geneva History Museum & *Geneva Republican*.

- **1941–45: Triangle Shell Service–**Paul Clement, a former Tri–City garage man builds a new station. Ph GEneva 3293
- **1945–54: Sullivan Shell Service Station–**Edward Sullivan Ph 838
- **October 27, 1954** St. Charles Chronicle: *"Shell Station for lease–2 bays–2 hoists on Highway No. 31, Geneva, IL. $5,500 investment required. Contact Shell representative, GEneva 1145 for appointment."*

Grand Opening FIGURE 7.7 Courtesy *Geneva Republican*

- **1955–62: Feece's Shell Gas Station**–Allan Feece–former manager at Avenue Deep Rock station.
- **1963–64: Carl's Shell Service**–Carl Pavlack, later went to Texaco location on Batavia Avenue, Batavia.
- **1965: Vacant**

The 1967 Grand Opening of Bentz Bros. Car Wash–Archie & Bernie Bentz congratulate each other with early 1967 Camaro at the pumps. *Aurora Beacon News* advertisement.
FIGURES 7.9 & 7.10 Courtesy Bentz family.

1970's photo looking South with railroad tracks in foreground. Bentz Bros. Mobil & Car Wash on the left, along with Duke & Lee's Phillips 66 on the former Roberts Drive–In site at right. At Bentz Bros., you can see the original Shell building in the middle, the long car wash building on the right, and the truck test lane addition on the left.
FIGURE 7.10 Courtesy Geneva History Museum.

Bentz Bros Firestone– "Free Car Wash with Any Service."
FIGURE 7.11 Courtesy *Geneva Republican*.

- **1965–66: Bentz Bros. Shell–**Archie Bentz, Sr & Bernard Bentz purchased the property with the intention of building the car wash that the City of Batavia would not allow on Randall Road. This was one of ShoDeen's earliest commercial projects.
- **1967: BENOCO/Bentz Bros. Car Wash/Illinois Truck Inspection Station** BENOCO, independent brand of Bentz Oil Company, the sign was an old Bentz Bros. Studebaker sign frame repurposed, Ph CE 2–8557.
- **1968–76: Bentz Bros. Mobil/Car Wash–**1968 jobber, Marcley Oil, original Shell supplier converted Mobil Oil. On a good Saturday we would wash 800–900 cars.
- **1971–76: Bentz Bros. Firestone–**signed on as Firestone store, still associated with Mobil, Car Wash and Illinois Truck Inspection Station. Archie Bentz, owner; Archie Jr, manager.
- **1976–77: Phil's Geneva Firestone–**Bentz sells to Phil Weimer on a contract sale
- **1978–79: Geneva Car Wash–**Phil Weimer with John Kerfoot partner/manager.
- **1979: Bentz Bros. Car Wash–**Archie had to take the station back after Kerfoot's failure and the station was leased to Ron Scheitlin.
- **1980–81: Ron's Mobil–**Ron Scheitlin, previously in business at 144 S Batavia Ave, Batavia; 102 W State, Geneva; Randall & Main, St. Charles; 215 E Main, St. Charles and then here, spanning 24 years.
- **1981–89: Geneva Mobil–Union 76–**Steve & Mary Ellen Camp purchased the property from Bentz.

Current CITGO with Bentz Car Wash building still present, original Shell station is gone.
FIGURE 7.12 Author's photograph.

Peter J. Armburst & B.J. Berg with employee John 'Jack' Leuer, 27 S. 1st St., Geneva. FIGURE 7.13 Photo courtesy of Ronald Rawson.

27 SOUTH 1ST STREET

NE corner 1st & James Streets

- **1885: Swedish Methodist Church**
- **Nov. 1921–22: Thompson & Berg Garage**–E.L. Thompson & B.J. Berg, head mechanic Pete Armbrust
- **May 1925–35: Fox River Central Motor Co; Agent for Studebaker,** then **Chevrolet** 1926; then in 1929, **Moon Motor Co,** featuring the **Windsor, White Prince motor cars, in 1932 a sub–agency for Plymouth. McCornack Texaco** supplied in 1934. Peter J. Armbrust & Bernhardt Johan Berg with employee, John 'Jack' Leuer. A story relayed by Sammi Maier King from her grandfather, Jack, "He told about helping someone along a dirt road one day. Three men in suits were stopped because of a flat tire. He rushed to help because it was an easy way to make a half dollar, the going rate. When he got close, he realized one of the men was Al Capone. He was really scared but he went ahead and changed the tire. When Capone asked how much he owed him, he said "nothing." He just wanted to get out of there as fast as he could. Capone reached into his pocket and took out a wad of bills and gave my grandpa $10. My grandpa said he was a "Helluva a guy!" Herbert White of Elburn worked here as a mechanic, starting in 1926.

Armbrust Garage Interior 1930s

FIGURE 7.14. Photo courtesy of Ronald Rawson, grandson of Peter Armbrust.

- **1935–43: Armbrust Garage/Texaco–**Peter M. Armbrust (Berg passed in 1934)
- **1940: Nelson John** 27 S 1st rear lower level, former blacksmith?
- **April 1, 1943** *Geneva Republican*: "Don Flynn Motors, having lost the lease at 12 E State to the railroad, Flynn leased this location and will sell Dodge and Plymouth. Peter Armburst and John Nelson will continue to be associated with Flynn. Morton of Flynn–Morton will enter the filling station business in Elgin."
- **July 9, 1943–1955: Armburst Garage–** Flynn passed from a heart attack on June 7, 1943 and Peter took over from the Flynn estate. Sumner R. Smith had a used car agency here during the war,
- **January 1955–58: Duke & Ray's Texaco–** Melvin A. 'Duke' Singer & Raymond Heiser–former Tri–City Garage employees.
- **1958–67: Duke's Garage,** Duke Singer––Repairs & Radiator shop
- **1967–74: Geneva Body Shop–**Harry Awalt and son, Gary. (Wide–plank wooden floors were still present in repair area). During this era, the Police Dept used the lower level as a parking garage for squad cars. Geneva Body moved to the former Chevy used car lot on NE corner of State and Bennett, now the site of *Geneva Place* retirement apartments.
- **1975: Soderstrom Radiator Repair and Taxi Cab Service**

- **1976–88: E&T Glass,** Ed and Tom Spriet, **Nova Communications**
- **Current: Chazio's Salon**

21 SOUTH 1ST STREET

Approximate location of the fire station)
- **1923–25: Fox River Central Motor Co, Studebaker–**Armbrust & Berg, (this was just north of their location at 27 S 1st) Later agents for **Studebaker and Chevrolet** in 1926, Ph 1149. September 1923 added **Samson & Ford trucks.**
- **1929: Windsor–White Prince Motor cars** Ph 1149. 1929 ad: "Windsor–White Prince motor cars manufactured by the Moon Motor Company, St Louis."
- **1929–30: Studebaker Garage–**George Ekdahl
- **Geneva Fire Station**

12 SOUTH 1ST STREET

Was built in 1913 on the west side of the street.
- **1913: Ekdahl Garage–**Jessica Strube, "We know that in 1913, Geneva's earliest garage proprietor, George Ekdahl moved the automotive portion of his business to this location from State and Third."

FIGURE 7.15 *1920 Geneva Republican advertisement*

- **1920: Geneva Battery Shop–** Gould Battery Service Station, Matthias F. Armbrust, formerly of Armbrust Bros.
- **1922: E.L. Thompson Garage–**corner First and James, stone building formerly Swedish M. E. church across from fire station of the day.
- **1939–40: Anderson Auto Exchange–**Used autos and tire shop Ph 3292. The City purchased this property in 1943 and the building razed in early 1950's

Business must have been booming for George Ekdahl as he and A.E. McIntosh have constructed a new garage directly across the street from his 12 South First Street garage in anticipation of more Lincoln Highway traffic. Previously thought to be Ekdahl posing at the pump identified with Standard Oil Red Crown before he stopped selling Standard products in 1922 as a response to Standard building the station across the street.
FIGURE 7.16 Courtesy Geneva History Museum.

Geneva Republican July 5, 1979: A close–up version of the above photograph was accompanied with this text: "Good Old Days; With Geneva's driver now paying $1 per gallon, or more, for gasoline, the days when a price increase put fuel up to 19 ½ cents per gallon really do seem like "the good old days." William C. Wood found this old photo of local sign painter Paul Esser changing a gas price sign at a service station that stood about where Geneva's police station is now. The exact year the photo was taken is not known, but it was probably sometime in the 1930's." This author is not aware of how Mr Wood identified Esser in the photo, possibly from knowing the subject or identification accompanying the photo. My original tag as Ekdahl, was provided by the Geneva Museum, but upon close examination the subject appears to be painting the sign. FIGURE 7.17 Courtesy *Geneva Republican*.

11-13 SOUTH 1ST STREET

On the east side of the street

- **1915–30: Ekdahl Garage Ford & Fordson Tractor, Standard gas**–George Ekdahl. August 1917; "Ekdahl has proven himself an automotive dealer by selling 78 Fords in the past 12 months." May 1926, Ekdahl switched to **Studebaker**; Arthur Carlson, head mechanic.

Interior Ekdahl Ford; round sign hanging from ceiling says STOCK MICHELIN TIRES, license plate on car is IL 1915, rectangle sign has the words "Not Responsible for injury or items left in car." FIGURE 7.17 Courtesy Geneva History Museum.

11–13 South 1st Street circa 1926. This photo must have been taken when the business was closing; a close–up reveals building is vacant; child inside watching photographer; awning is dirty; brand of gas had changed from Standard Red Crown, round globe replaced with oval; and price of gas was $.20. The vertical sign on front of building, visible to N–S traffic, has the correct number of spaces to spell EKDAHL. FIGURE 7.18 Courtesy Geneva History Museum.

- **1930–31: The Geneva Motor Co, Inc/Ford**–Carl Roach, Roy Phillips, and Ross O. Judd. *Geneva Republican* **February 14, 1930:** "Geneva has been without a Ford agency since 1926, when Mr. Ekdahl gave it up to devote more time to his other business. He has since handled another line of automobiles but quit the business last fall and offered the garage for sale. The building is owned by A.E. McIntosh." In the interim, Ross Judd had become the sole business owner and sold to Mitchell of Chicago about March 1, 1931.

- **1931–37: Mitchell J. H. Motor Co–Ford–**John H. Mitchell (In 1937 he moved the business to East State as Dodge & Plymouth) Arthur "Smash" Anderson in sales since 1933. March 3, 1934 "Lloyd Kautz …took delivery of a vermillion red panel delivery truck for the Unique Cleaners and Dyers, Geneva."

Stewart Cooper Motors, Inc. Tel 702. FIGURE 7.19 *Courtesy Geneva Republican.*

- **January 29, 1937–42: Stewart Cooper Motors Inc–Ford/Mercury–**Stewart Cooper announces purchase from Mitchell and retention of Miss Ann Oksas, bookkeeper; Joseph Petraitis and John Nelson, mechanics; and Arthur "Smash" Anderson as salesman. Cooper also operated the Ford dealership on Main St. in Batavia, and this leads me to believe that my first car in 1966, a 1937 Ford, was probably sold by Cooper at one of these locations.
- **1942: Anderson–Hickey Co.** cabinetmaker converted to defense materials while Cooper had moved auto repair garage across the street.

"Work has been going on for some months to transform the former A.E. McIntosh building... into a new police station. Plans were approved...to make the fronts of the police and fire stations conform." FIGURE 7.20 Courtesy *Republican* May 1965 photo.

- **1965: City of Geneva Police Station–**the original garage building was repurposed with a new façade and made it appear to be a portion of the same building as the fire department to the south.
- **1976: 9–1–1 Tri–Com Emergency Dispatch** added to Police Dept.

9 SOUTH 1ST STREET
- **1926–28: Studebaker Garage–**later moved to 21 South First as Ekdahl Studebaker, this would be the current Fire Station location.

102 WEST STATE
SW corners of 1st and State
- **1837–1872: Geneva House–**two story tavern house
- **1885: Blacksmith and Livery** per Sanborn map
- **1920: Lefborn estate sale of lot 65x104 to Standard Oil Co.** Standard Oil Co– The second purpose–built service station in Geneva. Standard lets bids for construction March10, and opens in June 1922.
- **June 1922–1924: Standard Oil** under the management of Roger Micholson. Lawrence Freeman worked as assistant salesman at Standard until Blue

Ribbon Station management was made available and he went on to manage the Blue Ribbon.

- **1924–28: John Nottolene Standard**
- **1928–29: H.I. Wagner Standard**
- **1930: Earl E. Schumacher Standard**
- **1932–33: H.J. Sudduth Standard** (he also operated 33 N Bennett)

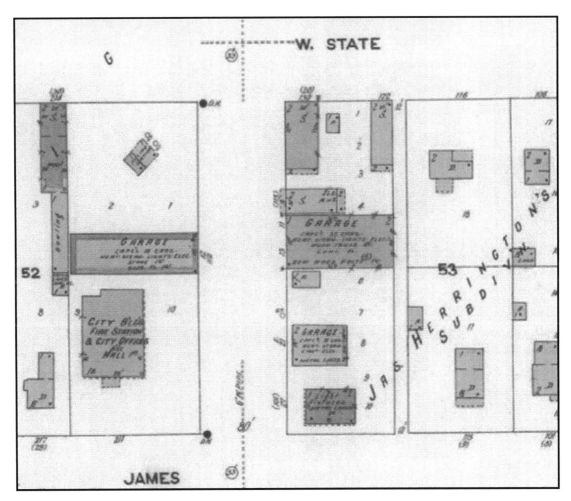

1923 Sanborn Insurance map of south First Street. On the left is the City Building with the fire station of that era, then the former livery turned garage by Ekdahl, followed by the new Standard service station. That building is located on an angle to the lot to provide ease of access to drive under the canopy (the dark portion is the actual building). On the bottom right is the Methodist Church, later converted to Armbrust & Berg's first garage. The large garage to the north of that was Ekdahl's new Ford Garage with estimated floor space for 35 automobiles. FIGURE 7.21 Courtesy Library of Congress.

- **1934: Richard Locke Standard**
- **1936–39: S.P. Wunderle Standard**
- **1939–42: Vogt & Guisti Standard**–Walter "Bob" Vogt, Roland P. "Rollie"

Guisti, Geneva boys that had previously operated a Standard in Elgin.

- **1942: Jigg's Standard**
- **1947: Standard Service**–Ernest Brandt, Manager
- **1948: Don & Bill's Standard Service, GEneva 3254**
- **1949–55: Stotler Standard Service**–Frank Stotler

Reents Grand Opening complete with clown.
FIGURE 7.22 Courtesy *Geneva Republican* June 13, 1957.

- **1956–59: Reents Standard Service**–William Reents Ph GEneva 3261, with Harvey Anderson, Tom Altepeter, & Lauren Hillquist.

1961 sign in window says 'Ron's Service Center' but it looks closed, when Scheitlin went to Randall Road and Main in St. Charles. FIGURE 7.23 Courtesy Geneva History Museum.

- **November 1959–61: Ron's Standard Service–**Ronald E. Scheitlin, formerly in Batavia, now moving to Randall and Main, St. Charles
- **1961–68: Bud's Standard Service–**Edward 'Bud' Ehlers, mechanic–Joe Parrillo, who was later in business at Shell station a few blocks west.
- **1968: Bentz Bros–**Archie Bentz Jr, manager–temporarily operated station for Standard Oil Company until a new dealer was found.
- **1968–73: Chuck's Standard–**Charles Fitzmaurice, later at Village Mobil, Elburn. Don Rasmussen night manager, Ed Costello mechanic.
- **1973: Bentz Bros–**Kee Moore, manager–temporarily operated station for Standard Oil Company until a new dealer was found.
- **1973–76: H & B Standard (Herbs' Standard)–**Herb Barnard & James Caldwell
- **1977: Herb's Standard–**Herb Barnard, Herb later went to work for Fox River Tire as outside salesman and at Way's Standard in St. Charles.
- **1978–80: Gene's Service Station–**Gene Jones & J. Robert Caldwell
- **1981–82: Geneva Standard–**Randy Marcellis, the former Standard Oil Field Supervisor was now working for Valley Petroleum.
- **March 1983: City of Geneva** has purchased the property, removed the tanks and razed the building to create a 21–space parking lot.
- 1982 saw the closing of 3 service stations on West State street, this AMOCO, the Texaco at 4th street, and the former CITGO/Marathon at 8th street. Only the Texaco was reopened in 1983 as a service station, and today, none of the downtown stations exist.

1 NORTH 1ST STREET

NE corner of 1st & State

- **1848: David Dunham's Store**
- **1917–25: Geneva Auto Tire & Harness Shop–**J.A. Matl, Ph 719. He installs a steam vulcanizing machine in 1917. A Sanborn map dated 1923 shows gas pump. FIGURE 7.35 reveals that the brand was **Indian Gas**. Matl's innovation is a great example of American Enterprise transitioning from horse and buggy to the automobile. With the early autos he was a supplier/maker of canvas tops and side curtains, thus making "open" cars year–round with winter enclosures. He evolved to being the prime supplier of tires and tubes to Geneva customers. After building the filling station in 1925, which he leased to McCornack, Matl continued business next door, east in the 29 West State tire and harness shop where he becomes an agent for Exide batteries and the **Rickenbacker** automobile in 1925. Even while Matl is building the

new filling station, he continues to ply the adapted harness–making to tops and side curtains for open automobiles.

Goodrich sponsored ad showing where you can make the purchase; J.A. Matl, Geneva; Foley & Redman, St. Charles; Guy & Son, Batavia; and Elburn Garage, Elburn.
FIGURE 7.24 Courtesy *Geneva Republican.*

"McCornack Texaco' in the Matl building on the righthand corner. The building on the left, is what we now know as "The Little Owl" and has a billboard painted on the side for the "Geneva Garage." The Warber–built facility selling Nash autos is north on this street. This dates this photo to about 1928 or later. FIGURE 8.25 Courtesy Geneva History Museum

- **October 10, 1924** *Geneva Republican*: "Work has started on a gas and oil filling station to be built by J.A. Matl at the northeast corner of State and First streets."

"The new building which will be constructed of a light–yellow colored brick, will be 12x24x20 feet. It will include an office, ladies' rest room and two toilet rooms. There will be a basement under the building and a first–class heating plant will be installed...is one of the most up–to–date and complete service stations in this vicinity. The exterior is attractively designed with two drive ways and four of the latest type Bowser electric pumps have been installed. In the evening the building and approaches are brilliantly illuminated with specially designed electric lights."

"The general building contract has been given to Harry Seastrom, local contractor. The concrete work which will cost over $2,000, will be done by Wren Holmberg."

"Charles McCornack, well known St. Charles oil dealer who operates in the jobbing and retail oil business on a large scale, has leased the proposed new station for a period of five years. He already has stations at St. Charles, Elgin, DeKalb and other localities in this vicinity."

"With the opening of the new South First street paving, the automobile traffic over the Fox River Trail will be considerably increased and the new station will be splendidly located to get a share of the business in addition to being on Roosevelt Road with the heavy Chicago traffic passing this point." Note that modern day State Route 31 was referred to as the Fox River Trail, as the Lincoln Highway had been relocated in 1919. The same newspaper announced the opening of the new Sixth Street School, Frank Gray, architect, and start of Rosenfelder's Hardware store in the Unity building.

- **February 1925–36: McCornack Texaco–**A.J. Dorsey, Manager–1925, Martin G. Hanson, manager–1933, Gilbert Larson–1934. Early advertisement is for **"Power–Full"** independent brand gasoline, then **Texaco.**
- **1937–41: McCornack Texaco–**Howard Crawford, Manager, enlisted in WWII.
- **1942–49: McCornack Texaco–**Bill Meltz, prop, Ph 1126–Arnie Gardner *(see page 151),* Bill Crook, Jack Watts, Henry Yokum 'hung out' and all of whom were sometimes employed there.
- **1949–53: Melby Texaco–**William Melby–Ph 1126. It is unclear as to whether Matl later sold the property to McCornack or if McCornack continued to lease. It would appear that Melby now came into ownership of the property and continued supply with McCornack Texaco.

A–OK Barbershop the 1960–70's. Lewis Insurance Agency, late 1970's.
FIGURE 7.26 & 7.27 Photos courtesy of Lewis Insurance Agency

Lewis Insurance, center portion of building was the original McCornack Texaco. FIGURE 7.28 Current photo sourced on Google Earth

- **1953: Anderson & Lindquist Real Estate–**Arthur "Smash" Anderson & Axel Lindquist, Ph 5924. Note that Smash has been in the real estate business in St. Charles for a number of years before this and will finish his career at 104 S. Batavia Avenue, Batavia.

   In three decades, Smash transitioned from his home–based garage to an agent for REO autos; to automobile sales for Mitchell and Cooper, then Tri–City Garage; and Davison Chrysler in St. Charles. He made the switch to a career in Real Estate and Insurance in the 1940's and retired in the 1960's. In 1959, he sold his personal home in Batavia to Archie Bentz.
- **1966–70's: A–OK Barbershop**
- **Current: Lewis State Farm Insurance Agency**

Arnie Gardner worked for McCornack Texaco at this location in the 1940's. The following is from his 2012 Illinois Stock Car Hall of Fame Induction: "Arnie was a multi–talented driver. He won races and Championships on Dirt and Asphalt, including Mance Park, Mazon Speed Bowl, Sycamore Speedway and Kankakee Fairgrounds. He won the Mazon 300 lapper two years in a row in 1956 & 1957. Santa Fe Speedway's NCTC 200 4 times in 1970, 1975, 1981 & 1986. Arnie was well known by his fans as "The Geneva Fox". On a national level he competed at Daytona, Atlanta and Charlotte Speedways! Arnie's gas station of choice in the late '50s was Lee Wallis Texaco in Batavia." The following information was gleaned from the website: https://mikethewelder.com/arnie-the-geneva-fox

The website belongs to Arnie's son, Mike Gardner, also a racer and former owner of America Auto Repair in Batavia. "Arnie Gardner, 'The Geneva Fox,' drove for many great car builders. A list of the local builders: Ray Weirich, Batavia; Bob Smith, Kaneville; John Fortman of Lou's Jeep, Geneva; Mike Hankes, Sugar Grove; John Kennedy, Villa Park; John Papp, Chicago; and Bob Novy, New Lenox."

A former livery stable converted to a garage with gas. This image shows Harold Miller, not one of the Miller Bros. in front of the building that was later replaced by the Lloyd & Raymond Warber Nash dealership building at 17 North 1st Street.
FIGURE 7.29 Courtesy Geneva History Museum.

17 NORTH 1ST STREET

- **1917–20: Klink Auto Livery & Teaming**–Louis Klink, Ph 27. We know of Louis Klink operating a wagon factory in the 1850's in St. Charles and this was his son.

- *Geneva Republican*–**March 19. 1920:** "Louis Klink sold his business and leased the barn and house at the N First St address to H.W. Skillin who will continue the St. Clair [Sinclair] Oil Service Station and conduct a 24–hour taxi service."
- **April 2, 1920–24: Metropolitan Garage–Sinclair Service Station–**H.W. Skillin Ph Geneva 827
- **1924–25: Miller Bros Garage–** Ph Geneva 627, previously on S Third St.
- *Geneva Republican*, **April 3, 1925:** "The L. Klink property in No First street has been sold to the Lloyd Warber and Raymond Warber and they will come into possession of it the first of May. Warber Bros, who have been conducting The Geneva Garage in the Hahn building in State street will move their business to the Klink garage building which until recently was occupied by Miller Bros."
- **1925–57: Geneva Garage Inc–Cities Service–Massey Harris Farm Equipment–**Lloyd A. Warber, pres, Eric B. Thorsen treasurer, I.A. "Ray" Warber, partner Ph 660. Lloyd bought out Thorsen in 1952. Lloyd also served with the Fire Department for 39 years and was Fire Chief for nine.
- **August 31, 1928** *Geneva Republican*: "...the new Geneva Garage nearing completion...repair shops in the basement, the main garage and office rooms on the first floor and there will be a seven–room apartment and a display room for radios on the second floor." The Grand Opening was embellished with a Barn Dance with music from the WLS Radio ensemble.
- **1925–30:** Gerhart N. Rasmussen of **St. Charles Oil Co,** was **Sinclair** supplier to Geneva Garage.
- **1929: DeSoto Agency–**Ralph E. Bartlett of Aurora leased space in the Geneva Garage
- **1934: Joyce Motor Sales–**Tom Joyce, former Batavia dealer, leased showroom space for a **Chrysler–Plymouth** agency, Ph 660

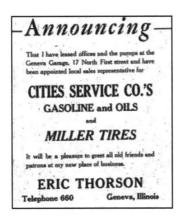

FIGURE 7.31 *Courtesy July 12, 1935 Geneva Republican*

- **1935: Thorson's Cities Service Station–**Eric Thorson leases the service station portion of the building. St. Charles Oil Co. was now the **Cities Service** distributor.

Geneva Garage building on the site of the former Klink building.
FIGURE 7.30 Courtesy April 18, 1947 *Geneva Republican*.

- **1935: Geneva Garage–Nash & La Fayette Agency–**Lloyd bought out his brother, Ray Warber
- **November 1936: Geneva Garage** is new home of **Dodge–Plymouth** along with Nash–La Fayette.
- **1956–57: Simon Motor Sales–used–** J.J. 'Jim' Simon
- **1960: Massie's Car Wash**

- **1962–1966: Wells Auto Service**–Russell Wells–19 address operated from lower level.
- **1960–80's:** *Geneva Republican* **and Republic Printing Co**
- **Current: ShoDeen Development**–now addressed as 77 North First Street.

17 N. 1st St.: Currently the ShoDeen Building. The capstone was added reflecting the Swedish origin of Kent ShoDeen's surname, SJODIN, and the establishment of his business in 1961. The red brick portion of the west side view of the building reflects the original Geneva Garage before additions. FIGURES 7.32 & 7.33 Sourced on Google Earth and ShoDeen website.

(1350) 1ST STREET

Approximate address of the corner of Stevens street.

FIGURE 7.34 Courtesy *Geneva Republican*

- **1930–31: Geneva Motor Company, Inc–Ford**

West State Street hill looking east to the river. In 1923, the north side of West State between 1st Street and River Lane. This photo and the map below show both Matl buildings, the E.J. Hahn garage, and the blacksmith shop at the bottom of the hill that has been converted to automotive. The shop identified as tire vulcanizing is the old Matl building, yet to be replaced with the Texaco and the garage at 125 is Matl's new garage.
FIGURE 7.35 Courtesy Geneva History Museum.

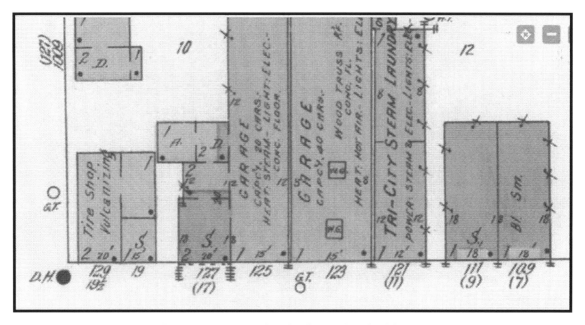

Through the decades addresses were randomly changed as buildings were built, then revised by the city in 1930 and again changed in 1947 when the post office revised their numbering system. FIGURE 7.36 1923 Sanborn Insurance map Courtesy Library of Congress.

April 20, 1978 *Geneva Republican*: when razing the 1850's limestone building was the topic of discussion. FIGURE 7.37.

7 WEST STATE STREET

109 later changed to 117, current address of 7

- **1867: Ward Rathbone Grocery–**also made Spruce Beer (Root Beer)
- **S.H. Henrikson–Blacksmith Shop–**Henrikson was also Geneva Fire Chief.
- **1920: Smith's Garage–Oldsmobile**
- **May 7, 1926: Red's Garage–Chrysler–**F.H. "Red" Swanson, proprietor, formerly with Ekdahl Ford and Tri–City Garage, Ph754. By June, Swanson had a partner, Vernon F. Modine.
- **June 4, 1926–1927: Swanson & Modine Garage–Dodge–**In 1927 he moved to the larger building up the hill to the west.
- **1960–68: Valley Auto Parts**
- **1968–78: Jim's Pizza**
- **Current: Buttermilk Restaurant**

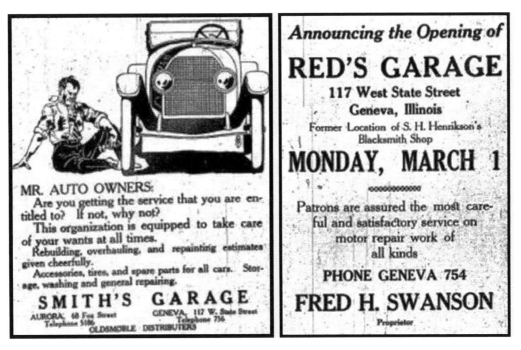

Smith's Garage followed by Red's Garage, 117 West State Street.
FIGURES 7.38 & 7.39 Courtesy *Geneva Republican.*

11 WEST STATE STREET (121)

- **1955: Valley Motor Shop**–Ph 3156

17 WEST STATE STREET (123)

- **1915–19: Emil J. Hahn's Garage**–Hahn purchased 70'x150' lot from Matl; Architect Frank Gray designed new building, also architect for McCornack buildings in St. Charles and Batavia. Hahn operated this garage in conjunction with his St. Charles garage.
- **1920–21: Sneller Garage**–Frank Sneller
- **1921–23: Smith's Garage–Oldsmobile**–P.H. Smith & Son, State Street new & used cars, Ph 758, second location on Fox Street, Aurora.
- **1923–24: Geneva Garage**–Warber Bros
- **1924–26: REO Garage Co.**– a branch of Aurora REO owned by Arthur "Smash" Anderson and his brother, J. Edward Anderson.
- **October 8, 1926** *Geneva Republican*: *"Swanson & Modine...formerly occupied Henrikson blacksmith shop two doors west, has succeeded the REO Garage Co."*
- **1926–28: Swanson & Modine Garage–Dodge–Graham–Page agent**–F.H. "Red" Swanson and Vernon F. Modine dissolved their partnership January 1927 with Swanson still conducting business from that point on.

- **June 27, 1930** *Geneva Republican*: "F.H. Swanson who had conducted a garage business in the Hahn building, 123 W State Street for several years, had leased the Emil Lundeen Garage, a new building just west of Fourth street at 415 West State and has moved his business to that building".

  "George E. Meyers who has been associated with Mr. Swanson with the **Graham-Paige** sales and service is moving with him and will continue to display these cars in the new location."

  "Omer Beal will take over the Hahn garage vacated by Mr. Swanson in addition to the Matl building next door which he now occupies. Emil Lundeen has made not announcement of his future business plans."

- **September 19, 1930** *Geneva Republican*: **Lundeen Motor Sales-Studebaker,** unsure of the physical locations in Batavia & Geneva.

- **1935: Relief Canning Plant**-Depression era cannery made available for individuals to can their own fruits and vegetables from gardens.

- **1936: Coryell's Radio Electric Shop**

- **October 8, 1937** *Geneva Republican*: "Charlie's Garage, which has occupied the Matl Garage on State street and Coryell's...located next door in the Hahn Garage building have exchanged locations this week...the local Studebaker sales agency is now in larger quarters."

- **1937-43: Charlie's Garage-Studebaker**-Charlie Bohleen, Ph 621. Later in 1957, opened D-X service station on East State.

- **1943-48: Cold Locker Storage**-WWII priority to create food storage.

- **Current: Foxfire Restaurant**

21–23 WEST STATE STREET (125–127)

Constructed in 1920

- **1920-26: J.A. Matl Garage 1922 Kelly-Springfield & Goodrich Silvertown,** added **Fisk Tires** in 1923, **Rickenbacker** automobile in 1925. August 1, 1926 Matl sold to W.S. Collins and E.H. Spiller

- **August 1926: Collins & Spiller Chrysler**-December 17, 1926 Omer Beal from Oquawka, IL took the lease on the building from Matl.

- **1926-32: Omer Beal Motor Sales-Chevrolet**- Omer Beal, later located at 12 E. State and then 415 W. State Street.

- **1927-32: Geneva Auto Laundry-F. Fuessel & Sons** Ph 661

- **1933-36: Charlie's Garage Dodge & Plymouth**-Charlie Bohleen Ph 661, in 1935 addressed as 61 W. State.

FIGURE 7.40 *November 1936 Republican*

- **1936–37: Charlie's Garage–Studebaker**–Charlie Bohleen, Ph 621, Charlie also built and raced cars at the "Farm Racetrack" outside Wasco.
- **1937–77: Coryell's Tri–City Radio Electric Shop**
- **1950: Blagg Motor Car Sales & Service**–George L. Blagg (Yorkville)
- **Current: Konicek and Dillon**

29 WEST STATE STREET (129)

- **1906–25: Geneva Auto Tire & Harness Shop**–J.A. Matl–harness maker and tires. Later, employee Clarence Smith buys into the business. Ph 719. Figure 7.35 shows a gasoline sign, possibly **Indian** brand gas, a brand that was eventually bought by Texaco. Matl purchased the lot to the west and constructed the Texaco station facing First Street with the 1 North First address on the combined properties. It was leased to McCornack Oil Co. in 1925.

FIGURE 7.41 Courtesy *1920 Geneva Republican*

The **Dort Motor Company** built cars from 1915–1924 and was at one time the thirteenth largest U.S. automobile manufacturer. No record of address for a Dort dealer so one would assume that Gust was working from his home much like Carl More had done in Batavia in the same era. "Phone Geneva 754 for a Demonstration"

 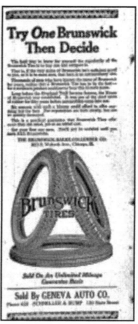

1920: Geneva Auto Co. Schneller & Bump, Brunswick Tires, Ph 720.
FIGURE 7.42 & 7.43 Courtesy *Geneva Republican*.

120 STATE STREET

South side of street

- **1916–20: Armburst Bros. Garage–** Matthias & Joseph Armburst, (brothers to Peter on First Street), Ph 70–R.
- *Geneva Republican* **March 1920:** "Armburst Bros. who have been in business the past 4 years on State St. sold their business **to Frank B. Schneller and Earl Bump**. Matthias Armburst will open a battery [Gould] service station in the McIntosh building on First St. where McIntosh was removing the horse stalls of **Geneva's last horse livery**." Matthias later moved on to Third street with his brother.

111 WEST STATE STREET

- **1950: Gordon & Funk Used Cars**: Elmer Funk (West Chicago) Robert Funk (Aurora)

NORTH 2ND STREET

- **1926–34: Smith's Auto Laundry–**Clarence Smith, "who for the past six years has been a mechanic for J.A. Matl...purchased the old Republican building... will put a cement floor and add large doors...install an electric steam car washing plant, as well as repairing outfit for autos." Later called "**Smith's Top Shop**", this building may have been incorporated with the B.F. Goodrich building shown below.

115 WEST STATE STREET

- **Frank J. Lennartz, Jr Grocery & Hardware**
- **1920: I.X.L. Tire Co.–Tire Manufacturer–**J.A. Skoglun, H.L. Naylor & Oscar Larson
- **1937–40: Western Auto Store–**Ralph Rea
- **Post–War: Western Auto Store**
- **1960–62: Geneva Tire & Auto Store–B F Goodrich–**Wilbur Willie

129 West State Street, Geneva Tire & Auto circa 1960's.
FIGURE 7.44 Courtesy Geneva History Museum.

129 W STATE NE

Corner of West State and 2nd St.

- **Hills Bros Dry Goods Store**
- **Aug 1946–52: Economy Home & Auto Supply–B. F. Goodrich–**Jerry Stejskal and brother–in–law, Robert Bradley.
- **1952–58: Jerry's Goodrich Store–**Jerry Stejskal
- **1958–60: Jerry's Store–**Frank Fernandez & Robert Thompson of Wheaton, retained the name and opened with Paul Evans as manager. They gradually turned this into a paint and wallpaper store.
- **1962–present: Geneva Tire & Auto Store–B. F. Goodrich–** Wilbur Wille merged with Jerry's. *Geneva Republican*, "the two firms will continue to operate independently under the same roof…Wille moving west a couple doors, has the franchise for Goodrich line of products, that were formerly handled by Jerry's when it was known as Jerry's Goodrich Store." Robert Wille, Jerry Wille, and now 3rd generation owners: Jeff and Taffy Wille.

204 WEST STATE STREET

Former Masonic Lodge in Oscar Nelson's Arcade building.

- **1928: Geneva Buick–**Elmer Johnson & Adley Schultz September 7. 1928 *Geneva Republican*: "...the local Buick sales and service agency recently relinquished by Tri–City Garage has been taken over by Johnson & Schultz of Hinckley...Buick dealers in Hinckley for the past ten years." Genevan Arthur Carlson will oversee sales and service. This was a temporary showroom and they relocate to 4 East State street. Ph 816
- **1937: Warner Motors–Hudson/Terraplane–**Ed Warner & W.W. Joyner, Ph 2428. per March 19, 1937 Republican article they temporarily located in the old Masonic building.
- **1939: Jewel Food Store**

July 14, 1922 *Geneva Republican*: "Never again will the gay joy rider wave farewell to motorcycle policeman Matt Armbrust. His old one–lung spark wagon has been replaced by a brand new up to date four–cylinder Henderson motorcycle."

Corner of State & 3rd St. Possibly the first garage in Geneva dates back to 1906, this photo from 1911 clearly shows the painted sign for 'GARAGE' towards the rear of Ekdahl's business building. There are newspaper advertisements for the introduction of the Excelsior Auto Cycle (early motorcycle) in 1911 *Geneva Republican*, followed by ads for Overland Model 59T in 1912. FIGURE 7.45 Courtesy Geneva History Museum.

230 WEST STATE STREET

SE corner State & 3rd

- **1904–1924: Automobile Sales & Repair**–George Ekdahl & John Skogland, also proprietors of billiard room, bowling alley, and purveyors of fine jewelry, cigars, Victrola phonographs, and sporting goods. 1912 agents for **Overland** automobile and **Excelsior** Motor Cycles. In 1913, Ekdahl moved the automotive garage to 1st St and later expanded that with new construction on the east side of 1st Street. 1917 **Willys-Knight "4"** sold by the Ekdahl–Mellander agency to Dr Marstiller. In 1924, the sporting goods portion of this business was moved to 311 West State and later 13 North 3rd street.

- **1925:** Oscar Nelson signed a 5–year lease with a major oil company and plans were to construct a red brick and stone gas and oil station. This was on the heel of plans to build a grand hotel across the street from the county courthouse. All of these plans will change with the expansion of Nelson's Geneva Hotel and another building to the corner.

- **1931–40: Maynard's Pharmacy**–H.C. Maynard

- **1941–2011: Merra–Lee Shop**–Sol Simon & Rose Becker Kozberg, started in 1929 on State by 2nd Street, then moved here in 1941. Eventually this shop would take over the entire block to the south as the **Merra–Lee Fashion Walk**, displacing all of the automotive shops.

Corner of State & 3rd Streets looking south toward Tri–City Buick garage, late 1940's. Note the Standard Oil gas pumps on the sidewalk. By 1989 the conversion of this entire block from "Automotive Row" to "Ladies Boutiques" had been completed with "The Fashion Walk Shops" comprised of Merra–Lee Shop, Bravissimo, Meeting Place, East Room, Petticoat Lane, Complete Petite, and Marion Court. FIGURE 7.46 Photo courtesy of Geneva History Museum.

Lincoln Highway (1st St) shared this underpass with the trolley cars.
FIGURE 7.47 Sourced from early postcard.

- In 1919, the Lincoln Highway route in Geneva had to change due to the danger of trolley cars and automobiles traveling through the 1st Street viaduct. 3rd Street became the new route and with that change almost an entire block was transformed to automotive service and repair. Women would surely persuade their husbands to stop in Geneva for service so they could shop at the *Little Traveler* whose address was simply 'The Lincoln Highway'.

3RD STREET NEAR STATE

- **1918:** "The old Cedarstrom livery barn is to be replaced by modern 50x135 brick garage if the plans of Mrs J.A. Peterson and Albert Anderson are carried out."
- **1920: Geneva Battery & Electric Co–**R.G. McNew, **Willard** Battery Ph 1138.

11 SOUTH 3RD STREET

- **1917–24: Miller Bros. Garage–**first names unknown, (probably shared the same building as Armburst), relocated in1924 to the Klink property on North First Street.

FIGURES 7.48 & 7.49 Courtesy March 28, 1919 *Geneva Republican.*

15 SOUTH 3RD STREET

Partial building just showing on the left side in Figure 7.50

- **1919–1925: Armburst Bros. Garage**–Matthias and Joseph Armburst, originally at 120 West State Street, agents for **Sampson and Model 'A' Ford trucks**. Brothers to Peter on South First Street.
- **1926 this property was razed, and Tri–City made another addition.**

17 SOUTH 3RD STREET

- **1905: Peterson Livery**
- **1905–17: August Cedarstrom Livery**–frame building razed and replaced by brick structure erected by John A. Peterson and leased to Tri–City Garage.

Tri–City Garage circa 1922–26 before the Armburst Garage on the left was acquired.
FIGURE 7.50 Courtesy Geneva History Museum,

- **1917–19: Tri–City Garage**–Lundeen Bros, Emil & Frank Lundeen. In 1925 Lundeen Bros were at 12 East State (Charles M. Hansen worked for them as a mechanic).

FIGURE 7.51 Courtesy March 21, 1919 *Geneva Republican.*

- *1919:* **Tri–City Garage**–B.E. Richardson, (ex–sheriff) proprietor, Ph 785. Sold in October to returning veterans, Howard S. Bauder & Fred W. Hillquist, who had served for two years in the U. S. Army doing auto–repair work in France.

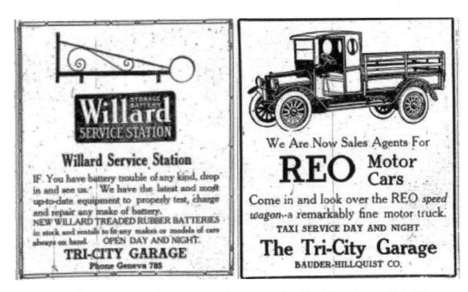

Willard Batteries and REO Speed Wagon plus Taxi Service at Tri–City.
FIGURE 7.52 & 7.53 Courtesy *Geneva Republican.*

- **1920–23: Tri–City Garage**–Howard Bauder & Fred Hillquist, March 1923,

announced **Chevrolet** agency, Ph 785. Bauder sold to C.M. Hanson in Sep 1923. Tri–City Cab was retained by Bauder and Ernest Soderstrom was taken on as partner and will operate as the Geneva Cab Co.

- **1923–1931: Tri City Garage–1924 Buick–**F.W. Hillquist & C.M. Hanson. A matching humped roof portion to the north was added in 1926 when the Armburst location at 11–15 South 1st Street was acquired. Tri–City was addressed as 9–45 S 3rd Street, occupying all but the corner building on the north facing State Street. In 1928, the Buick contract was relinquished and **Chrysler** automobiles were added. Neal G. "Clem" Clement was the mechanic in 1926 and went on to manage Hillquist Bros (Fred, Vincent, & Iver) Fargo Garage in Sycamore in 1928.

- **February 14, 1930** *Geneva Republican*: "Articles of Incorporation have been issued...to the Tri–City Garage...Fred Hillquist, Charles Hanson, and George Lyle Miller with Miller to assist with sales and office work." (G. Lyle Miller sold his share to Charles Hanson Nov. 13, 1931). "The latest style of electric gas pumps installed."–November 1931

Tri City Garage interior. FIGURE 7.54 Courtesy Geneva History Museum.

- **1932–58: Tri City Garage Buick–**Fred Hillquist & Charles M. Hanson, father of Dr. Charles Hanson. Re–acquired the Buick franchise when **Geneva Buick** folded during depression. The **Packard** line was added shortly thereafter but was dropped in favor of the **Pontiac**. They had 2 **Standard Oil** gas pumps on sidewalk for curbside service until 1958; sidewalk sign is Standard's Permalube Oil. "Smash" Anderson came here from Cooper Ford in 1937.

Ross Judd, former St. Charles dealer and salesman since 1916, was salesman here in 1952. Hillquist retired from this business in 1955.

- **1937: The Pabst Blue Ribbon Cafe–**Opens in the large automobile showroom formerly used by Tri–City Garage.
- **1958: Tri–City Garage–**closed the doors with the retirement of 73–year–old Charles Hanson. The building had been sold to Sol Simon and Sam Korberg.
- **Garage–**Howard Bauder and his father
- **Year unknown: Grove's Auto Repair–**Bob Groves
- **1946–74: Valley Auto Parts & Machine Shop–**45 S 3rd St. (southernmost building)–Chet Nespril prop. Dave Balance & John Smith machinists, while Rich Warber, Bob Groves, & Ed Carlson were countermen.

Tri City Garage Parts Department. FIGURE 7.55 Courtesy Geneva History Museum.

In 2018, the Geneva History Museum hosted a 100th Anniversary recognition gala for the inception of the Tri–City Garage. The following is directly from their presentation on the evolution of the facility which was a mainstay for the community and a source for many of the mechanics who passed through the doors of Tri–City Garage. "Capitalizing on the automobile craze, the Peterson family decided to replace their livery barn with a service station. The 30–year–old livery barn of South Third Street, operated by Gust Cedarstrom, was demolished in March 1918 and local contractors, the Wilson Brothers, began building an $8,000 modern brick garage."

"The garage's early business years transferred hands several times from the Lundeen Brothers, to former Sheriff Beebe Richardson and then to Howard Bauder and Fred Hillquist. Hillquist would remain the garage's proprietor until its closing in 1958."

"In 1919, Geneva's Lincoln Highway changed street routes due to the danger of trolley cars and automobiles traveling through the First Street viaduct [FIG. 8.45] The route would now travel along South Third Street. It is no doubt that the increased traffic led to the large south addition of the Tri–City Garage. In 1922, construction of a 60x100–foot structure was built for $15,000. This addition more than doubled the floor space."

"Oscar Nelson, also State Treasurer, built an addition to the north of the Tri–City Garage in 1926. The new garage building would be 50x75 feet *and connect, as well as mirror, the original rounded brick facade design of the 191*8 building. It had a large basement for stock and supplies and a fine display room for cars in the front."

"By 1928, Tri–City Garage was being touted as one of the largest and best equipped in northern Illinois. This status and increased business created the need for enlarging the garage's mechanical department. A 25x82–foot addition was constructed in the rear of the buildings and extended east along James Street. This addition allowed for six car repairing pits, a painting booth, wash racks, oiling and greasing racks, battery room and tire repair room."

"The Tri–City Garage remained a staple on South Third Street until it closed in 1958. Then the buildings were leased to various businesses including Bentley's Camera Shop, Baird and Warner Real Estate and Valley Auto Parts until the early 1960's, when the Merra–Lee clothing store expanded from the corner of State and Third Street."

The Tri–City Garage began with the middle–humped portion of the garage being built first in 1918 and then the long rectangular portion to the south, being added in 1922. A matching humped portion to the north (left) was added in 1926 when the Armburst location at 11–15 S. 1st was acquired and razed. In 1928 another addition was made to the rear of the building, so by that time, everything you see under black roof was Tri City Garage along the new Lincoln Highway on 3rd Street. FIGURE 7.56 Courtesy Geneva History Museum.

Tri City Garage, South 3rd Street c. 1928.
FIGURE 7.57 Photo courtesy of Geneva History Museum.

Chief of Police Ruben Anderson shown with Fred Hillquist c. 1937.
FIGURE 7.58 Courtesy Geneva History Museum.

TRI-CITY GARAGE
OPEN DAY AND NIGHT
Phone Geneva 785

J. W. Hillquist   C. M. Bassett

188 Proof,
Alcohol
for radiator of your car
70c a gallon
In 5 Gallon Lots
1 Gallon in Can 75c
WITH SERVICE

1 gallon 85c
3 quart 70c
½ gallon 50c
1 quart 25c

FILL 'ER UP!

HARK! Hark! Yes, it's your gas tank, gurgling for joy as it fills to the brim with fine, pure gas from a Texaco visible-measure pump. You get more gallons per dollar, and more miles per gallon by buying this Superior Gas from us.

Armbrust & Berg
TELEPHONE GENEVA 1149

Alcohol was the early form of antifreeze and was also used in a carpenter's level; hence the name for early levels was a "whiskey stick". While alcohol lowered the freezing temperature, at the same time it lowered the boiling temperature. That necessitated the removal of alcohol from the radiator of a car prior to very warm weather because the auto would overheat and boil out all of the alcohol. My father told the story of saving each customer's alcohol in glass gallon jugs and storing same in the attic of Clark's Pure Oil. That service was provided free of charge but also insured the customer's return in the fall of the year. Later Prestone Antifreeze, was one of the prominent names in permanent antifreeze derived as ethylene glycol and that product raised the boiling temperature of the coolant, a product still used in modern cars.
FIGURES 7.59 & 7.60 Courtesy *Geneva Republican.*

223 JAMES STREET

- **1961–62: Shorty's Garage–**Clyde Gum, Ph Central 2–4256

317 JAMES STREET (REAR)

- **1974–76: IMP–**Import car repair specializing in Volkswagen. Ph 232–2722

523 SOUTH 3RD STREET

Directly across from the train depot

- **April 1954: Pack Ford–**Harry Pack, also North 2nd Street in St. Charles, while this was a short–lived venture, a portable office building was located on what was a vacant lot. The intent was to offer rail commuters sales & service with new cars parked in this lot across from the train depot. The customer cars were then driven to St. Charles for service.

17 NORTH 3RD STREET

- **1946–49: Valos Motor Sales–Kaiser/Frazer & Graham/Paige**–William T. Valos, Alton Cherry service dept. A 1947 advertisement is touting the desirable wage of $1.25 per hour for experienced mechanics.

Valos Motor Sales. FIGURE 7.61 Courtesy *Geneva Republican.*

- **June 17, 1949–50: Valos Motor Sales–Studebaker**–Bill Valos, owner, service men; Alton Cherry, Carl Pugsley, Bill Gescke. Valos also owned movie theatres in the area.
- **1950–53: Gregg Motor Sales–Studebaker**–John P. Gregg Ph 792
- **March–September 1953: Hanson Motor Sales, Inc–Studebaker**–Willis M. 'Skip' Hanson, Ph 792. Skip was the former owner of the news agency purchased from Ekdahl. Valos was still owner of the property and he had a new tenant; Skip made the move to east State.
- **1953–73: Gibbs Shoes**

Brilliant Bronze at 330 West State Street, this brand was supplied by Johnson Oil 1938–1959, the photo was dated 1953. FIGURE 7.62 Courtesy of Lencioni family & Geneva Historical Museum.

330 WEST STATE STREET

SE corners of 4th and State

- **August 1939:** Johnson Oil Co purchase empty lot from Oscar Nelson.
- **1939–41: Brilliant Bronze–Johnson Oil Co.–**Justin "Jud" T. Young, manager
- **April 1942: Hillquist Brilliant Bronze–**Fred S. Hillquist later went to Aurora Brilliant Bronze at Lake & Holbrook Streets. He was a longtime Geneva contractor and passed away in January 1943.
- **July 1942: McDonald's Brilliant Bronze–**Tom McDonald, Ph 3241
- **December 1942: Bobert's Brilliant Bronze–**Morris Bobert, also proprietor of Aurora BB station at Walnut & Wilder Streets, Tom McDonald attendant.
- **1943–44: Bobert's Brilliant Bronze Service Station–**Bob Lemke, Manager
- **1944: Bobert's Brilliant Bronze–**August '44, Elmer Gordon, Manager
- **1945–48: Bobert's Brilliant Bronze–**January '45, Clarence Boyer came here after operating Boyer's Pure Oil on east State street in 1943–44.
- **March 1949: Brilliant Bronze Service Station/A.A.A. Chicago Motor Club,** Elmer Jahreiss
- **September 1949: Lemke–Cundiff Brilliant Bronze**
- **1950–55: Jerry's Brilliant Bronze–**Jerry Lencioni
- **1955–56: Jerry's Cash Discount–**Jerry Lencioni
- **1956–57: Jerry's Bonded–**Jerry Lencioni
- **1958–61: Jerry's OK Oklahoma–**Jerry Lencioni

Circa 1960–61: Jerry's OK Oklahoma. FIGURE 7.63 Courtesy of
Lencioni family & Geneva Historical Museum.

Jerry Lencioni at the OK Oklahoma pump. License plate is 1961 and the movie at the Fargo
Theatre is "One Hundred and One Dalmatians." FIGURE 7.64 Courtesy
of Lencioni family & Geneva Historical Museum.

In 1962, the original station was demolished and Jerry built a new modern Enco Humble service station with pump islands on each side. This was part of Geneva '62, a civic program to beautify the downtown. The building served as a service station until the late 1970s when the it was repurposed and later demolished. FIGURE 7.65 Courtesy of Lencioni family & Geneva Historical Museum.

Jerry's Enco in the 60's. FIGURE 7.66 Courtesy of Lencioni family & Geneva Historical Museum.

- **1962–65: Jerry's ENCO Service Station–**Jerry Lencioni
- **1965–67: Gene's ENCO–**Eugene F. Boudreau
- **1968–77: G & B ENCO,** Gussie W. and Betty Langston, also provided Geneva

Cab Service. Greg Cryer started his career here with his in–laws, until it turned to OK (Oklahoma Gas).

- **1977: OK Oklahoma Gas**
- **Current: Aurelio's Pizza**

402 WEST STATE STREET

SW corners of 4th and State

The property at the southwest corners of 4th and State opened as a small masonry construction Texaco service station in 1928 and was later remodeled in 1952 reflecting the oblong–porcelain style shown above, followed by another remodel in the 1970's reflecting the trending 'Matawan' roof style, named by Texaco after the town in New Jersey where it was introduced in 1964. One more facelift in 1984 with the familiar red T, white star in a red circle prominent on a black background. This station was managed by the Clark family from 1928–37 in the original brick building. This was also the location where Bette Davis, famous movie star, and her husband had their car greased and gassed on route from Hollywood to Boston in 1934. Bob and George Clark would go on to lease the cottage–style Pure Oil service station one block west. FIGURE 7.67 Courtesy *Geneva Republican* February 1942.

- **May 28, 1928** *Geneva Republican*: "Brick work is nearly completed...the new station is being built by John Ellis and has been leased to the Texas Company."
- **June 1928–1932: Clark's Texaco Station**–Alexander Clark Ph Geneva 2431
- **January 26, 1934** *Geneva Republican*: "Alexander Clark succumbed to heart trouble...In the spring of 1928, he came to Geneva with his family and took the Texaco station business. He was the active head until last July when his sons, Robert and George took over the business and Mr. Clark was obliged to retire due to ill health."

"Son of Rev. Dr. Alexander Clark, a Methodist minister and the founder and editor of The Methodist Recorder, Mr. Clark often told how his father, as a young man, went to Gettysburg, heard President Lincoln deliver his famous dedication and having a knowledge of shorthand, he took down the only authentic report of the speech which later became a famous masterpiece of eloquence."

FIGURE 7.68 Courtesy October 19, 1934 *Geneva Republican*.

- **1932–37: Clark Bros Texaco Station**–Robert "Bob" & George Clark. Dick Shewalter was the author of this April 14, 1994 article in *The Republican* based on the memories of **Nellie Clark–Graham**, daughter of Alexander Clark.

While most Genevans relate the Clark's with their Pure Oil Station as depicted in this drawing, Nellie's story below starts with their Texaco Station.
FIGURE 7.69 Courtesy *The Republican*.

NELLIE CLARK GRAHAM

"My dad had been advised by his doctor to leave the smog and soot of Pittsburgh for a clean air climate because his heart condition made breathing difficult. His sister lived in Oak Park, and a brother in Elgin, so he came for a visit to try on the climate for size. One day, he and his sister were on their way to Elgin through Geneva and he fell in love with the town. Spotting a Texaco station under construction on the south corner of State and Fourth, he stopped and inquired, and soon became its original owner and operator.

That was in 1928 and Mother and I moved out here that summer under protest! Neither of us wanted to leave Pittsburgh, but we decided to give it a try. I was so lonesome that summer. School was out and I didn't know anyone my age. I spent a lot of time with my Dad and brother, Ken, who worked at the station.

Dad would try to keep me busy with little chores, one of which was pumping up the gas tanks. There was a glass container at the top of the tank, and it took a lot of pumping before the gas reached it! As I remember, gas averaged about 12 to 15 cents a gallon. Dad insisted the station always be clean and attractive and he planted petunias in front each spring.

Strictly a gas and oil station, it offered no towing or mechanical repairs except for simple items. The lift was outdoors, so grease and oil jobs were at the mercy of the weather. As a full-service station, cleaning windshields, looking under the hood, and checking tires were all standard procedure.

Situated on the old Lincoln Highway, many tourists traveled through Geneva—including Bette Davis and her husband making a coast-to-coast journey. It was summer, and she told dad she drove in because the station was so clean and the flowers so pretty.

In those days, if people had car trouble and needed a place to stay overnight, dad often would call mother and tell her "set a couple of extra plates and get the guest room ready.

Among the amazing things that happened at the station was the incident of the cattle truck which stopped for gas and to have the tires checked. With people waiting at the pumps, dad asked my brother to help put air in the truck's tires. My brother wasn't too happy about it as he was all dressed up to go to the Saturday night dance. While he was bending over a tire, one of the steers yielded to nature's call. Needless to say, my brother never made the dance!

In 1938, a Pure Oil station opened a block up the street on the corner of Fifth and State. Dad had died in 1934 and my three brothers had taken over the business. Leaving the site of the first enterprise, the family acquired the new station which boasted two bays and a wash rack, all inside! For good service, they always tried to maintain two men for each car at the pump where most people would buy six gallons for about a dollar. The station was open 24 hours a day, including Sundays, until World War II.

The grease and wash racks were always busy and four gas pumps were available. "Service Right Away" was the slogan. There was no automatic shut-off on the [gas] nozzle, so one person had to stay with the hose until the required amount was put in the tank. In the days before automatic transmissions, station staff would push cars up State Street to start the engines. One auto of 1926 vintage, had just driven into the station with the battery hanging by the cables under the floor boards, when the battery promptly dropped off and started a fire in front of the gas pumps.

In 1951. The Pure Oil Co tore out the small underground storage tanks and replaced them with larger ones capable of holding 1,000 gallons. Most service calls were a dollar, regardless of the location. One time, we were called to push a car to get it started and after we did, he pulled into another station for gas!"

Shewalter closed his 1994 article with; "Today, progress spells out a new moto, "Self–Service Right Away."

- **1937–48: Lennartz Texaco Service**–Lawrence "Lonnie" Lennartz, a former Omer Beal salesman. "As Clark Bros depart in December to Pure Oil station, a new ten year–lease has been signed by Texaco with property owner John Ellis of Geneva and Lennartz is new dealer."
- **1949–52: Kolar Texaco**–George & Thomas Kolar

State & Fourth Streets. FIGURE 7.70 *Geneva Republican* February 7, 1952.

- **1952–54: Wallis Texaco**–Lee Wallis, after 14 years with B. F. Goodrich, Ph GEneva 3292, assisted by Jerry Jobe & Hans Hubbard. (Lee had already opened Texaco in Batavia).

FIGURE 7.71 *Geneva Republican* March 11, 1954

- **1954–56: Jack's Texaco**–Jack Manny & Jack Ryan, who later founded Ryan Auto Parts.

Two Dalmatian puppies were part of the give–away. FIGURE 8.71
Geneva Republican November 1956.

- **1956–1960: Dick's Texaco**–Richard J. Walls
- **1961–62: Dick's Texaco**–Richard Walters
- **1962–63: Dick's Texaco**–Maynard H. Gray, prop.
- **1964–66: Gray's Texaco**–Maynard H. Gray (West Chicago)
- **1966–67: Dixon's Texaco**–David 'Jr' Dixon, formerly at Bentz Bros
- **1968: Village Texaco Service**–Mike Carter, Manager
- **1969: State Street Texaco**–Chuck Fehr & 'Jr' Dixon, Junior later went on to Union 76 on East State.
- **1969–70: Runge's Texaco**–Erl Runge came here from Shell, Ph CE 2–2739.
- **1970–72: Steve's Texaco Service**–Steve Stack Ph 232–2739
- **1973–75: Walker's Texaco**–Floyd Walker
- **1975: Geneva Texaco**–Jim Newman & Bill Shearer Ph 232–7454
- **1977–78: Geneva Texaco**–William Joynt & Mick Biskup
- **1979: Geneva Texaco**–Mike Biskup
- **1980–81: Service Texaco**–Tony Daniello Ph 232–8280
- **1982–83 vacant**

Geneva Texaco 'Matawan' roof style circa 1983.
FIGURE 7.73 Courtesy Geneva History Museum.

- **1983–86: Geneva Texaco**–Timothy Steinmetz
- **May 1986: Texaco turned Mobil**–Tim Steinmetz
- **1986–93: Geneva Mobil**–Tim Steinmetz & Paul Lukac, Nate Pritt manager.
- **Currently** an empty lot, building was razed in the 1990's?

415 WEST STATE STREET

- **September 21, 1928** *Geneva Republican*: "Albert Kraft of Batavia has been awarded the contract for the erection of a new garage for Emil Lundeen... who has the Oakland–Pontiac automobile agency in Batavia.

Grand Opening crediting the local contractors for their part in the construction.
Emil Lundeen photograph gleaned from a later advertisement.
FIGURES 7.74 & 7.75 January 18. 1929 *Geneva Republican*.

- **1929–30: State Street Garage–Hudson–Essex**, Emil Lundeen, with a second location in Batavia. July 1929, switch to **Ford**, then **Studebaker–Erskine** in 1930. Ph 2288

FIGURE 7.76 Courtesy 1930 *Geneva Republican*

- **1930–36: Swanson–Meyers Garage,** agents for **Graham–Paige, Sinclair Gas–**F.H. Swanson and George E. Meyers. George passed in 1936 of a cerebral hemorrhage.

FIGURE 7.77 Courtesy 1941 *Geneva Republican*

- **1936–47: Omer Beal Motor Co–Chevrolet & Oldsmobile–**Omer Beal dealership w/**Blue Ribbon D–X** gas pumps, Ph 799. **Cadillac–LaSalle** added in 1937. Beal purchased this property from Lundeen and the Stimple home to the west with plans to make that a parking lot. He formerly had a garage at 21 West State from 1928–32, and then in 1932–36, the Chevrolet dealership 12 East State. In 1947, Omer died of a heart attack at the age of 52 in 1947.

The Gates Motor Co sign is apparent with the letter G blocked by a tree, then the car lot sign to the left, and the Standard Oil station in the background.
FIGURE 7.78 Courtesy Geneva History Museum.

- **1947–53: Gates Motor Co–Chevrolet/Oldsmobile/Allis–Chalmers Tractors, Sinclair gas.** Joe Gates, Ph 3254. Adam Sande, head mechanic, Bud Gates, & Don Lynch in sales
- **1954–55: Fanning Chevrolet**–Edward J. Fanning Ph 605, John F. Cahill, (Oldsmobile franchise had gone to St. Charles). Earl Judd was Service Manager. Then Fanning trades Chevy dealerships with Ralph Knight of Aurora in 1955.
- **1955: M & K Chevrolet**–H.H. McClellan & Ralph Knight Ph 605, May 1955, then Chevrolet was picked up by Skip Hanson on East State in August 1955.
- **1956: Rabb Ford Motor Sales**–Carlton A. Rabb, Paul McMahon, Ph 8077. Rabb Ford was also on 3rd Street in St. Charles 1955–56.
- **1956–57: John Norris Ford**–John B. Norris Ph 8077, 1956 Christmas Greeting acknowledged employees; Paul McMahon, Russell Nystrom, Oscar Christensen, and Bob Rogers; some of whom worked at the St. Charles location of 25 North Second Street.
- **Jan–Mar 58: Lloyd Drury Used Cars**

"Harry Weissehnur Auto Sales" on edge of awning, circa 1960's. F
IGURE 7.79 Courtesy Geneva History Museum.

- **April 1958–62: Weissehnur Used Auto Sales**–Harry Weissehnur, former Zimmerman & Pack Ford sales manager, later owned Village Motors in former Chronicle building, on First Avenue, St. Charles.

- **1962: McDermott–Zimmerman Ford**–new and used cars, CE 2–7553
- **1964: J & R Used Car Sales**
- **1966: Aud's Auto Clean Up & Used Cars**
- **October 1973–current: Riley Drugs** (In 1957 Riley address was 113 W. State St.)

427 WEST STATE STREET

NE corner 5th and State

Standard Station which was built in 1928 by Lawrence Freeman. Many people petitioned against a station at this location because of the city's over saturation of stations. This may be why the popular English Tudor masonry style with a large clock hanging at the top was chosen so as to blend in with the residential neighborhood. In this photo, there is a two–bay addition to the right side of the building and I would speculate that is when the original brick and stone structure was painted. After the original was built it was said that, "The Standard Oil station on the Lawrence Freeman property...is one of the most attractive buildings of its kind along the Lincoln highway in this vicinity."
FIGURE 7.80 Courtesy Forni Grand Opening *Geneva Republican*.

- **June 1926:** *Geneva Republican*: "Lawrence Freeman has given John Bloomdahl the contract for building a gas and oil service station...will be very attractive in design and will be constructed of brick veneer. The Freeman residence which stood on that corner the past sixty years or more, has been moved to the rear of the lot and faces Fifth street."

   The delays in construction were due to locals protesting the construction of "another service station" and finally opened in September 1928.
- **1928–29: Standard Oil Co**–I.O. Sandberg, proprietor. Carter Randall was the third victim/attendant of armed robbery April 1932 as Alvar Lindahl

had been September 1931. During the Great Depression, there were almost weekly newspaper reports of filling stations being robbed up throughout the Fox Valley.

- **1936: Standard Oil Co–**R.W. Bartholomew, proprietor, C.T. Bartholomew Manager.

Gideon R. Danielson–427 East State–c. 1940. This photo shows the beautiful brick and stone work of the original cottage–style station. Most gasoline purchases at this time would be in the range of less than a dollar or two and would require that change be refunded in exchange for a couple dollar bills so attendants wore coin changers on their belts. The attendant would make change "on the spot" using the tubes loaded with pennies, nickels, dimes, and quarters and dispensed into the palm of his hand while depressing the appropriate levers.
This device was also very popular tool for the gals working at the A&W drive–in restaurants while tending to their duties as car–hops on roller skates.
FIGURE 7.81 Photo Courtesy of the Danielson Family.

- **1936: Carlson's Standard Service–**C. Arthur Carlson, he left to manage bulk plant.
- **1936–42: Danielson's Standard Service–**Gideon Danielson, he formerly managed a Standard Oil station in Elgin, but returned to Geneva where he

had previously been an attendant.

- **July 1942: Soderstrom's Standard**–Ernie Soderstrom Ph 3254, Geneva's Yellow Cab. Rumor has it that he bought a gas station to secure a supply of gas and tires for his cabs during World War II rationing. He also had the Standard at 11 East State.
- **Apr 28, 1944 Soderstrom's Standard**–George Dietrich, manager, reopened after closure during WWII.
- **1944: Rigg's Standard**
- **1946–47: Ben & Howard Standard Service**–Ben Paoletti & Howard Neal
- **1948–52: Bud's Standard**–William "Bud" Stuebinger Ph 3243
- **1952: Pete's Standard Service**–Peter Cesari Ph 3243
- **1953: Bob's Standard**
- **1955–56: Ray & Don's Standard Service**–Ray Schuett & Don Sims Ph 3247
- **1956–58: Don's Standard Service**–Don Sims, November 1956

FIGURE 7.82 Courtesy June 26, 1958 *Geneva Republican*

- **1958–59: Forni Bros**–John and Hugo Forni
- **1960: Rioux's Standard Service**–Ronald V. Rioux
- **1962: Don's Standard Service**–Donald Kuntz
- **1964–68: Burton's Standard Service** John R. Burton
- **1968: Bentz Bros**–managed station for Standard Oil
- **1969–72: Rothecker's Standard**–John R. Rothecker
- **1973–74: Bob's Standard**–Robert Caldwell

- **1974–77: Caldwell's Service Corp**–Bob Caldwell
- **1978–79: Ron's Service Center**–Ronald L. Wade
- **1980–Current: Marberry Dry Cleaners**

Current photo of the former 1928 Standard Oil station at 427 West State Street. The right-hand portion of the building that is now brick was originally porcelain panels and housed the service bays. FIGURE 7.83 Photo sourced on Google Earth.

501 WEST STATE STREET

NW corner 5th and State

- **1944:** Plans are made to move homes from the Derrick property and the Shell Oil Company will build a service station.
- **1950–55 Doring Shell Service**–Joe Doring, sold in April 7, 1955
- **1955–58 Rumsey & Trybull Shell Service**–Billie Rumsey & George Trybull Ph GEneva 3297
- **June 1958–Vacant**
- **1963–65: Rumple Shell**–Mike Rumple
- **June 1965–69 Runge's Shell**–Erl D. Runge, CEnter 2–9797, he later went to Texaco.

Runge's Grand Opening announcement caused confusion since the Bentz Bros. Shell address of First & Cheever was listed in the advertisement instead of Runge's at 501 West State. FIGURE 7.84 Courtesy June 24, 1965 *Geneva Republican.*

Ranch Style Shell: designed by famed industrial architect Raymond Loewy. Included in Loewy's broad portfolio were also the bullet nosed Studebaker of the 50's and the Avanti automobile design for Studebaker in 1963. This photo is gleaned from the internet and is representative of the Geneva station built in 1966. Geneva's was a mirror image with the bays on the left. FIGURE 7.85 Photo from *Wikipedia.*

- **1970–92: Parillo's Shell**–Joe Parrillo and wife, Carole, retired from this location after 22 years with Shell. He was a former mechanic at both Clark Pure Oil and Bud's Standard. Parillo was also a victim of his own company competing directly, when in 1987, Shell constructed a company–run facility about two miles east and sold gasoline at wholesale prices. That new station was also the first in the area to have the new pumps with credit card readers.

Joe was a consistent advertiser and supporter of the community.
FIGURE 7.86 *Geneva Republican.*

- **1992–2002: Beyer's Shell**–Brian and Alice Beyer with long–time mechanic, Dale Snyder.
- **2002: Dennis Shell**–Dale Snyder also worked for a year with new owner but could not remember his full name.

502 WEST STATE STREET

SW corners of 5th and State

The *Geneva Republican* featured a drawing of this gas station on the front page of December 03, 1937 edition. The following are quotes from the lengthy article. "The attractive, thoroughly modern and completely equipped new Pure Oil Co. service station was opened for business Wednesday Dec. 1, by the Clark Brothers, 'Bob' and 'George.' Their brother, Kenneth who recently came here from Washington, D. C., is also associated with them in the business.

"The main portion of the new building includes the office and rest rooms. Then comes the room where cars are serviced and greased and oiled. This room is equipped with two Rotary hoists operated by air compressor, and a complete assortment of air 'guns' used in greasing operations. Storage space is also provided for tires and batteries. Next to this room is the wash rack where...a tank with 150 gallons of hot water is available... and cars may also be given waxing finishes."

"Four of the newest type Tokheim computing pumps provide the various brands of gasoline desired by the motoring public. The concrete driveway extending from east to west is lighted at night by 1000 candle power flood lights. A large Pure Oil neon sign is hung at the corner just east of the station"

"Employees of the new station are Stanley Beesley, Donald Larson and Vernon Hanson. The boys were all decked out in their new Pure Oil Co. suits and put in a might busy day..."

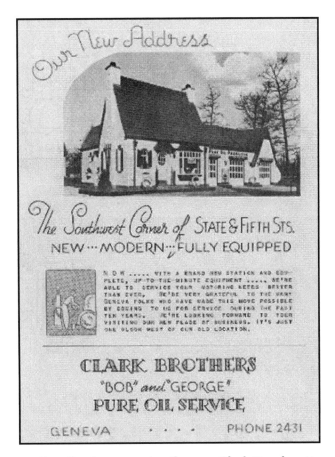

1937 Post Card announcing the new Clark Bros location.
FIGURE 7.87 Courtesy Geneva History Museum.

The article went on to credit August Wilson, General Contractor, and a long list of local sub–contractors and suppliers used in the construction.

This location has been a Pure Oil Company icon since 1937 with having the distinction of only two operators over a 69–year history of service. The Clark family, with Bob the surviving sole proprietor, spanned the first 39 years, transitioning from Pure Oil to Union 76. Joe Kuchera operated for an additional 30 years as a Union 76 and then as an auto repair facility with no gasoline until his retirement in 2006. This building became the subject of preservation as presented by a passionate local group to block demolition by a bank for expansion.

The lives touched in these stations vary from Bette Davis, actress; Chester Gould, the author of Dick Tracy; Paul Harvey, radio commentator; and Lenny Cash, who after his own business venture in Batavia was the mechanic whose tenure bridged both Clark and Kuchera.

Archie Bentz worked here in the 1940's and 1950's with time off to serve in the Army, and Joe Parrillo similarly started his career here and the two of them had a combined tenure of over 80 years in the business.

- **1937–45: Clark Bros Pure Oil**–Bob, George & Ken Clark, Ph 2431, Paul Clement left Tri–City Garage to come here as a mechanic. Don Graham, brother–in–law, work here in 1945 and later became a respected local insurance broker.

In 1939, Clark Bros opened another Pure Oil in Aurora at South Lake and Gale streets under Ken Clark's management and that building, with similar architecture, still stands today. Both George and Ken Clark left the business during WWII.
FIGURE 7.88 Current Google Earth view.

- **1945–72: Clark's Pure Oil:** Bob Clark
- **1972–76: Bob Clark's Union 76**

This very undeniable identification with the building superimposed over the Pure Oil logo was used by Clark throughout his tenure. This Christmas greeting is from Bob, George & Ken Clark, with Stan Beesley, Don Larson, Vern Hanson & Bill Christensen.
FIGURE 7.89 *Geneva Republican.*

I had to include the picture of what could have been my father shoveling snow
at the Clark station. In 1945, at 16, he was "low man on the totem–pole."
FIGURE 7.90 Courtesy Geneva History Museum.

The steep sloped blue tile roof combined with the quaint charm and warmth of the English
Cottage and trademark blue "P" on the chimney were unmistakable as the iconic beacon for a
Pure Oil gas station amongst the many restored homes with wooden shutters and
flower boxes in the neighborhood. FIGURE 7.91 Copy of original Peterson
drawings in American Gas Station.

The entire 6th chapter of *The Gas Station in America"* epitomizes the Pure Oil English Cottage style of gas station as designed by C.A. Peterson and that significance is attributed as to setting the industry standards for developing buildings that bridged a corporate standard that blended with the neighborhood culture. It is my contention that if the preservation group had presented just this chapter to the Geneva Historic Preservation Commission, it would have cut to the chase and the resulting vote would have been unanimous for preservation. I would still support a movement for the property owner and the community to band together to further restore the window and door nomenclature to reflect the original as depicted in Peterson's early drawing shown above.

This former Rockwood, TN station retains the radius top entry door and copper–topped bay window. The canopy over the pump area, is a feature more prevalent in the south. While the two bay doors have been eliminated, there was a plague on the front door reading: " Hines Bros Service Station, c. 1937." FIGURE 7.92 Author's photograph.

The Geneva station had an early addition (overhead door) across the rear of the building making room for 2–3 more service bays, with access to the front of the building. With the removal of that addition shown in the picture on the right, the doorways are now used for access to the current drive–up bank facility. FIGURES 7.93 & 7.94 Courtesy *Wikipedia*.

MARCH 1955: SUBURBAN MOTORS, LTD-VOLKSWAGEN-BOB CLARK.

During my research for this book I had the occasion to speak to many "Genevans" in the museum's brown–bag lunch round–table discussions and always took the opportunity to ask if anyone had any memory of the Clark Pure Oil station selling Volkswagens. At that time, no one there could corroborate my memories of VW cars lining the sidewalk in front of the station or remember seeing any advertisements or Volkswagens. I remembered the VW introduction at the Burgess Norton Family Picnic at what I recall may have been at Good Templar Park. My father worked at both Clark's and Burgess Norton and had worked out a plan to sponsor the ice cream for the picnic in exchange for displaying Volkswagens on the picnic grounds. As a 6–year–old, I can remember riding in a VW bus which was unlike anything we had seen before, a predecessor to modern minivans. An entire book could be written about the challenge of selling a German–made car in post WWII America.

Years later, conversations on the subject with my father recalled that Clark was the second VW agency in the State of Illinois. The other very significant recollection was that Pure Oil Company was not happy with an automobile sales lot in conjunction with the service station and insisted on the immediate termination of the dealership relationship. Additionally, if you peruse the advertisement below for the sale of VW's in Geneva, Clark had avoided tying the auto dealership to either Pure Oil or Clark names by creating the Suburban Motors Ltd. moniker under which to do business, in an effort to avoid detection by Pure Oil Co. This all helps to explain the short–lived dealership and the lack of awareness. Later, Bob Clark sold the VW franchise to a fellow that intended to re–establish the dealership in Aurora. That individual had also appreciated Archie's product knowledge and salesmanship skills and in turn offered Archie a partnership. Archie was skeptical and passed on an opportunity to become a part of what was to become Springbrook Motors, Inc., Volkswagen, 417 South Lincolnway, North Aurora.

Bob Clark was a local resident, doing business over the decades, but as is often the stigma with gas station operators, they were perceived as just "grease monkeys" and not entrepreneurs. It may be difficult for many people to truly comprehend the cutting–edge of this entrepreneurship displayed by Clark and others to the point that I opened this book with Clark's "Free Air–Free Enterprise" from 1944.

I was thrilled to find an advertisement on the last page of a 1955 *Geneva Republican* and a corroborating announcement in the *St. Charles Chronicle* to validate my memories. The second advertisement is dated in June of 1955, combined with the knowledge that BN family picnics were traditionally in July, which tells me the dealership lasted about six months.

- **March 3, 1955** *Geneva Republican*: "If any residents of the Fox Valley observed last week while driving out West State Street in Geneva a display of small cars of unusual design, they may not realize that they are looking at the product of the fourth largest automaker in the world. With the opening of a Volkswagen agency, valley residents will have an opportunity to buy any of a complete line which includes not only the sedan and sunroof convertible, but also a station wagon, bus, ambulance and four different truck models. Robert Clark of Geneva is the sales outlet on display at 502 West State...many Americans who have grown tired of pushing around unneeded tons of metal will find much to recommend..."

FIGURE 7.95 *Geneva Republican* March 10, 1955. See text and ad on next page.

FIGURE 7.96 Courtesy June 9, 1955 *Geneva Republican*

VOLKSWAGEN—NOW IN GENEVA—THE IDEAL 2ND CAR—HERE'S WHY . . .

35 miles to the gallon...5 pints of oil at an oil change...air cooled engine therefore no radiator, no need for anti-freeze...minimum "bump shop" bills (a new fender costs $14)...rear engine drive plus all four wheels are independently suspended giving outstanding traction in snow, mud and on ice... the latest thing in comfort and ride is the torsion bar suspension—again on ALL four wheels...normal cruising speed 60–70 miles per hour...easy to drive, park, and maintain...complete SERVICE facilities and PARTS department right here in Geneva.

And Here Is What They Say About It . . .

CONSUMERS REPORT, OCT. 1954 – "For the American small-car buyer who wants novelty in design, stamina over the road and above all quality and good workmanship, the VOLKSWAGEN stands practically alone at its moderate price."

ROAD AND TRACK – Summed up, the VOLKSWAGEN as "the most amazing and versatile car in its class. It combines satisfactory traffic performance with ample highway cruising speed and remarkable all-around economy not only in fuel consumption but also in all things including first cost, depreciation and repairs."

WIKIPEDIA: "Volkswagens were first exhibited and sold in the United States in 1949, but sold only two units in America that first year. On entry to the U.S. market, the VW was briefly sold as a Victory Wagon. Volkswagen of America was formed in April 1955 to standardize sales and service in the United States. Production of the Type 1 Volkswagen Beetle increased dramatically over the years, the total reaching one million in 1955."

ST. CHARLES CHRONICLE, March 9, 1955: "Selling Volkswagen: A new foreign car agency has opened at 502 W State St, Geneva for the sale a small German car called the 'Volkswagen'. It has a rear drive engine."

1939 Memorial Day Parade, note Pure Oil 'P' on chimney. Where the cars are parked facing the street is where the later Volkswagens would be on display. That parking area would diminish when the highway was widened in later years.
FIGURE 7.97 Courtesy Geneva History Museum.

Geneva Republican photo announcing the change of ownership in 1977. Note that the Pure Oil 'P' on the chimney is no longer highlighted in blue. Also, the unique architectural elements of the earlier radius top door and bay windows have been eliminated in favor of a larger, more modern window. FIGURE 7.98 Courtesy Geneva History Museum.

- **1976–95: Kuchera's Union 76–** Joe Kuchera, eventually stopped selling gas about 1995 but still operated as a repair facility until his retirement in 2006.

2007 Pure Gardner Florist shop FIGURE 7.99 Courtesy Pure Gardner

- **2007–12: Pure Gardener Florist**

In 2012, it was repurposed as a drive–thru bank and subsequently recognized on the National Register of Historic Places and received a City of Geneva Historic Preservation Award. FIGURE 7.100 Current Google Earth View.

- **2012–Current: Geneva Bank and Trust**

29–33 SOUTH 8TH STREET

- **1960–85: Olie's Garage**–Ralph L "Olie" Olson had a history of wrenching in Geneva and St. Charles since 1945. Herb White worked with him in the beginning. He moved to a new shop next door and leased his former garage to Ed Eakins.
- **1974–2016: Ed's Garage**–Ed Eakins, a former employee of Duke & Lee took over the building where Olie had been when Olie retired.

23 SOUTH 8TH STREET

- **1973: Tri–City Transmission**–Ph 232–2517 Ed
- **1985–2018: Gorecki's Service**–James F. Gorecki, Jr, formerly at ARCO on East Main in St. Charles.

501 EDISON STREET

- **1968–71: Shorty's Garage**–Clyde E. Gum
- **1975–80: SVD&D–Special Vehicle Design & Development**–Gary Severson
- **1980–81: Auto–Truck Garage**–Ken Poellauer & Chuck Fehr
- **1982–2017: Ken' Automotive**–Ken Poellauer
- **2017: Theresa Fairbank**

511 STEVENS STREET

- **1971: Chuck's Automotive**–Chuck Fehr
- **Year unknown: Chuck Augustine**
- **1985–86: Myron's Auto Repair**–Myron Stevens
- **Ron's Automotive**–Ron Erickson

522 STEVENS STREET

- **1981–1983: Chuck's Garage**–Chuck Fehr

728 WEST STATE STREET

SE corner 8th and State

- E.D. Jones of Chicago built in 1922. The **first purpose–built** service station in Geneva. February 24, 1922 *Geneva Republican*; "Taylor Gibbs has the contract for the construction of a new gas and oil filling station just west of the W.H. Martin Lumber Co on West State street." The station was completed mid–April.

FIGURES 7.101 & 7.102 April 28, 1922 & October 22, 1926 *Geneva Republican*

- **1922–33: Blue Ribbon Filling Station–Diamond Gasoline–**L.H. Freeman, manager. Jones managed his station for a short time until he took on the construction of another location in Wheaton and then turned this station over to Freeman. Oscar Swanson, night employee, was robbed at gunpoint June 1930.
- **1933–35: D–X Service Station–**L.H. Freeman, branding changed to **D–X** gasoline in 1933 as distributed by **Blue Ribbon Oil Co/Mid–Continent Petroleum Co.**
- **1935: D–X Service–**Art Johnson
- **November 1936: D–X Service –Floyd "Toots" Anderson**
- **August 1937–40: Martin's D–X Service Station–**Paul & Claire Martin, Ph 619
- **1940: Cities Service Oil Co–**leased the site from John Wheeler, with a new station to be built by local contractor, August Wilson, will be operated in the meantime as Cities Service.

The new station was completed December 1941.
FIGURE 7.103 Courtesy Geneva History Museum & *Geneva Republican*.

- **January 1942–75: Dick's Cities Service/CITGO–**Dick Rydquist, formerly with McCornack Oil St. Charles, Ph 3299. Jack Leuer employee, formerly with Armburst Garage/Texaco. It was the beginning of WWII and gas rationing was about to begin. Dick did not have an established monthly volume of gasoline purchases and the branding had changed from D–X to Cities Service. It wasn't long before he became a statistic of the 25% closures due to rationing. I do not know if he sought employment elsewhere or if he served in the armed forces. Dick did reopen after the war and when he closed this location after 34 years, he was hired at Bentz Bros. Mobil to pump gas and greet his old customers.
- **1975–78: Geneva Quick Mart–**Rasmussen Oil–Howard & John Rasmussen, manager.
- **1978–81: Geneva Marathon–**Rasmussen Oil
- **1982: Carlson's Flooring**

There was one more gas station heading further west of Geneva that was located at **1401 Prairie Street** and while technically in St. Charles, the customer base was largely "Genevans." Earlier I touched on the subject of the Lincoln Highway and also discussed one route change in Geneva from 1st to 3rd street in order to avoid trolley traffic under the trestle. Again, another change to the Lincoln Highway route through Geneva resulted in the building of this gas station. Initially, to travel this highway one turned left off of westbound State St and followed Kaneville Road to Keslinger Road. Now, however, State Street extended to 14th Street and one turned right, north, to Prairie Street and then left in order to continue west to DeKalb. The road then ran through the area where the St. Charles Moose building is currently located. Eventually, in the 1965, State Street was paved farther west which straightened out the route. That new road now bypassed the gas station on 14th and Prairie.

You may, at times, be confused with the highway name or nomenclature for State Street which we now know as State Highway Route 38 or Lincoln Highway. This road has had route numbers of 30, 330 and Alternate 30 all assigned to it in days gone past. This was further complicated by another State Route 30, (Galena Street) running parallel to the south through Sugar Grove and Aurora; hence the Alt 30 nomenclature. To get a better picture of the local route and its changes, go to the following website for a map.

www.lincolnhighwayassoc.org/map

As was the case in most stops along the Lincoln Highway, there were many overnight "Tourist Camps" for overnight rest. The primary needs of the traveler were being met with food, gas, and affordable place to stay overnight. At this intersection, the camp was called the McDonald Tourist Camp.

Current photo of a former Filling Station/Barbeque Stand with an 'off the beaten–path' location on Prairie & 14th St. The original building is the portion with the pitched roof and had living quarters upstairs. There had been gas pumps with a canopy where the flat roof addition is now. FIGURE 7.104 Sourced on Google Earth.

1401 PRAIRIE STREET

SW corners of Prairie and 14th St.– a "Y" intersection on the former Lincoln Highway.

- **1929–34: "Y" Barbecue and Pure Oil Filling Station/General Store**–Emmett Phillips. Ph SC 2733 A large illuminated "Y" sign could be seen for miles.
- **1936–40: Bell's "Y" Barbecue**–a **Pure Oil** gas station on the old State Route 330 and the Lincoln Highway heading west to Dekalb. Charles Benns became manager in 1937.
- **1939: Busse's "Y" Barbecue**–they were from a popular Yorkville restaurant.
- **1940–43: Wally's "Y" Barbecue**– "1 mile west of Geneva on Route 330"
- Ph St. Charles 3535
- **1944–45: Al's "Y" Barbecue** "Roast Duck Sat & Sun, Liquors & Beer"
- **1946: Bud's "Y" Barbecue**
- **1954: "Y" Barbecue**–Sherm & Clarence, April 1954
- **1954–61: Sherm & Pat's "Y" Bar–B–Que,** August 1954

FIGURE 7.105 *Geneva Republican*

- **Nov 1962–66: "Y's" Owl–Bar/Restaurant**–Ben Paoletti and Bill Arbizzani. Many often confused the "Y's" Owl with the downtown "Little Owl" restaurant name, but I discovered an article that explains that both restaurants were now under the same management. So now the former "Y" Bar–B–Que is the "Y's" Owl, pronounced "Wise Owl", featuring family dining and a separate bar area. There was no mention of the gas pumps that I remember seeing there in the early 1960's. St. Charles phone; JU 4–9535
- **1966: The "Y"**–Harvey and Vera Giese
- **Current: One Stop Liquors**

DID YOU KNOW THAT WE HAD OIL WELLS IN KANE COUNTY? May 16, 1930 *GENEVA REPUBLICAN* HEADLINES: STRIKE OIL AT "Y" BARBEQUE– "The furor of excitement which swept Geneva Wednesday is spreading all over the state today as news is broadcast of the discovery of a miniature oil gusher in the basement of the "Y" barbeque station..." FIGURE 7.106 Courtesy *Geneva Republican*.

- **Republican–May 16, 1930:** The article goes on to detail the flow of high–grade oil filling augured holes that had been drilled to rid the basement of seepage but were instead filling with oil that "when filtered through a chamois skin resulted in a product that when introduced into the tank of a Model T, the "flivver," purred as smoothly as though it was using high test gasoline." Experienced oil men, engineers, and geologists offered opinions that the property owner, Phillips, would soon be very rich man with offers from Standard Oil, Indian Refining and Purol taking samples that revealed high–grade oil. Phillips had declined an offer of $125,000 for his place to include the oil rights. The rumors abound with many farmers west of Geneva noticing a scum of oil on creeks and ponds and one farmer near Wasco reporting sufficient natural gas coming from his well water to burn two lights in his home. There was definitely a strong feeling of an "Oil Boom Era" about to begin in the area.

- **Republican–May 30, 1930:** Oil continues to flow into the basement of Emmet Phillips "Y" Barbecue and operations are at a standstill pending definite analysis from laboratories. Each night the oil is bailed out but by morning it reaches the top of the nine shallow wells that have been dug in the basement floor. While geologists and farmers were arranging to sink holes in nearby farmland a report came from South Elgin that a well driller there had stuck what appeared to be oil. Mr. Phillips appeared unwilling to finance the sinking of a deep well on his property and was still chiefly concerned with getting the oil and gas out of his basement.

- **Republican–June 27, 1930:** Called by Fox Valley Federation, State Geologist, M.M. Leighton makes a thorough survey and study of the so-called "Y" filling station oil well on the westward outskirts of Geneva and St. Charles. His report notes a remarkedly close similarity between the discovered "oil" and the plain gasoline in the nearest underground tank on the property. It was his intent to prevent a serious explosion from the tank's leakage into the basement and to put an end to "get rich quick" dreams and schemes where attempts might be made to secure investments in promoting unwarranted drilling. In other words, there is no question but that the "oil" seepage came from the gas station tanks.

- **Republican–July 25, 1930:** Emmett Phillips, owner of the "Y" Barbecue west of Geneva and several local men associated with him have been visiting farmers in the past two weeks in an effort to get them sign leases for oil rights on their lands. A Wheaton geologist contended that there was considerable oil to be found hereabouts despite the unfavorable reports made by the state geologists.

- **Republican–August 15, 1930:** Encouraged by a geologist using a radium instrument and opinions that there was certainty of much oil to be had, local men Emmet Phillips, Taylor Gibbs and J.A. Tallman secured oil rights and leases on practically all farms in this vicinity and have announced their intentions to drill three wells in the near future; one to be sunk at the "Y" station, another at Bald Mound, and a third on the Scott farm near LaFox. The radium instrument which is said to have a proven record in oil fields in southern states encouraged the investors to ignore the state geologist's opinion.

- **Republican–September 12, 1930:** "Considerable water in the test bore being sunk on the Scott farm near LaFox has halted the drilling for oil at a depth of about 200 feet…several oil men from Creston, Iowa have been watching the work this week."

- **Republican–September 19, 1930:** "Driller for oil on the Scott farm near LaFox 'shot' the well with a heavy charge of the dynamite the first of this week. Just what the result has not been determined, according to Paul Scott."
- **Republican–September 26, 1930:** "Oil continues to flow in the Phillips "Y" Barbecue basement, reliable sources say they are driving their cars with the oil that they dip daily from an inverted section of sewer pipe."
- **Republican–November 7, 1930:** "Dr. H.J. von Hagen, widely known geologist and oil engineer, to locate four wells for Phillips Syndicate." *The Republican* is informed of a trust that was enlisting financial support of some of the shrewdest and best–known business men of this and nearby cities and a that a sum of $60,000 will be raised to insure the drilling of four wells. Mr. Neely of Batavia, a driller who has had 15 years' experience in the Oklahoma oil fields has his equipment in place and operations will start next Monday.
- **Republican–November 14, 1930:** As the oil frenzy continues, Mayor H.C. Hanson and City Engineer E. Roy Wells are called upon to deny rumors that traces of oil are in the new city water well on North Logan Ave. State Inspectors have been called in to confirm this. In the meantime, C.W. Crosby who drilled the well on the Scott farm at LaFox emphatically denies that any oil has been found in that drilling which is now down to 635 feet.
- **Republican–December 5, 1930:** Dr. H.J. von Hagen, PhD wrote a lengthy opinion noting full justification for the exploratory oil wells. He also stated that he examined the seepage or "as the experts called it; leakage." His further evaluation of the basement oil seepage versus the contents of the "leaking" tanks bore no resemblance and the "young experts" were inexperienced with oil products.
- **Republican–December 12, 1930:** W.J. Neely of Batavia has drilled to a depth of 140 feet in the second well, that being sunk on the Murphy farm, some four hundred feet southwest of the well where natural gas was struck Thursday evening at a depth of 108 feet. Dr von Hagen stated this well was producing 150,000 cubic feet of gas per day and that half dozen such wells would produce natural gas sufficient for light and heat in Geneva. All of this fed the furor of excitement in this section of the state.

The winter of 1930–31 must have taken its toll on the finances and fortitude of those involved in the oil fever speculation. I found no further references to oil wells until the July 15, 1932 edition that picks up a story from the

DeKalb Chronicle that speculates there is oil on the Ed Wyman farm near Sycamore. In the meantime, the Republican staff remember the speculation of the so-called experts two years before. Over the next ten years speculators will drill wells at the "Y", Bald Mound, LaFox, Sycamore, Sheridan, and even by a new St. Charles water well on 7th Avenue where a pocket of oil was discovered. During the Great Depression, people were also scammed by the "Rainmakers" offering, for a fee, to make the heavens open and bring forth the rejuvenating rain. Needless to say, no one got rich from oil wells in Kane County.

- **Republican–August 13, 1937–**The problem of oil and gas seeping into the basement has reoccurred with concerns about fire prevention from owner Bell. A spark from the electric pump installed to pump out the seepage started a fire that was quickly extinguished. D. Howard Davis, district manager for the **Pure Oil Co**, has checked the tanks and says positively there was no loss of gasoline from that source.
- **November 26, 1937–**State Fire Marshall ordered the gas tanks to be removed, and relocated to front driveway area.

1505 LINCOLN HIGHWAY

SW corner State St. and Bricher Rd., St. Charles
- **1992: BP–**pumper built by ShoDeen, leased by AMOCO Oil
- **Current: Pride of St. Charles BP**   ·

855 RANDALL ROAD, ST. CHARLES
- **Current: Meijer Gas**

530 LARK STREET
- **1993–current: Stevens' Automotive Repairing–**Dave Stevens Ph 232–9440 His father, Avery Stevens, who had worked for Reber & Foley in St. Charles for 50 years before joining his son here in 1995 until his retirement in 2006.

560 LARK STREET
- **1979: Alpha Beta Werks–**Rex Chalmers & Robert Sanderson

561 LARK STREET
- **1979: Kern Brake & Alignment–**Richard L. Kern had moved from Prairie Street
- **1988: R-S Automotive–**Steve Anderson Ph 232–2113

EIGHT

GENEVA EAST SIDE

5 EAST STATE STREET

- **1922–33: East Side Auto Parts and Service Station**–Lloyd Bogart prop. Ph 635, Agents for **Oakland & Pontiac** sales in 1926. In 1922 new and used parts advertised from auto wrecking yard. The Auburn–Cord–Duesenberg Museum confirms that there is record of an Auburn Dealership doing business as **Geneva Auburn** at 5 E. State in 1931, which would then have had the same proprietor, L. Bogart. While I found no evidence of any attempts to sell Auburns via advertisements, there were notices for the sale of new automobiles. October 5, 1928: "R.W. Holmberg is the owner of an attractive new Auburn sedan purchased from the East Side Auto Parts." November 22, 1929: "Arch Richards is the first owner in Geneva of one of the new Cord front wheel drive automobiles...It is powered with an eight–cylinder Lycoming motor similar to the one used in the Duesenberg." May 29, 1931: "Maynard Skogland is driving an attractive new Auburn sport roadster."

Bennett St. (Rt. 25) looking north to State St. Sinclair on north side of State St with Chrysler garage on left. FIGURE 8.1 Courtesy Geneva History Museum, circa 1939.

11 EAST STATE STREET

- **1928: George Tronto Filling Station–**East State Ph Geneva 2428
- **1932–45: Johnson's Sinclair Service**–Clarence C. Johnson. **March 30, 1945** *Geneva Republican*: "William Johnson of Johnson's Sinclair was charged with passing 476 counterfeit A12s [gas ration coupons] for 1,428 gallons. He was suspended for the duration."
- **1945–47: Joe's Service Station**–Joe Petraitis, Ph 3644, former Ford mechanic
- **1950: Stotler's Standard**–Frank Stotler
- **1952–56: Soderstrom's Standard Service–**Ernie Soderstrom, formerly with Tri–City garage, he also had the 537 W State Standard in 1943.
- **1980s': Mill Race Cyclery**

15 EAST STATE STREET

NW corner State and Bennett (Rt. 25)

- **Netter Garage–**with gas pumps
- **1934–37: Fox River Sinclair Service**– Herman Baselsoder, Ph 1013
- **1940: East Side Conoco–**Clyde Young

19 EAST STATE STREET

- **1932–41: John Zaranka Service–**McCornack Oil converted to Texaco in 1934. Zaranka also operated a tavern at this location.

12 EAST STATE STREET

SW corner State and Bennett–Rt 25 (17 S. Bennett)

FIGURE 8.2 Courtesy October 10, 1924 *Geneva Republican*

- **1926–27: Lundeen Bros Hudson–Essex–**Emil & Frank Lundeen, Ph Geneva 635 and Batavia 1571. Formerly at Tri–City Garage and other endeavors. In July 1926, Lundeen Bros. purchased this property from Lloyd Bogart of East Side Auto Parts, who had started constructing this large garage the previous year but had not finished. Upon completion of the building Lundeen also offered **Oakland/Pontiac.**

- **July 27, 1928** *Geneva Republican*: Lundeen has sold the building to the C A & E Railroad/Bus Garage (Chicago Aurora & Elgin) *"...having sold to interests controlling motor coach lines...[Lundeen] has purchased the fine large lot in W. State street between Fourth and Fifth streets...will soon start the erection of a modern brick garage at a cost estimated at near $18,000."* Apparently, the bus lines will utilize the rear of the building while leasing the front to various dealers.

- **1928–32: Geneva Buick–**Elmer Johnson & Adley Schultz, both from Hinkley, also sold **Standard Oil products** including **Atlas tires**.

- **1932–36: Oldsmobile 6 & 8–Omer Beal Motor Co–Chevrolet & Oldsmobile,** Ph 719. Blue–Ribbon Oil Co. supplied **Diamond Gas**, a precursor to D–X gas, then Beal switched to **Mobilgas**, a **Socony–Vacuum** product in 1934.

When Beal announces his switch to Mobilgas in 1934 the *Geneva Republican* quotes him as saying: "The Socony–Vacuum Corporation is a unit of eight great oil companies...Standard Oil of New York; Vacuum Oil Co; Lubrite Refining Corp; Wadham's Oil Co; Magnolia Petroleum Corp; White Star Refining Co; White Eagle Corp; and General Petroleum." In a previous chapter, I discussed the 1911 break–up of Standard Oil and this quote emphasizes how in spite of that so–called break–up, Standard Oil continued to grow. Even so, Congress decontrolled the oil companies in 1981 and now we have Exxon–Mobil and a handful of other major oil conglomerates.

In 1932, Beal had moved to this location from 21 West State Street. During his tenure here from 1932–36, he became concerned that the new landlord, the C A & E Railroad was looking to expand with the future evolution from electric trains to buses and would want to use the entire building for themselves, so he opted to move again to Lundeen's building at 415 West State.

12 East State St., 1937 J.H. Mitchell advertisement, and circa 1943 photo of Flynn–Morton Dodge & Plymouth with Standard Oil gas pumps. Note the Mill Race Inn sign in background, the well–known restaurant which was started in 1933 by Ann Forsyth with the help of her sister Marjorie. The restaurant building incorporated the structure of the 1842 Alexander smithy and a former mill raceway, hence the name. She sold to Ray Johns sometime in the 1940s. FIGURE 8.3 & 8.4 Courtesy *Geneva Republican* & Geneva History Museum.

- **1936–40: Mitchell Neighborhood Service Station & Garage, Dodge & Plymouth–**John H. Mitchell, Ph 888 (moved here from Ford on First Street), Jack Frost, (Jack's Garage–Batavia) manager, Ray Murray, sales. In 1937, a large addition was made by contractor, August Wilson, to house, wash, and repair buses for the C A & E bus service. The buses will replace the third rail electric trolly system serving the Fox Valley.
- **1940–1943: Flynn–Morton Dodge & Plymouth–**Donald Flynn & E.M.

Morton, also sold **Standard Oil & Gas, Ford Ferguson** tractors. The dealers lost the lease at 12 East State to the property owners, C A & E Railroad. Flynn leased Armburst Garage and will sell Dodge and Plymouth. Peter Armburst and John Nelson will continue to be associated with Flynn. Morton will enter the filling station business in Elgin.

- **1943–1953 C A & E Railroad/Bus Garage (Chicago Aurora & Elgin).** There were multiple changes to Geneva in February 1953. A huge fire on the west side, devastated multiple businesses. Rosenfelder's Ace Hardware needed an alternative site while rebuilding on his original site, so the railroad leased part of this building to him. In August, the Illinois Commerce Commission terminated the Fox Valley buses and with Rosenfelder moving into his new building in September, the building became vacant.

  Also, in August, Valos, the owner of the dealership building where Skip Hanson is conducting his Studebaker business on north Third street, was making plans to lease his building to a new tenant. So, Hanson buys the former bus garage and moves the Studebaker dealership in October while still remodeling this new location.

- **1953–1955 Skip Hanson Studebaker & Packard** "Willis 'Skip' Hanson was a successor to George Ekdahl in operating the local News Agency…then succeeded John Gregg as the local Studebaker dealer on Third street, now is remodeling this building back to retail showrooms and service repair."

Hanson Chevrolet in the early 1970's–SW corner State and Bennett.
FIGURE 8.5 Courtesy Geneva History Museum.

Hanson Chevrolet in the early 1970's–NE corner, this sales lot was added in 1962. When the dealership moved to St. Charles, this became the site of 'Geneva Body Shop' and is now the 'Geneva Place' retirement apartments. FIGURE 8.6 Courtesy Geneva History Museum.

- **1955–72: Hanson Chevrolet–** Willis 'Skip' Hanson *"Then at this location, recently added Packard to the line when Packard and Studebaker merged. Now in 1955, Hanson Motor Sales has acquired the Chevrolet Agency and returns to a brand he is quite familiar with."* 1961 service manager–Art Wullbrandt, my cousin's father–in–law.

   Here is a great example of why local ownership of businesses benefits the community. *Geneva Republican* July 16, 1959: "Willis M. Hanson, Geneva Chevrolet dealer, who was awarded the grand prize at the St. Charles VFW Fourth of July carnival, in turn presented the Chevrolet Brookwood sedan to St Peter's Catholic Church." How many large corporations even purchase a ticket?

- **1972–1974: Jim Wulff Chevrolet–**Wulff was a former defensive halfback with the Washington Redskins for three years; then district manager with GM. He moved this dealership to East Main in St. Charles where Don McCue is now.

   By the mid–1970's, Geneva, which had historically been served by multiple car dealerships, found itself with one remaining hometown dealer, Lou's Jeep. The dealers from surrounding communities recognized that the needs for Genevans were not being met and the following companies were now advertising in the *Geneva Republican* in 1976: Greg Chrysler–Plymouth, Zimmerman

Ford–Mercury, Jacobs Chevrolet–Buick, Davison Buick–Pontiac, Fanning Chevrolet, Fran Wibbs Cadillac, Krumpholz Chevrolet, and Avenue Chevrolet. At the time of this writing, there are no new–car dealers in either Geneva or Batavia.

9 SOUTH BENNETT STREET

Rt. 25, SE corner State and Bennett
- **1848: H. & Wm. Miller Distillery**
- **1929: Adolph's Shell**–listed as both Auto Dealer and Filling Station/Garage
- **1930: Parkside Service Station–TYDOL** addressed as Bennett south of State
- **1931: Shell Service**–managed by Peter Arbizzani
- **1932–33: Hakes Service Station**–Clyde Hakes former McCornack employee
- **1936–37: Swanson's Service Station**
- **1940: Cleland's Shell Service**
- **1965: Geneva Cycle Shop–Ducati**–Ph 232–4883

12 NORTH BENNETT STREET

- **1931–32: Gentry Service, Lawrence Gentry** Ph 1106
- **1938–40: Cutrite Oil Co** *"50 feet north of Stop and Go signal"* –Orlan "Orie" Therrien, Manager.

    The City of Geneva had purchased land along the east bank of the river, north of State street, to create a city–funded tourist court to encourage travelers in the early days of automotive travel. *Geneva Republican* August 1924: *"The Chief of the Opekchia Indian tribe, nine bucks, one squaw and two papooses from Central Arizona are camping in the auto camp on the east side of Geneva. Among them are the medicine man, snake charmers and fancy paper cutters."*

EAST–SIDE STOP LIGHT

No specific address given in the ad
- **November 1940: D–X Service**–Bill Schnulle (former City of St. Charles Electrician)

33–35 NORTH BENNETT STREET

- **1924–32: Frank Lundeen & Lloyd Bogart Garage** (new construction) later just Bogart.
- **1932–33: H.J. Sudduth,** also 102 West State, Standard Oil
- **1936–37: Kirkey Service Station**, Nelson J. Kirkey

FIGURE 8.7 Courtesy July 1938 *Geneva Republican*

- **1938–40: Judd's Cities Service–**Earl L. Judd, prop, Ph 2071.
- **1942: Swanson's Mobile Station**
- **1962: Grubb's Cities Service–**the only reference to this station was a mention of bowling team sponsorship w/American Legion 342 league.
- **1970's: Zabel Auto Electric–**Al Zabel was a specialize company rebuilding starters, generators, and alternators. He moved to Stevens St in the 80's
- **1980's–90's: K & D Sales & Service–**small engine shop

34 NORTH BENNETT STREET

- **1975–82: Rothecker Automotive–**Auto parts, Jon E. Rothecker Ph 232–8318

Hilltop Sinclair Service, 206 East State. FIGURE 8.8 Courtesy *Geneva Republican*.

206 EAST STATE STREET AND CRISSEY AVENUE

1949–Batavia Road was renamed for prominent Geneva author and Saturday Evening Post contributor, Forest Crissey. There had been confusion between Batavia Road and Batavia Avenue on the west side.

- **1950–62: Hilltop Sinclair–**W.D. "Bill" Rourke, manager with Don Seyller, Jim Marian employees, added Ben Chesley as mechanic in 1958.

Author's note: The following news article was probably in response to yet another gas station being built at the corner of State and Crissey, the Hilltop Sinclair Grand Opening was in December 1950. All of this is just the tip of the iceberg for communities looking to limit the number and locations of future gas stations over the next four decades.

- *Geneva Republican* **July 28, 1950:** "Twelve of the 13 gas stations are on State street, the lone exception being Sullivan's Shell station on First street, south of the North Western tracks–––Two of the garages are on First street, two on Third and one on East State–––With Sinclair, the Geneva motorist will [now] have eight different [brands] of gasoline to choose from–––Standard may be purchased at four places, Cities Service, Pure Oil and Texaco at three each, Shell at two, Mobilgas and Brilliant Bronze at one each–––Three stations have gone out of business in recent years and one garage has discontinued selling gas, so the increase in numbers of stations is probably very small in the last few years–"
- *Geneva Republican* **August 4, 1950:** "Harry C. Hanson, Geneva city attorney, has received a reply from the Illinois Municipal League in reference to the matter of limiting the number of filling stations in a city. "They do not know of any municipality which has limited the number of filling stations which may be established–––These businesses may by subject to regulation and licensing, but there is apparently no authority for limiting the number–"

  Ironically, this same location is the very site of protests three decades later, but then the protesters were service station dealers fighting a jobber taking this location and selling gas at wholesale prices. The demise of your locally owned service station started here in 1981 and it was not due to the natural attrition process, but instead, the takeover by the oil companies themselves.

- **1963: For Lease**
- **1964–66: Robinson Service–**Neil A. Robinson
- **1966–68: Wallace Sinclair–**Mike Wallace, also Phillips 66 on W. Main, St. Charles.

- **1970–72: Geneva Sinclair**–David Marellis manger
- **1972–75: Geneva ARCO**–David Marellis manager, the building had been changed to a kiosk.
- **1975–81: Geneva Standard**–David Marellis, manager, now the building has evolved to more of a convenience store.
- **1981–89: Geneva Amoco**–Randy Marcellis, manager, former Amoco Field Supervisor is now working for Valley Petroleum as this location evolves into a wholesale pumper location
- **Current: CITGO/Vacant**

537 EAST STATE STREET

NW corner State and Harrison (441 East)

- **July 13, 1928** *Geneva Republican: "Mead & Mikesell of Aurora have leased a lot at the corner...and have engaged contractor Gibbs to erect a modern building for the sale of Shell gasoline."*
- **1928–33: Mead & Mikeselle Service Station–Shell,** Ph Geneva 2485
- **1936–37: Standard Oil Service Station**

In 1947, Einar (Andy) Anderson and Glen Pierce built Andy and Glen's Cities Service Station at 537 East State. Andy's career started in 1924 at Tri–City Garage where he worked until partnering with Glen in 1947. Glen had worked at Carlson Texaco in Batavia for 15 years. FIGURE 8.9 Courtesy Geneva History Museum.

- **July 1948–69: Andy and Glenn's Cities Service**–Einer 'Andy' Anderson, Glen Pierce, Ph 3283. In 1969, they built a beautiful modern 3–bay service station to replace the old one and then opted to retire. Andy and Glenn had achieved a combined record of 48 years of service in the automobile industry.
- **1970–73: Ed's CITGO**–Edwin Vodvarka Ph 232–9783

- **November 73–74: Lowell's CITGO–**Lowell Hager, Jr, assisted by Joe Madison.

Gen Hoe restaurant in remodeled CITGO gas station. FIGURE 8.10 Picture Post Card.

- **1977–Current: Gen Hoe–**Shee Yee Lee & Jenny Lee remodeled the station and moved their Cantonese restaurant here from 732 East State where they had been since 1967.

"EAST END OF STATE" IN 1932
No address which generally would have meant the city limits which was located around Harrison street in the 1920's.
- **1932–33: Texaco Service Station–**Marchesechi Bros.–Raymond & William

605–611 EAST STATE AND HARRISON STREETS
Multiple businesses at different times in the same complex
- **1928: L.M. MYERS–**Ph Geneva 2206
- **1930–31: Phillips 66–**G.L. Shornden Ph 2485
- **1932: State Street Garage** Ph 754

605–611 East State and Harrison. FIGURE 8.11 Courtesy Geneva History Museum.

- **1949–53: State Street Motors–Hudson/Mobilgas–**John L. Joynt & Edwin Beeth, Ph Geneva 859, in 1950 the gas station was let to Joe's.

FIGURE 8.12 Courtesy *Geneva Republican*.

- **1950–58: Joe's State Street Mobil–'53 Standard Oil** Ph GEneva 4128, was this Joe Petraitis from Cooper Ford and 11 East State?
- **Date unknown: Roy Joynt State St. Motors**, separate operation from gas
- **Date unknown: Phillips 66–**Don Creeden and John Cryer, separate operation from auto dealership in the same building.
- **Date unknown: Meyer's Phillips 66–**A.Z. Meyer
- **September 1953: Myer's Phillip 66 & Auto Laundry–**Clarence C. Myers, the same Myers at 313 North 5th Street, St. Charles.

July 1955 Valley Motor Sales Grand Opening. FIGURE 8.13 *Geneva Republican*.

- **1955–59: Valley Motor Sales–Ford Lincoln Mercury Edsel–**Sam Franscona Ph 7270, as of May 1, 1955
- **1958: Jake & Curt's Mobil–**Jake Thomas & Curt Bartle, former deputies, bought out Joe's September 11, 1958, Ph 4821. Thomas had worked nights at Reber & Foley.
- **Date unknown: J&L Gas**
- **1977–80: Wayne's Discount Service–**Wayne Caldwell
- **1980–84: Caldwell's Service Inc–**Wayne Caldwell, Ph 232–7222
- **1980–85: Dewey's Garage–**Dewey Sartos from ARCO station in St. Charles, then moved from here to 520 South 14th Avenue in St. Charles around 1985.
- **Date unknown: Jet Transmission**
- **1983: Omega Car Wash/Detail shop in rear**
- **Current: Music Store/Mall**

600-602 EAST STATE (502)

Corner of East State and Kansas Streets

600 East State––Howard Davis Pure Oil in the 1920's. Under 'Gas' the sign reads: ENERGEE 'DETONOX' GASOLINE which would date this photo circa 1927. Near the grease pit to the left of building the sign says: Crankcase Service, The Pure Oil Co. The glass globe on the central pedestal reads: Purol Gasoline. FIGURE 8.14 Photo courtesy of John Fortman and Geneva History Museum.

Geneva Oil Company ad and early tank delivery truck with solid rubber tires. FIGURES 8.15 & 8.16 *Geneva Republican* May 27, 1927.

- **1922–23–Geneva Oil Co. Service Station–Wadhams Oil–**William Brandt & Eric Thorson had started gasoline delivery in October 1922, Ph 1191.
- **1923–26: Geneva Oil Co. Service Station–**Howard Davis, one of the older purpose–built service stations in town, had an outside service pit. Davis went

on to be the District Manager for Pure Oil.

- **1926–29: Geneva Oil Co. Inc. Pure Oil & Tiolene Oil** –Elmer Nungerson, Harry C. Hanson, and partner/manager, Eric Thorson, set up four large storage tanks with a total capacity of 40,000 gallons.

Purol Premium with the new addition of Ethyl additive. Geneva Oil Co. with Stations in Geneva, St. Charles, Batavia, North Aurora. FIGURE 8.17 *Geneva Republican* Nov. 7, 1930.

- **1930–33: Geneva Oil Co**–Eric B. Thorson pres, Ehmer Mungerson sec, Ph 1911 Wholesale and Retail sales w/bulk storage tank facility. Thorson was an entrepreneur and had filling stations in the Fox Valley that extended from Aurora to Algonquin. He was also a partner with Warber in the Geneva Garage on north First street 1925–1952.
- **1933–34: Purol Service Station**–Douglas F. Keiser, prop. Ph 1191
- **1934–42: Valley Pure Oil–Wholesale**–Ph 1911 **June 19, 1942** *Geneva Republican* "The Pure Oil Co offices and station...have been closed. Ernest Huntley, who has been in charge of bulk sales is now out of a job." The bulk tanks were removed in 1946.
- **1944: Boyer's Pure Oil Service**–Clarence J. Boyer, former mechanic with Tri–City Garage; later he operated the Brilliant Bronze.

Geneva Pure Oil dealers; Clark Bros and Chesley's.
FIGURE 8.18 Courtesy October 1945 *Geneva Republican*.

- **1945–46: Chesley's Service Station–**Ben Chesley (Formerly employed in 1943 as a mechanic at Houser Motor Sales, Wheaton) Ph 1016
- **1947–53: Ben and Lou's Garage–** Ben Chesley & Lou Fortman as new partner, Ph 1016. This location operated as a Pure Oil service station until 1963

FIGURE 8.19 *Geneva Republican* May 1955.

- **1953–58: Ben & Lou's Jeep/Willys**–Lou Fortman became a Jeep Dealership and sold some Fords as a secondary location for the Wheaton Ford Agency and Val's Lincoln–Mercury. Ben left the partnership in 1958 and worked at Hilltop Sinclair, later joining Bentz Bros in 1959. Apparently, the dealership was gone with Ben's departure and Lou advertised as just a service station in 1958.
- **1958–59: Lou's Pure Oil Service**
- **1959–89: Lou's Service "Your Jeep Dealer"**–Lou Fortman and his son, John Fortman. The first new Jeep advertisement I found was December 1959. Gas pumps were eliminated with a transition to new station further east.
- **1989–99: Lou's Jeep/Eagle Inc.**–Eagle automobile line added. **Lou's Jeep ultimately became Lou's Used Cars**–John Fortman. All car dealers were threatened with the loss of their franchise if they refused to build a grand new building to project a modern, prosperous image. Other prior examples of this were: Avenue Chevrolet, Hansen Chevrolet, Farrell Oldsmobile, and Richard Buick which had also experienced this corporate pressure and moved to new facilities.

Geneva Republican newspaper photo from 1949 for new crossing guard light which also shows Ben & Lou's Pure Oil Station. Close inspection reveals Pure Oil & AAA signage, along with tow truck and bulk delivery truck in background. FIGURE 8.20.

637 East State was typical 'Small Box' design, as depicted in Figure 4.1, used by Clark Oil throughout the Midwest. Founded by Emory T. Clark in 1932 as a single filling station in West Allis, Wisconsin, Clark Super Gas sold only premium gasoline. Unlike most service stations, Clark stations did not offer mechanical maintenance and tire changing, but were well known for low–price cigarettes. FIGURE 8.21 Courtesy *Wikipedia*.

637 EAST STATE AND SANDHOLM

- **1965–66: Dave Carter's Super 100 Station–Clark Oil Co–**David Carter
- **1967: Dine's Clark Service**
- **1970–1990 Clark Oil Co–**Damian Toledo (also operated West Main Clark in St. Charles & West Chicago Clark across from DuPage Airport)

802 EAST STATE AND EAST SIDE DRIVE

South side of State street

- **1966–69: State Street Motors–**Used cars; had pumps for their own use, formerly at 611 East State as the Hudson dealer.
- **1970–80's: State Street Body Shop**
- **1982–84: Caldwell's Service Inc.** Ph 232–7222
- **1985–98: Black's Auto Rebuilders–**Bob Black
- **Current: State Street Collision–**Bill White, cousin to White Bros Trucking, Wasco

801 EAST STATE STREET

NE corner State and East Side Drive

NE corner of State Street and East Side Drive. The D–X station was built and operated by Charlie Bohleen in 1958. FIGURE 8.22 Courtesy Geneva History Museum.

FIGURE 8.23 *Geneva Republican* May 15, 1958.

- **1928: Blue Ribbon Oil Station**
- **1957: Carl Osland & Charlie Bohleen D–X** Ph 3272

- **1958–68: Bohleen's D–X Service**–Charlie Bohleen, former owner of Studebaker Garage, 1956 mechanic at Tri–City Garage.
- **1969: Charlie's DX**–Charlie Bohleen Phone CE2–9772 1963–70's
- **1970–72: Erv's D–X Service**–Erv Konen also Konen Bros. Standard in Aurora
- **1972: J's Sunoco**–James Martin
- **1973–74: Vacant**
- **1974: The Tire Ranch**
- **1977: Buy–Rite Gas for Less**–Jack Gervase & Don Flexman (Gervase was also on West Main and Fourth Street in St. Charles)
- **1984: J & M Budget Pantry–Gas for Less**
- **1985–90: Don's Gas for Less**–Don Flexman

1009 EAST STATE STREET

Corner of Longview Drive

1009 East State Street, Lou's Pure Oil. Per John Fortman: Lou had eliminated gas pumps at the Jeep location and Pure Oil Company built this station with a permit issued in 1964. This later pre–demolition photo is all that we have. I do recall that the two bays, while equipped with lifts, were also two–car lengths in depth. FIGURE 8.24 Courtesy Geneva History Museum.

FIGURE 8.25 July 1, 1965 *Geneva Republican*.

- **1965: Lou's Pure Oil–** Lou Fortman. The opening of this station was lacking fanfare due to pending lawsuit of Clark Oil seeking a permit in the same time frame. He employed Bill Kerfoot, Don Seyller (Hilltop Sinclair), Leland Smith, Wayne Johnson, and Bill Blakely. Ph 232–9763
- **1970–71: Roger's Union 76–**Roger Smuda
- **1972–73: Chuck's Union 76**
- **1973–78: Dixon's Union 76–**David 'Junior' Dixon, former Bentz Bros. employee until 1968, then he went to Texaco on W State, followed by this location.
- **1980: First National Bank of Geneva**
- **Date Unknown: U S Bank**
- **Current: Fox Jewelers**

1166 EAST STATE STREET
- **Current: Mobil & Car Wash**

1491 EAST STATE STREET
NW corner East State and Kirk Road
- **1987–Current: Circle K Shell Pumper**

1501 EAST STATE STREET

NE corner E. State and Kirk Road

- **1986–94: Geneva Amoco Food Shop**
- **Current: Marathon now Amstar Pumper/U–Haul**

Checker Gas. FIGURE 8.26 *Geneva Republican*

RT. 38 AND THE RAILROAD TRACKS EAST OF TOWN

- **1971: Checker Gas–**while technically a West Chicago address, this station directly competed for the Geneva commuter traveling to Chicago.

NINE

McCORNACK OIL COMPANY

1901: Charles Samuel McCornack was first in business as McCornack Oil d/b/a Elgin Oil Company with retail locations in Elgin and Dundee. I found records of this date in the attic of the former main office at 215 East Main, St. Charles.

1904: Main & 11th Avenue, St. Charles–Henry Delno was St. Charles' first wholesale purveyor of oil products starting in 1899. In 1904 Charles S. McCornack along with partner Sherwood R. Moore, a cousin, purchased the St. Charles Oil Distribution Company and became McCornack & Moore Oil Company. His business journal has the following April 9, 1904 entry: "Purchase Stock of Oils for $2,000 to be paid upon sale of such, purchase of Business for $4,400 to include shed, 10 oil tanks, 3 wagons, 4 horses, 2 sleds and various harness, pumps and containers."

The partnership was short lived and Charles formed McCornack Oil Company. He became one of the primary suppliers of kerosene and coal oil in the Tri–Cities, utilizing horse drawn wagons to haul barrels of the product to be dispensed with hand pumps. From what I have been able to piece together, the McCornack Oil Company constructed three filling stations in St. Charles and Batavia; leased the Matl location in Geneva, and

constructed at least one more in DeKalb. The earliest structures, though made of stone and brick, were quite small shelters for the attendant with maybe a restroom and minimal inventory. There were no indoor service areas for vehicles; at best there might be an outdoor electric hoist, with the most common option being a pit to drive a car over to allow the attendant to service the undercarriage.

Movie Theatre 'Magic Lantern style' slide showing attendant in grease pit.
FIGURE 9.1 Courtesy Bentz family & St. Chas History Museum.

The attic of my former service station, a McCornack building, housed a small treasure trove including multiple boxes containing six glass advertising slides each. I have estimated their age to be in the range of 1928–1932 based on two criteria; one, the Batavia location is not listed, while the Geneva station is; and two, there are no slides referencing Texaco. Note that the McCornack name is followed by the Independent Dealer Logo. The slides were used in local theatres, such as the Fargo and Arcada, during prelude and intermission of the movie.

In the slide advertisement, McCornack states they had service stations in Geneva on 'State and First,' and in St. Charles on 'Main & Third'. We know that the Third Street location came first in 1920. The Geneva station was leased in 1925 and the second St. Charles location was constructed in 1928 so that would date this slide between 1925–28. The Batavia location was built in 1930. After 1928 they no longer attempted to list their numerous locations, but instead just referred to themselves as *The Home Company, established in 1904.*

1939 Sky Chief sign and early electric pump face. FIGURE 9.2 Author's collection.

More attic treasures from my 215 East Main Street location include one of three 1939 Sky Chief signs found in the original box. Another of those signs is in the collection of the Filling Station restaurant at West Main and Third Street. The framed pump face is from a 1930's Wayne electric gas pump; and the photos of this location span 90 years of history.

MCCORNACK RETAIL LOCATIONS IN ORDER OF CONSTRUCTION

Charles S. McCornack at 300 West Main Street, St. Charles circa 1920.
FIGURE 9.3 Photos Courtesy of McCornack family & St. Charles History Center.

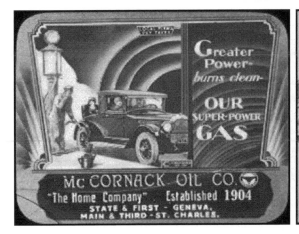

Another glass advertising slide and different view of
300 W. Main Street, St. Charles. FIGURES 9.4 & 9.5.

1925: 1 North 1st Street, Geneva built by J.A. Matl and leased to McCornack. The October
10, 1924 Republican article states that McCornack "already has stations in St. Charles, Elgin,
Dekalb, and other localities in this vicinity." FIGURE 9.6 Courtesy Geneva History Museum.

215 East Main Street, St. Charles (1928 address: 74 East Main).
FIGURE 9.7 Courtesy Bentz family archive.

The 1928 McCornack Oil location at 215 East Main Street in St. Charles, designed by Geneva architect Frank Gray, was constructed on a grand scale to accommodate the filling station with an overhead canopy, two heated indoor service bays, separate restroom facilities, and a corporate office overseeing five service stations and bulk plant deliveries. The building itself stands as an historic icon, with solid stone and brick masonry construction, clay roof tiles, and copper gutters and downspouts. The leaded–glass windows are the only feature not remaining in the building 90 years later. The third bay and hydraulic hoists were added in 1941. I believe Gray was also the architect for the Batavia location based the timing and the architectural elements repeated in that structure.

The building was still very viable to serve the industry into the next millennium. The publication titled "*Pump and Circumstances*" refers to "the golden age. . .when humble curbside stations evolved into palaces of petroleum. Then, the whole experience became much more than filling the tank: attendants in spiffy uniforms bustled about among gleaming pumps, eye–catching signs, and strings of pennants flapping in the wind."

ST. CHARLES CHRONICLE, DECEMBER 20, 1928

McCORNACK TO OPEN NEW GAS STATION DECEMBER 24

"The new super service station of the McCornack Oil Company, located at Third Avenue and Main Street will be opened for business Monday, it was announced yesterday.

The new station, one of the most attractive in northern Illinois, has been under construction for six months.

Designed by Frank Gray, it is English in architecture. It is constructed of rough brick with stone pillars.

The building fronts on Main Street. There are three driveways for cars, six gasoline pumps have been installed.

The offices of the McCornack Oil Company will be moved this week to the new station from the old station at the corner of West Main and Third Streets. Spacious offices have been built in the station.

The old station will continue in operation, Charles S. McCornack, president of the company, announced. Rumors have been circulated that the old station would be discontinued.

One of the features of the new station is the greasing room. Two grease pits have been constructed under cover, and the room will be steam heated. This will make it possible to thaw out cars with frozen radiators in winter. The pits are located in the west end of the building."

FIGURE 9.8 *St. Charles Chronicle*, December 20, 1928

Late 1920's McCornack station with no history of location. FIGURE 9.9 Photo Courtesy of McCornack family & St. Charles History Museum.

Surviving McCornack family members are unsure of the actual location of the above gas station also shown from the side in the next photograph. While someone had written "Geneva" on the back of one photo, there had been some mistakes made in the identification of others. To my knowledge, this building does not match anything in Geneva's history. I had thought it might be an Elburn location but again, in my research, there were neither links to any site, nor to any history of a McCornack owned retail gas station in Elburn. We do know that McCornack had a presence in Elgin, St. Charles, Geneva, Batavia, Elburn, and DeKalb as a wholesale supplier.

Hopefully someone may either recognize this building or the surrounding buildings to help with location. The brands of gas on the pumps are "Blue Seal" and "Hi–Test" independent brands, and this station pre–dated McCornack's conversion to Texaco.

FIGURE 9.10 Photo Courtesy of McCornack family and St. Charles History Museum

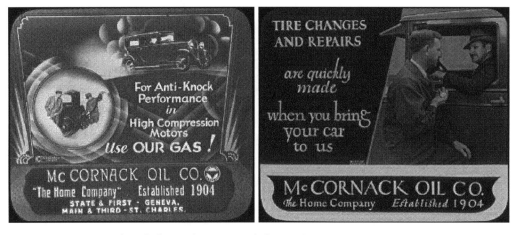

McCornack Oil glass advertising slides. FIGURE 9.11 & 9.12 Courtesy
Bentz family archives & St. Charles History Museum.

Constructed in 1924, McCornack d/b/a DeKalb Independent Oil.
FIGURE 9.13 Courtesy McCornack family & St. Charles History Museum.

Located on the SE corner of the Lincoln Highway and Fourth Street in DeKalb, Illinois. If you look closely you will see DeKalb Independent Oil is painted on adjoining building wall. This is similar in architecture to the 1920 St. Charles location, but not identical. This building has the clay tile roof and a double island which was used one year later in the 1928 St. Charles structure. Note that this photograph is during a gas pump transition period where the front pump is still a hand pump and the 3 center island pumps are very early electric pumps.

By May of 1924, DeKalb had ten filling stations on the Lincoln Highway. DeKalb Daily Chronicle, May 5, 1927: "Wrecking an old building that stood for years on the south–east corner of Lincoln Highway and Fourth street resulted in the building of a model service station by the Independent Oil company in the charge of Richard Barbour. The station has enjoyed a prosperous business from the start and service with high quality products has enable the large volume of business to be maintained week after week."

42 East Wilson in Batavia built 1930, 3 electric pumps featuring Globe, Red Hat, and Aviation Gasolines. Mobiloil pedestal sign on right. FIGURE 9.14 Photo Courtesy of McCornack family & St. Charles History Museum.

112/116 East Main Street Firestone Store and McCornack Oil Company office–1947–1957. FIGURE 9.15 Photo Courtesy of McCornack family & St. Charles History Museum.

Note that the signage in Figure 9.15 is split between the Firestone Store and the McCornack Oil Co. Office. The Firestone Store had two entrances while the company office door was at the far left. The building still stands today.

Up until this time, McCornack had been a loyal supplier of Goodyear tires. Later I will talk later about the early days and the arrival of the predecessors of what we would now call the "big box" stores in the automotive supply chain and the resulting effects on the local service station. McCornack takes notice of that trend in the early post–war years and will meet that competition head–on with this move.

201 South Third Street September 1957 Grand Opening of new McCornack Firestone Store– Donald and Elmore McCornack. FIGURE 9.16 & 9.17 Courtesy of McCornack family & St. Charles History Museum.

St. Charles Chronicle: "The roomy, modern one–story store is situated on the south–west corner of S. Third and Illinois St. It is joined to a building formerly used as a warehouse. The remodeled warehouse will have space for the storage of 2,000 tires. Its main feature will be a large service department for the mounting and repairing of truck, automobile, and tractor tires...able to handle five vehicles at a time if necessary. The main offices of McCornack Oil Company, now on E. Main St., will be situated in a modern wing on the south end of the store."

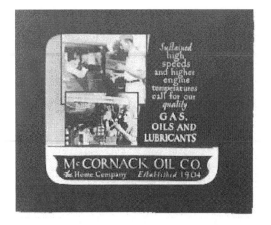

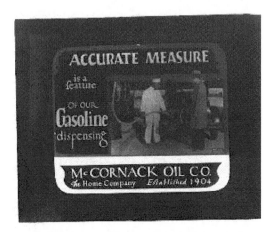

Additional McCornack Oil Co. advertising slides. FIGURE 9.18 Source Bentz family.

MCCORNACK CORPORATE OFFICE LOCATIONS

- **1904: 528 South 6th Avenue, St. Charles–**McCornack Oil home–based office
- **1920: 220 East Main, St. Charles–**McCornack Oil home–based office, this is the old address for corner of 8th Avenue and Main
- **1921–27: 300 (91) West Main, St. Charles–**first gas station also served as office.
- **1928: 215 (74) East Main, St. Charles–**built as a state–of–the–art gas station

also housing the corporate offices. Operated as an independent oil company until 1934 when they went with Texaco.

Charles S. and Martha McCornack. FIGURES 9.19 & 9.20
wedding photographs courtesy of McCornack family.

- **1932–35:** Officers of the corporation were listed as C.S. McCornack, Herb Borman and Carl Anderson. Friday, June 21. 1935 Charles S. McCornack, civic, business, and religious leader passed on the Country Club golf course of which he was a charter member. Having a business history of over 30–years in St. Charles, his widow, Martha, will continue at the helm of the company until her passing in 1960.
- **1947–57: 112/116 East Main, St. Charles –**One block west and on the opposite side of the street from current headquarters was Price's Economy Auto Parts, located at 116 East Main. When an opportunity to open a Firestone Store in that building became available, McCornack proceeded to do just that. McCornack subsequently moved their corporate offices to 112 East Main. With that decision, they leased the Texaco station at 215 East Main to long–time employees, Bob Henningson and Len Askeland.
- **1957: 201/203 South 3rd Street, St. Charles** (SW Corner of 3rd Street and Illinois)–While the Firestone store front facility at 116 East Main was ideal for selling tires, batteries, parts, accessories, refrigerators, washers, dryers, radios, TV's and bicycles, there weren't adequate facilities for servicing the automotive side of the business. McCornack already owned this Third Street property and was utilizing the garage facility on it to service vehicles from

the Firestone store. Needless to say, this was less than convenient so the decision was made to build an all new McCornack Firestone facility on that site that would also house new corporate offices.

- **1956: McCORNACK OIL CO.**– Officers of the corporation were listed as: Martha S. McCornack–Pres, Carl A. Anderson–V. Pres, Elmore L. McCornack–Sec, Donald C. McCornack–Treas– Ph 28
- **1962:** In the fall of 1962, Elmore McCornack, the president of McCornack Oil Company, decided to sell the oil business, and approached Texaco. An agreement was reached and signed on December 22, 1962, and McCornack Oil Company transferred the business to Texaco Oil Company on December 28, 1962, for a total consideration of $500,000. Texaco wanted the use of the McCornack name locally for obvious reasons, and it was agreed that Texaco would be assigned all trade names used by McCornack in the business. For additional consideration, goodwill and trade names were sold for $54,629.

On December 28, 1962, pursuant to its agreement, McCornack Oil Company assigned to Texaco "the right, but only in connection with the sale and distribution of petroleum and related products, to use and to do business under the names, `McCornack Oil Company' and `McCornack Oil,' excepting and reserving, however, to the Assignor the right to use said names in connection with its Firestone dealer store operation."

The new distributorship was set up at the same time with Herb Borman, who had been an officer of McCornack Oil Company. Warren Munson, Texaco's representative in that area, participated in negotiating this agreement, which described the new distributorship as "Herb Borman, d/b/a McCornack Oil Co", not Inc

During these negotiations, Munson had arranged to join Borman in the distributorship, which in fact, was known to Elmore McCornack, but unknown to Texaco. Munson did join Borman in January of 1963 and assumed a leading role in the business at that time. Subsequently, in September of 1964, he incorporated the distributorship under the name "Kane County Oil, Inc." The business continued to operate under the McCornack name until August of 1965, when the distributorship was cancelled by Texaco. At that time, Texaco appointed a new distributor, the Collins–Locke Group, conferring upon it the right to use the McCornack name.

There were also obscure properties that were sold to Texaco which many locals were not aware of, such as the NW corner of Main and Dunham, St. Charles. That property was still a grassy field in the 1980's and I had proposed building a pumper/convenience store for my own operation there, although that was in the era when oil companies were building stations for themselves, not dealers. Texaco did not, however, purchase the Batavia and Lily Lake locations because they were outdated, so they were liquidated independent of this transaction. Holdings in Elgin Oil were also sold in 1963.

McCornack business listings in 1966 Polk Directory showed family retention of Firestone while the bulk plant had been sold to Texaco in 1962.

- **1966: McCornack Oil Co/Collins Group Div.** James H. Collins, Pres; Charles A. Locke, V–Pres; 203 South 3rd Street (office in Firestone building)–James Collins was a son–in–law of Lester and Delora Norris, major stockholders in Texaco.
- **1966: McCornack Tire & Service Inc.** Officers listed as: Robert C. McCornack, Pres; Richard V. Weagley, V–Pres; Warren Kammerer Sec–Treas; 201 South 3rd Street (McCornack Tire & Service was later sold to Firestone Corporate and Warren Kammerer and a new store was built at 1645 East Main).

The Wallace Evans Game Farm had this McCornack Oil fuel pump like this on the farm still in service in 1947 as many area farms were serviced by the bulk plant. The brand of pump is a Fry that has been called the "Mae West" for its shapely design and is a highly regarded collectible. At the request of the St. Charles History Museum, a pump like this was acquired by the author for display at the museum. FIGURE 9.21 Courtesy of McCornack Family & St. Charles History Museum.

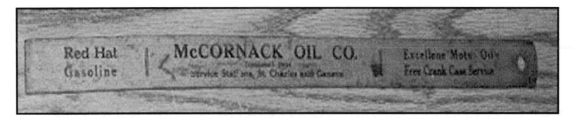

Model T Gas Tank Dip Stick. Opposite side was a gauge showing gallons in inches.
Circa 1920–1931 based on Red Hat Gasoline and locations available.
FIGURE 9.22 Photo courtesy Bentz family archives.

The Ford Model T had no gas gauge and the tank was located in the cowl between the engine and passenger compartment with the tank fill in front of the windshield. In order to know how much gas was in the tank, a stick such as this would be introduced to measure how many gallons were present in the tank. A free handout, such as this stick, was very popular with Ford drivers and the stick usually sat on the floor in front of the driver's seat for easy access.

MCCORNACK BULK PLANT LOCATIONS

- **1902: Elgin Oil Company–375 N. State Street–**bulk plant with pumps, and a station located at the NW corner of State and Highland and operated by Herman Bunge.
- **1904: 13th Avenue & Great Western tracks, St. Charles–**Original Henry Delno location
- **1910: Aurora Oil Company,** established in 1910 by H.H. Hoyer and C.S. McCornack Vine and North River Streets, Aurora with a second bulk plant built by the railroads tracks in Hinckley, Illinois.

Charles S. McCornack on one his delivery wagons. The long strips of leather hanging on the horses' sides were to shoo flies and avoid a run-away wagon.
FIGURE 9.23 Courtesy McCornack family.

FIGURE 9.24

Aurora Daily Beacon article dated June 29. 1912: boasts 4 storage tanks each holding 13,000 gallons, 2 tank wagons with 450–gallon capacity, and an auto car with a capacity of 530 gallons. Local Garages supplied: The Coats Garage, Wolf & Parker, George Arnold, The River Street Garage, and the LaSalle Street Garage.

National Petroleum News, Vol.9, June 1917: "R.M. McCornack, who together with his brother, C.S. McCornack, owned and operated the Aurora Oil Company at Aurora and Hinckley, Illinois, is now with Anderson & Gustafson, Chicago, in their refined oil and gasoline sales department. The McCornack brothers recently sold their business at Aurora and Hinckley to the Sinclair Oil and Refining Corporation."

- **1926: McCornack Oil Co. Bulk Plant, Harrison Street, Elburn**–50,000–gallon storage capacity.
- **1932–62: 402 North 2nd Street, St. Charles–McCornack Oil Co. Bulk Plant**–250,000–gallon storage capacity.

There were numerous partnerships that C.S. McCornack was involved with in the early years, such as Elgin Oil, Aurora Oil, DeKalb Oil and possibly in Naperville. The man was an entrepreneur in a grand style in the early Twentieth Century.

C.S. McCornack. FIGURE 9.25 Courtesy McCornack family and St. Charles History Museum

The possibility of ownership in Naperville Oil comes only from this photograph with C.S. McCornack posing with a Naperville Oil Co. truck while it is parked at the West Main Street location. The Independent Oil logo on the door appears fresh while at the same time the lettering on the tank is faded. I found no record of his involvement with an oil company by that name and it could be that he had acquired the truck as "used" and was yet to change the name.

EARLY MCCORNACK LOGOS AND BRANDS BEFORE BECOMING TEXACO IN 1934

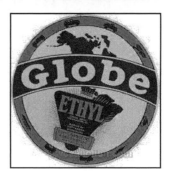

Left to right, top to bottom: FIGURE 9.26, FIGURE 9.27, FIGURE 9.28, FIGURE 9.29

The Independent Oil Eagle symbol, FIGURE 9.08, was displayed at all early McCornack facilities regardless of which gasolines were being pumped. It signified that the company was part of an organization of independent dealers banded together for protection against the large oil companies. The Red Hat and Aviation brands are clearly visible in photos on the St. Charles pumps. The Globe Ethyl gas was present in the Batavia 1932 photo. In FIGURE 10.8 the ad announced the opening of 215 E. Main, and the Anti–Knock brand of gas is also mentioned. In July 1933 McCornack's "Power–Full" gas was introduced. The branding on the pumps in DeKalb was that of Independent Gas and Motor Oil. The Indian brand of gasoline was also identified on St. Charles pumps; Indian Oil, an Illinois based company, was later acquired by Texaco Oil in 1931. This expanded Texaco's refining and marketing base in the Midwest and also gave Texaco the rights to Indian's Havoline motor oil, which became a trademark Texaco product.

In Elburn, the brands identified on the gas station pumps were "Blue Seal and Hi–Test," both independents. The only association known with a major brand were the October 31, 1929 advertisements in the *St. Charles Chronicle* and *Elburn Herald* announcing Phillips 66 as supplier. By 1930 the change was made to Globe Ethyl.

FIGURE 10.29 Courtesy *St. Charles Chronicle*

FIGURE 9.30 & 9.31 Courtesy *St. Charles Chronicle*

We have always assumed that one of the key reasons for McCornack rebranding to Texaco in 1934 was the local association with both the Norris and Baker families, but it went deeper than that. Delora Norris' maiden name was Angell and the two families, McCornack and Angell, had indeed been friends for years before Dellora's inheritance of Texaco stock from the John W. Gates estate in 1918.

Ever wonder how the moniker Fire–Chief for a gasoline brand came about? "The Gasoline Fire Engines Depend on! Meets US Government specifications for use in emergency equipment." Albany–Democrat Herald, May 1932. In 1938, Texaco introduced Sky Chief gasoline, a premium fuel developed from the ground up as a high–octane gasoline rather than just an 'ethylized' regular product. In 1939, Texaco became one of the first oil companies to introduce a "Registered Rest Room" program to ensure that restroom facilities at all Texaco stations nationwide maintained a standard level of cleanliness to the motoring public.
FIGURE 9.32 Courtesy *St. Charles Chronicle*

The following announcement for McCornack's transition to Texaco would not transfer from archived newspapers in a readable format so I have transcribed the article as follows:

ST. CHARLES CHRONICLE MARCH 15, 1934

(I have expanded the addresses for the readers' ease of understanding the location.)

Announcing–McCornack Oil Company's
Association With Texaco Petroleum Products

We are pleased to announce that we have been given a franchise for the wholesale distribution of TEXACO products throughout this and surrounding territory.

Recognizing the unquestioned quality and nationwide acceptance of TEXACO products, (The TEXAS COMPANY is the World's largest independent Refining and Marketing Organization), we chose them and their products only after months of careful consideration of several other brands.

This acquisition of TEXACO products will in no way change the present ownership, management or personnel of the McCornack Oil Company.

A complete line of TEXACO products will be carried at our stations in St. Charles, Geneva and Batavia and distribution will be made through the following dealers:

FISKE SERVICE STATION
E Main, St. Charles

W. C. MASTERSON
Main St & Bliss Rd, Bald Mound

EAST SIDE GARAGE
N First Ave, St. Charles

POTTER & CO.
La Fox

MODDE SERVICE STATION
W Main, St. Charles

RAY READ
Rt 47 & Empire Rd, Lily Lake

THOS. WILCOXE.
St. Charles

M. ABRAHAMSON
Rt 47, Lily Lake

ARMBRUST & BERG
S First St, Geneva

PETER LEUER GARAGE (Chevrolet)
Main St, Elburn

JOHN ZARANKA
E State St & Rt 25 Geneva

SNYDER SERVICE STATION
Maple Park

H. E. TRAVIS
Rt 64, Wasco

SOUTH SIDE GARAGE
West Chicago

BERGLAND & CO.
Rt 64, Wasco

FRANK HUMMEL
East Elgin Rd [Rt 25, Valley View]

USE TEXACO FIRE–CHIEF GASOLINE
Developed for Fire Engines . . . Yours at No Extra Cost.
McCORNACK OIL COMPANY–Established 1904

When growing up in the Fox Valley, the names McCornack and Texaco appeared to be synonymous. There were multiple versions due to many folks' limited understanding of Col. Edward J. Baker's, along with Lester and Dellora Norris's, major holding of Texaco Oil stock shares. When I started my business in the McCornack building, many locals would share their interpretation of the lineage of this character called "Bet–a–Million" Gates. Prior to the internet, I found the best resource for laying to rest the rumors was a copy of the book, *"Bet–A–Million"– The Story of John W. Gates,* authored by Lloyd Wendt and Herman Kogan and first published in 1948.

An abbreviated version of his biography is as follows: John W. Gates was born in 1855 and his family farmed in Turner Junction, modern day West Chicago. He desired the hand of Dellora Baker, daughter of Edward H. Baker of St. Charles, but Baker refused Gates quest for his daughter's hand based on his lack of a stable job and place in the community.

Gates then went to DeKalb where a couple of new entrepreneurs, Glidden and Elwood, had invented their own versions of barbed wire; wire that was intended to keep fencing costs down while maintaining a herd of cattle or horses in their dedicated pens. Elwood hired Gates and assigned him the task of selling the company's barbed wire that was sitting idly in Texas warehouses. Local ranchers had previously refused to buy the lowly wire, convinced that nothing so trite could impede the wild and rangy Texas Longhorn. Elwood also offered Gates a bonus to rid the company of the wire because shipping to other markets was too expensive. Gates went to Texas, but did not try to sell the wire. Instead, he became involved in one of his favorite hobbies: poker. While playing cards, he asked his tablemates why all that wire was sitting on the rail side and he was promptly met with many a disparaging remark.

It was then that he came up with a plan to conduct a rodeo, with all of the traditional roping and bronco riding, and take advantage of that gathering to prove to the ranchers that a barbed wire stockade could contain the meanest longhorns they possessed. He bet that if none broke out overnight, the ranchers would buy the wire.

Gates made short work of selling the existing barb wire and sent orders to the company for more. Elwood, while thrilled with the sales, refused to pay the extra bonus believing that the prior salesmen were simply incompetent. Gates, not to be discouraged and still needing to prove his metal to Baker, saw opportunities to make profits other than just being a traveling salesman of barbed wire. One of his first transactions was to purchase a controlling interest in the company that provided the strand wire to Elwood. The biography goes on in great detail about the beginnings of a great barbed wire trust that would go on to develop the steel industry from mining to the forges, and the owning of railroads to control shipping rates in the late 1800's. Gates' Illinois Steel Company would later become an integral part of U S Steel in a hostile takeover by J.P. Morgan and Gates' own lawyer, Elbert Gary.

Gates also became a keen stock manipulator and later, an early investor in a start-up oil company called the Texas Company, which we now know as Texaco. He became one of this country's "most audacious financial tycoons in all history," matching wits with the likes of Morgan, Carnegie, and Rockefeller. He owned mansions in Chicago, St. Louis, and Port Arthur, Texas, maintained a penthouse in The Plaza Hotel, New York City and a chateau in Paris, France.

Gates passed in 1911, leaving his widow, Dellora, and son, Charles, with very substantial holdings. At the time of his death, Gates "penthouse" at the Plaza encompassed an entire floor of the hotel in order to house his extensive art collection. After John's passing, Charles was engaged in building a $1,000,000 mansion in Minneapolis, modeled after a French palace, to house his father's art collection. That mansion was said to surpass the cubic foot displacement of the White House. Then, in 1913, at the age of 37, Charles passed away from a heart attack while on a hunting trip and never saw the completion of the mansion. His widow did complete the home, but moved away. With an annual maintenance cost of $50,000, accompanied by a tax bill of $7,000, very few could afford the property even as a gift, so the largest and grandest home in Minnesota was razed just twenty years after it was built.

When Dellora Gates passed in 1918 at the Plaza Hotel, New York, the heirs to the fortune were her brother, Edward J. Baker and a favorite niece and namesake, Dellora Angell, both of St. Charles. Dellora Angell was a teenage millionaire and later married Lester Norris. Forty years later, in 1959, they became the sole heirs to Baker's share of the estate.

That is the short version of why we in St. Charles are so familiar with the generosity and philanthropy associated with the family names of Baker and Norris and their ties to Texaco ownership. *The Story of St. Charles, Part III*, is available on YouTube and the video will share more of the details of the Gates, Baker, and Norris families.

TEN

ST. CHARLES EAST SIDE

As we travel through St. Charles it is important to note that because the city is split into the east and west sides by the Fox River, all roads on the east side of the river are designated as "avenues" and those on the west side as "streets." To complicate matters, however, early addresses did not have this designation. For example: Second Avenue was called "E. Second Street," and Second Street was called "W. Second Street."

.

EAST MAIN IN THE VICINITY OF PHEASANT RUN & DUPAGE AIRPORT
- **1960–1980's: Clark Oil**–Damian Toledo. While a portion of St. Charles is in DuPage County, this station may have been in West Chicago.

4200 EAST MAIN STREET
- **1970: Farrell Oldsmobile**–Don Farrell relocated here from the Baker Garage.
- **1973–84: Town & Country Oldsmobile**–Max Cohen, Jr
- **1984–86: Dennis Oldsmobile**
- **October 1990: Don McCue Lincoln/Mercury** Ph 584–6200
- **Current: Used Car Lot**

2651 EAST MAIN STREET

Toyota West, 2651 East Main Street, St. Charles.
FIGURE 10.1 Photo courtesy St. Charles History Museum.

- **1985–92: Toyota West**–Ed Basil who had previously been further east on Rt. 64 in West Chicago Ph 584–6655.
- **1987–92: Chrysler Plymouth West**–Ed Basil
- **1993: TORCO Dodge**

2500 EAST MAIN STREET

NE corner of Dunham Road

Humble Oil, NE corner of Dunham Rd., c. 1961.
FIGURE 10.2 Photo courtesy Joe Jakubaitis.

- **1961: Humble Oil (Enco)**
- **1968: ENCO Gas Station**–LeRoy McDowell of St Chas & Lonnie Burkett of Batavia.
- **1970: Norway ENCO Service**–Wayne Neeley & Norm Westenbager

- **1975–83: Phil's Phillips 66–** used to be known as 'Philthy' Phil's
- **1984–88: Wise's Family Service–**Michael E. & Ellen F. Wise
- **1991: Shell Oil Co Pumper–**new construction, Sandy Gratchner manager.
- **Current: Circle K Shell**

2525 EAST MAIN-FORD

SE corner of Dunham Road, 2535 East Main–Pontiac

'Close out on all 1976 models'–construction is expansion to accommodate both dealerships.
FIGURE 10.3 Photo courtesy St. Charles History Museum.

- **1964–2017: Zimmerman Ford and Zimmerman Pontiac–**William P. "Bill" Zimmerman, with sons, Mike, and Jack Zimmerman. The son of Issac Zimmerman, a junk and scrap metal dealer, Bill worked himself up from bell boy to entrepreneur.

  While most of us can relate to this Zimmerman location of the past 55 years, I have researched his business biography through my most utilized sources: Polk Directories, Bell Telephone books, and both the *St. Charles Chronicle* and *Geneva Republican*. I will summarize that biography here so the reader can relate to the many locations where Bill did business as both a dealer and gas station operator. I will not attempt to include the real estate investment and rental property history, but suffice it to say that he had many endeavors.

  As we geographically travel through St. Charles, Zimmerman's locations will not be in chronological order. For ease of understanding how his businesses progressed, I have listed his locations below in order of date. Full details, descriptions and histories of these locations can be found later under each address as we travel west through St. Charles.

- **North 2nd and Cedar Streets**–Zimmerman's first place of business across from Baker Garage on the SW corner.

     St. Charles Chronicle, **March 31, 1938: W.P. Zimmerman Used Motors** "for the last 7 years [he] has been employed as a salesman at the Hotel Baker Garage...he is opening his own used car business, being located at the used car lot, corner of North Second and Cedar street, directly across the street from the Hotel Baker Garage."–Ph 479 or 2118. (Zimmerman's first business was started with inventory sourced from Hotel Baker Motors.)

- **708 South 3rd Street**–Second place of business–not to be confused with the later 3rd & Prairie Street location.

- **September 1938–August 1942: W.P. Zimmerman Motor Sales–Pontiac** Ph 2719 William P. "Bill" Zimmerman's first new car dealership.

- **August 27, 1942:** Bill Zimmerman announced the closing of this business. He was compelled to close due to the lack of new autos and war rationing. Over the previous eleven years Bill estimated that he had sold around 2500 cars and trucks. He was confident that employment would be found in war work given his mechanical knowledge. According to his obituary he went to work in Chicago at the International Harvester building that had been converted for war production, but it wasn't long before he was back in the used car business.

- **307 West Main Street**–third place of business.

- **June 3, 1943:** By the Spring of 1943 Bill has set up a used car lot at Fred's Brilliant Bronze on west Main Street. Fred Utroska was the manager of the service station and Bill is placing used car advertisements in the Chronicle every week to buy and sell used cars.

- **North 2nd and Cedar Streets**–fourth place of business.

- **August of 1944:** Fred Utroska is no longer the Brilliant Bronze manager and Zimmerman has relocated the used car lot back to his original corner across from the Baker Hotel Garage.

- **Baker Hotel Garage, 2nd and Cedar Streets**–fifth place of business.

- **September 1944: Baker Hotel Garage**–Bill Zimmerman proprietor, **Pontiac** franchise is back in anticipation of post–war production. Zimmerman has taken over all operations of the garage and **Texaco** gas station from Baker.

- **423 South 2nd Street and Prairie Street**–sixth place of business.

- **Apr 1951–55: Zimmerman Used Car Annex**–Fred Utroska manager. The annex originally supplemented the Baker Garage facility and later adjoined the new dealership building on south 3rd street.

- **440 South 3rd Street and Prairie Street**–seventh place of business.

- **November 1953: Zimmerman Pontiac–GMC:** new building constructed.

- **October 1957: Zimmerman Pontiac–Rambler** was added. He was a Rambler dealer for less than three months when both Pontiac and Rambler were dropped in favor of Ford.
- **January 1957–September 1964: Zimmerman Ford Inc**, seven more years here, followed by the move to East Main and Dunham Road.
- **413 East Main & 5th Avenue** –SW corner Rt. 64 and Rt. 25–Eighth place of business.
- Zimmerman had purchased E.J. Baker's home at this high traffic corner and applied for a zoning change from residential to commercial. In the early 1950's he wanted to construct his new car dealership building but was denied zoning by the city.
- **2525 East Main Street**–SE corner of Dunham Road–ninth and tenth place of business.
- **1964–2017: Zimmerman Ford**–tenth place of business.
- **September 1976–79: Lincoln Mercury**–franchise added as another building
- **1979: Zimmerman Pontiac**–October 1979 Lincoln Mercury dropped
- **2017–Current: Hawk Ford**

CONTINUING OUR JOURNEY WEST ON MAIN STREET...

2015 EAST MAIN STREET
- **November 1974–80: Jim Wulff Chevrolet**–moved here from Geneva. Shelly Solomen, service manager.
- **October 1980–current: McCue Chevrolet**–Don McCue

1845 EAST MAIN STREET
- **1980: Richard Buick**–Richard Massarelli, moved here from former Davison Buick Pontiac dealership address of 212 West Main.
- **1988: Richard Buick/YUGO**–the Yugoslavian auto was added through GM
- **Date unknown: Richard Jeep**–when Lou's Jeep gave up the franchise.
- **Current: St. Charles Toyota**

1745 EAST MAIN STREET
- **1985–86: St. Charles Enterprises**–Robert F. Szweistis/James R. Weiland–Car Wash/Pumper. Bob was former partner in Fairview Mobil/Car Wash.
- **Current: BP**

1645 EAST MAIN STREET

- **August 30, 1971–present: Firestone of St. Charles–**new corporation formed to take over the McCornack Firestone operation at 201 South Third Street. Warren Kammerer, president and general manager was in partnership with the Firestone Company in the construction of a 10–bay service facility with additional dedicated area to service large truck and agricultural with storage for 6,000 tires. Robert Hawkins, commercial and dealer sales; Richard Nelson office manager; and Charles Stewart, manager of passenger tire sales. Wes Mallady and Don Read were later outside sales. Wes went on to work at Bentz Texaco.

1619 EAST MAIN STREET

- **St. Charles Kitchens**
- **Fox Valley Chrysler Dodge Jeep**

1421 EAST MAIN STREET

- **1985–86: Dennis Oldsmobile**
- **McGrath Buick GMC**
- **Fox Valley Buick GMC**

520 SOUTH 14TH AVENUE

- **1985: Dewey's Far Better West–**Dewey Sartos garage after Geneva location & ARCO on west side of St. Charles.

14TH AVENUE & OHIO AVENUE

- **1985: Caldwell's Service Inc–**Wayne Caldwell Ph 377–6252 or 232–1023

1351 EAST MAIN STREET

- **McGrath Honda**

1360 EAST MAIN STREET

- **1926–42: Johnsen Service Station,** Raymond C. Johnsen, business name changes to **Purol Service Station** in 1930 and **Pure Oil Service** in 1936.

1312 EAST MAIN STREET

NE corner 13th Avenue

- **1946–65: Cunningham's Sinclair Service–**James L. Cunningham Ph 3135
- **August 1965–Sinclair Refining permit issued for $40k new building**

Sinclair, 1312 East Main Street, NE corner 13th Avenue, c.1965.
FIGURE 10.4 Photo courtesy Joe Jakubaitis.

- **1965–81: Olsen Sinclair/ARCO–**Bob Olsen. This will be his second location, with his first at the 'Triangle' formed by First, Second, and Prairie Streets. Jim Gorecki, worked as mechanic until Bob retired.
- **1981–86: Gorecki's ARCO–**James F. Gorecki, Jr, Dave Stevens mechanic. While ARCO would not sell stations to their dealers, Standard Oil purchased the property and announced their intention to eliminate the pumps and tanks, offering a lease only to repair cars with no petroleum sales. Jim moved to a garage on 8th Street in Geneva.
- **1987–93–Steve's Repair–**Steve Pederson
- **1993: Car–X Muffler & Brake–**Steve Pederson
- **Current: Action Auto Clinic–**Steve Pederson

1280 EAST MAIN STREET

1280 East Main Purple Martin, c.1961. FIGURE 10.5 Photo courtesy Joe Jakubaitis.

- **December 1956–84: Martin Oil Service–** *"S'Martin up with Martin"* 1956–Donald Hitz mg; 1964–Aldon McGee manager; 1966–Bobby Lacefield manager; 1972–James Duff manager; 1973–Floyd Fox manager; 1977–Terry Hufford manager
- **1985–89: Valley Lube** "10–minute oil change"–no gasoline.
- **Current: Pit Stop**

1303 EAST MAIN STREET

FIGURE 10.6 *St. Charles Chronicle* June 4, 1931

- **1931–32: Harold Morter's Texas Service Station–**Ph 449

FIGURE 10.7 Courtesy *St. Charles Chronicle*

- **1932–34: Fisk's Service Station–Texaco–**Glenn C. Fisk Ph 3129, McCornack Oil supplied in 1934. Assisted by Ernest Weber July, 1932.
- **May 1934: East End Service–**Herb Reimers, manager for McCornack, property leased from Mr Mattsen.

FIGURE 10.8 Courtesy *St. Charles Chronicle* May 30, 1935

- **1935: Fisk's Mobilgas Service–**Glenn Fisk, Ph 3128
- **1936: Vernon Hansen's Mobile Station–**June 1936

FIGURE 10.9 Courtesy *St. Charles Chronicle*

- **1936: St. Charles Mobilgas Station–**W.R. Dawdy, Manager, July 1936
- **1943–46: Dailey's Mobiloil Service Station–**John Dailey, later in West Chicago, as Dailey's Phillips 66 well into the 1970's.
- **1947–56: Ferry Mobilgas Service Station,** Paul E. Ferry Ph 3533
- **1958: Schulz Service Station**

1303 East Main, c. 1961 Morgan's D–X/Freeway Station.
FIGURE 10.10 Photo courtesy Joe Jakubaitis.

- **1961–69: Morgan's D–X Service–**Morgan Davis
- **1970–77: Morgan's Freeway–**Morgan Davis, later a partner in Stan and Morgan's Texaco on Second street.
- **1977: Wallace's Freeway–**Thurman Wallace & Norman Moore
- **1977–78: Bob's Freeway–**Bob Eastman
- **Current: Vacant office building**

904 EAST MAIN STREET

NE corners of 9th Avenue and Main Street
- **1933: Standard Oil Service Station–**construction contract; Max Lehmann

904 East Main Street, c. 1938. FIGURE 10.11 Courtesy Reber & Foley website. Photos and quotes from Reber and Foley History website, "The original Standard Oil station on our site, circa 1938; notice the classic outside car lift, and tool box on the left side of the building. Also spot the 'Atlas' tire sign on the right edge of the photo. They were Standard Oil's own private tire brand. Look in the background, and you'll see the DuKane 'Operadio' factory."

- **1939–41: Phillip's Standard Oil Service Station**–Harold E. Phillips went on to the Post Office.

FIGURE 10.12 Courtesy *St. Charles Chronicle*

- **1941–43: Cunningham's Standard Service**–James L. Cunningham, formerly with Judd Motors and Hahn Pontiac. He later relocated to Sinclair at 1312 East Main Street.

FIGURE 10.13 Courtesy *St. Charles Chronicle*

- **April 1945: Reber & Rothecker–**Vic Reber & John Rothecker. Avery Stevens, started wrenching while he was still in high school, the beginning of a 50–year career at this location, taking time off to do battle in the Korean War. A separate garage was added behind the gas station in the early 60's and that was considered to be Avery's domain for many years.

- **June 1946–49: Reber, Rothecker & Foley–**Vic Reber, John Rothecker & Bud Foley Ph 440. In 1950, Rothecker left to start John Rothecker Standard in Batavia

"904 East Main Street, c. 1961 The station was renovated and received an enclosed service bay and a new porcelain exterior. If you look underneath 'Standard', you can see the original portion. Main Street/Route 64 was only a two–lane road at the time and this building was partially demolished to facilitate four lanes and rebuilt farther back."
FIGURE 10.14 Courtesy Reber & Foley website.

- **1950–62: Reber & Foley Standard**–Vic Reber and Bud Foley
- **1962–78: Reber & Foley Standard**–Ken Carlson and Bud Foley. Dave Stevens, Avery's son, started his career here in 1976 along with Ken Carlson's son, Nick. Dave did leave in 1984–86 to work for his friend at Gorecki's ARCO, and then came back until opening his own shop.
- **1978–96: Reber & Foley Standard**–Mark Foley and Bob Hughes
- **1996–01: Reber & Foley Amoco**–Mark Foley and Joe Jakubaitis
- Joe was a Bentz Texaco employee in 1980's. Brian Farley, a former Bentz Mobil technician, came here in 1990.
- **2001–present: Reber & Foley Service Center**–Mark Foley and Joe Jakubaitis purchased the property from Amoco and ceased selling gas in 2001.

Reber & Foley Service Center–904 E. Main Street, c. 2017.
FIGURE 10.15 Courtesy Reber & Foley website.

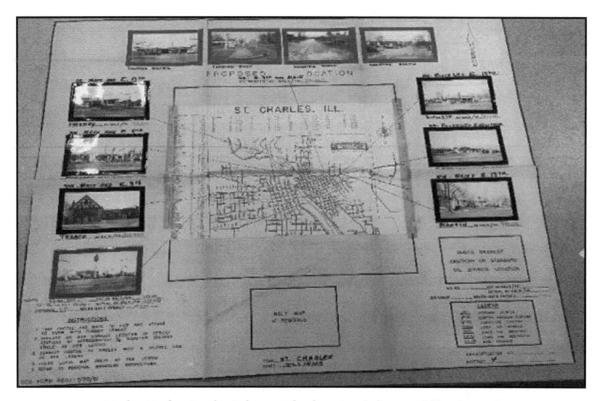

1961 Market Evaluation for Reber & Foley location (what would be deemed poor
quality photos by today's standards, were if fact high–tech Polaroid photos,
"film developed in a minute"). FIGURE 10.16 Courtesy Joe Jakubaitis.

Joe shared this 1961 archived market evaluation with those of us at the first round–
table discussion. The Standard Marketing Representative in 1961 spent considerable
time evaluating the St. Charles market, taking pictures, noting addresses and locations on the map along with estimates of annual gasoline gallonage based on traffic
volume. It is dated 7/20/61 and the new (1962) Standard station on Randall Road had
to be estimated for gallonage. That new location was estimated at 350,000 gallons and
a similar gallonage was expected of Reber & Foley. All of the estimates would soon
become enhanced as the city grew. For example, the gallonage for Bob & Len's Texaco
was estimated at about 315,000 gallons in 1961 and by 1989, my actual gallonage at the
same location was 960,000, a number that was barely acceptable by the ever–increasing
corporate standards.

800 EAST MAIN STREET

NE corner at 8th Avenue

Phillips 66, NE corner 8th Avenue and Main Street, c. 1961.
FIGURE 10.17 Courtesy Joe Jakubaitis.

April 1, 1953 Ted Larson advertisement was for spring tune up with Ture Paulson as chief
mechanic. Ture was later in business at Pure Oil in Batavia.
FIGURE 10.18 Courtesy *St. Charles Chronicle*.

- **November 1952–56: Ted Larson Service–Phillips 66–**Ted had been in business at his Batavia station on the Avenue for 9 years, and while his requests for a new modern facility had gone unanswered, Phillips Oil Co. offered him this new station in St. Charles.

- **1956–62: Robinson Sixty–Six Service**–Neil A. Robinson, JU4–9559
- **1962–65: Morris Sixty–Six Service Station**–Willard L. Morris

June 29, 1966 Neil Robinson "after 4–year absence."
FIGURE 10.19 Courtesy *Geneva Republican*.

- **1966–69: Robinson's Phillips 66**–Neil Robinson, owner w/Mike Wallace, manager, JU4–9550. Wallace also operates Sinclair on E State, Geneva 1966–68.
- **1970: Randall's Phillips 66**
- **1970–71: Gene & Dave's Phillips 66** Gene Schaffer & David Odell
- **1972–73: Gene's Phillips 66**–Gene Schaffer
- **1974–79: Earl's/E&M CITGO**, Earl Mustard and Mike Szot
- **1979–80: E & M Union 76**
- **1980–90: Citgo & Class Truck** Rental–Mike Szot & Larry Katkus, gas tanks were taken out in 1990.
- **Current: Gill's Automotive**–Mike Gill

EAST MAIN STREET & 7TH AVENUE

NE corner (619)

- **1929–40's: Polly's Store**–Jerome Polly grocery store with a gas pump Ph 472

413 EAST MAIN STREET

SW corner at 5th Avenue

- **March 1957–64: Zimmerman Pontiac Used Car Lot** *(eighth place of business)*

Mid 1960's Zimmerman Ford Used Car Lot on SW corner 5th Avenue and Main.
FIGURE 10.20 Courtesy St. Charles History Museum.

The home on this car lot was the former homestead of Col. E.J. Baker, while the home on the right was the former home of H.T. Rockwell, Mrs. Baker's father. The Rockwell home became the Yurs Funeral Home and later, the Baker home was relocated to State Avenue and the original site became the parking lot for the funeral home.

In 1954, having been previously denied the car dealership zoning for this location, Zimmerman again approached the city for zoning for a service station and possessed plans already approved at the State Highway Department level. A 2–year battle ensued ending with Bill again being denied approval for the development of his property.

By 1957 the location was used as an annex for the overflow of used cars from the dealership located on south Third Street. The city could not legally deny him this conforming business use.

NORTH 5TH AVENUE

Unsure of brand or address

- **1934–35: Bumgarner's Service Station**– Leslie G. Bumgarner, Ph SC 2923

FIGURE 10.21 Courtesy *St. Charles Chronicle*

805 SOUTH 5TH AVENUE

Rt. 25 and Riverside

- **1929: Roxana Star Co**–distributors of Shell Oil products
- **1931: Wheeler's Shell Oil**–Roy Wheeler and son, Irving
- **1932–45: Murphy's Shell Oil Station**–George D. Murphy
- **1946–47: Bohl's Shell Service**–Edwin Bohl, Ph 3182
- **1948: Riverside Shell**
- **1949: Riverside Shell Oil Station**–George D. Murphy resumed operations
- **1950: Jack's Riverside Shell** Ph 3182
- **1952–53: Smitty's Shell**–Ph 2747
- **December 1953–54: Riverside Shell**–James D. Joslyn, Ph 6478
- **1956: J & L**–new pumps & tanks. Owner Lester Wright (this is his sixth station); and lessee Oscar Mosely of Chicago.

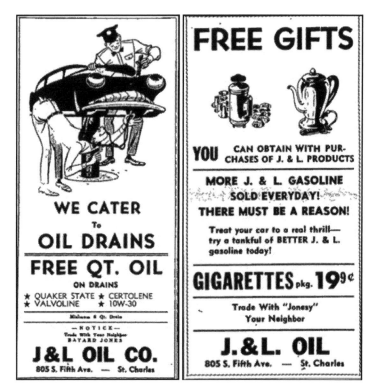

"Trade with your neighbor, Bayard Jones."
FIGURE 10.22 & 10.23 Courtesy *St. Charles Chronicle*.

- **1956–58: Jonesy's J & L Service–**Bayard Jones (author's uncle), formerly at Brilliant Bronze on West Main.
- **1959–61: Riverside Shell–**Joe Murphy & Jerry Lencioni from Geneva.
- **1961–66: J & L Oil Co–** Chase lease 1962
- **1966–69: J & L Oil Co–**Gary Tierney Manager., Gil Tierney on the lease.
- **1969–72: J & L Oil Co–**Gerald Elliot Manager.
- **1977: J & L Oil Co–**Rick McKiness, Manager.
- **1985–87: St. Charles Marathon–**Div. of Rasmussen Oil–Ron Larson manager.
- **December 1987: Shack's 5th Avenue–**Robert Ketelson–gifts and collectibles

215 EAST MAIN STREET (74)

McCornack Oil Co, 215 East Main Street, Circa 1928.
FIGURE 10.24 Photo courtesy Bentz family & St. Charles Museum.

The above photo of the McCornack Oil Co station and headquarters was also the location of the author's dealership from 1977–1990. The story as related to me by Elmore McCornack in 1977 when he entrusted me with this photo was that Charles McCornack, prior to building at this location, had originally attempted to purchase the building across the street, far left of this photo, from blacksmith Carl Nelson. Nelson saw his opportunity to reap a large profit from the McCornack Oil Co. and demanded an outrageous price. McCornack then approached Ira Minard's son, George, at this location, made the $40,000 purchase in December 1927, and moved the Minard home to what had been a forgotten location until recently. Ira Minard who had previously lived in a cabin along the river, then above his store, is considered to be one of the earliest settlers of the community.

This early photograph shows the west end of the service station and the original two–bay construction. Each bay was designed with in–ground service pits that the automobile would straddle for servicing. The very unique design had the pits joined with a low headroom connection and an additional connecting passageway that led into the basement where more supplies and tools could be accessed without the bother of climbing in and out of the pits. The outline of the access passageway is still visible in the current museum basement. Note the west–facing wall has five leaded–glass windows, but the original windows were drafty and were replaced at least three times over the past 90 years. The elevated pediment corner was home to a flagpole. To this date, the original clay tile roof remains along with copper gutters and downspouts. The home purchase of $40,000, relocation costs associated with the move, and new construction cost of about $25,000 would make this the most expensive gas station in northern Illinois when average new–cost construction would have been around $5,000.

During the author's tenure in the building, there were at least three occasions that painters would show up at the direction of the oil company with orders to repaint the building in a current company color scheme. Those painters were given orders to paint all of the brick and sometimes even the beautiful limestone pillars. Each time the painters were turned away, much to their chagrin, until I could contact the company and secure the painting variance to maintain the original integrity of the building.

Ira Minard home, constructed in 1838. Mr & Mrs George Minard on porch.
FIGURE 10.25 Courtesy St. Charles History Museum.

In 2019, the research of Amanda Helfers and Tim Kirsininkas, managers for the St. Charles History Museum, disclosed the 1928 location of the long–lost Minard home as 1201 Illinois Avenue, the same neighborhood where the C.S. McCornack family had lived.
FIGURE 10.26 Author's photograph.

Ira Minard, 1809–1876. Early pioneer that later, as Illinois State Senator in 1842, brought the railroad to St. Charles. FIGURE 10.27 Courtesy St. Charles History Museum.

- **1838–95: Ira & Sarah Minard–**2nd home of early settler (1834) in Charleston (St. Charles), with Sarah surviving her husband until 1895.
- **1895–1927: George Minard, son**–when George sold the home to McCornack, the old address was 74 East Main Street. George was born in this home in 1845 and passed on Dec 15, 1928 at the age of 83 which was just days before the opening of the service station on the former family homestead. As told to Lina Paschal, Chronicle Editor: "a revelation from George Minard who well remembered seeing Mrs Lincoln when she would pass the Minard home after a visit to Mrs [Caroline Esther] Howard who had become noted for her clairvoyant messages. Mr Minard, Sr served as a state legislator and personally knew the Lincoln family at their home in Springfield. George stood near when his father and Mrs Lincoln talked and she shared that she was so broken up over the tragedy of Mr Lincoln's death and the passing of her son, a young lad they called "Tad," that she came here hoping to get some calming word from the beyond. She stayed at the Howard House on the west side [under an alias, Mrs. May] and made daily trips to the east side home [516 S. 6th Ave.] of Mrs Howard."

St. Charles Chronicle Grand Opening advertisement for December 24, 1928.
FIGURE 10.28 Courtesy *St. Charles Chronicle*.

215 East Main Street–circa 1928, Architect Frank Gray of Geneva, William J. Johnson, contractor. The wall, which impeded the mobility of trucks with trailers, was eliminated in the early years. FIGURE 10.29 Photo courtesy Bentz family & St. Charles History Museum.

- **1928–34: McCornack Oil Co.**–Charles S. McCornack. Independent–Red Hat, Aviation, Anti–Knock, Indian & Globe Gasolines –Ph 28 & 30. Corporate office
- **1934–1951: McCornack Oil Co.**–As of March 1934, McCornack is now a Texaco distributor. In June 1935, Charles McCornack died of a heart attack, leaving his widow, Martha and two sons, Donald and Elmore, to operate the company over the next four decades.

McCornack Texaco in the late 1930's as the backdrop to a photo of the inter–urban trolley which operated from 1896–1937; like the horse and buggy, it was another casualty of the transition to the automobile. Sign next to Texaco reads: Goodyear Tires, Rest Rooms. FIGURE 10.30 Courtesy St. Charles History Museum.

1934–51: McCornack Texaco. FIGURE 10.31 Courtesy March 1938 *St. Charles Chronicle*

FIGURE 10.32 Courtesy Bentz family and St. Charles History Museum

In 1941, the station had been remodeled with the addition of the third bay to the west end of the building and two hydraulic lifts to replace the in-ground pits. Those are hot water radiators on the far wall.

FIGURE 10.33 Courtesy *St. Charles Chronicle*

• **1951–60: Bob & Len's Texaco–**Robert Henningson and Leonard M. Askeland, leased from McCornack. April 4, 1952 Grand Opening

Bob and Len's Texaco in 1952, left to right: Preston Askeland, Fred Utroska, Kent Blackman, Ron Scheitlen, Gil Nelson, Len Askeland, Bob Henningson, Howard Proper, and Bob Eastman. Note that apart from the owners, Askeland and Henningson, three of these young men were later businessman in the community and their names are repeated in this publication. FIGURE 10.34 Photo courtesy of St. Charles History Museum.

The photo above is a great example of how significant Service Stations were as employers. There were at least 9 families dependent on either full-time or part-time employment in this photo. I have also seen mention of Jim Minard, Bob Thompson, and David Nielsen working here.

"Bob & Len, Your Texaco Men" Texaco sign hung on building in place of the original clock, c. 1951. FIGURE 10.35 Photo Courtesy McCornack Family & St. Charles History Museum.

- **1960–61 Bob's Texaco–**Bob Henningson (Len had moved to Florida)

Bob Thompson at the pumps working for Bob & Len.
FIGURE 10.36 Courtesy St. Charles History Museum.

Bob & Dick's Texaco c. 1961, the Texaco sign is no longer on front of building, but the clock will not be restored until the building is the museum in 2001. It was always my plan, once I came into ownership of the building, to restore the clock and the flag pole on the right pediment . FIGURE 10.37 Courtesy Joe Jakubaitis.

FIGURE 10.38 Courtesy *St. Charles Chronicle*.

- **June 1961–72: Bob & Dick's Texaco–**Robert K. Eastman, a former Bob & Len employee, and Richard I. Manda, first leased from McCornack and then Texaco Oil Company when on January 1, 1963 McCornack Oil assets were sold to Texaco.
- **1972–1973: Dick's Texaco–**Dick Manda
- **1973–1976: Ron's Texaco–**Ron Scheitlen, former Bob & Len employee, also sold Allis–Chalmers lawn equipment.
- **January 1977–1986: Bentz Texaco–**Archie L. Bentz, Jr, Ph 584–6800
- **1986–1990: Bentz Mobil–**Archie Bentz, Jr, Texaco property was sold to Mobil 1986
- **1990: Archie and Linda Bentz obtain historical plaquing of the building**
- **1990–2000:** Location was boarded up for remediation, details cited in Chapter 5
- **2001–2002:** City of St. Charles purchased, remodeled and opened the **St. Charles Heritage Center/St. Charles History Museum**

Bentz Texaco c. 1977, note gas price was $0.599. FIGURE 10.39 Photo courtesy Bentz family.

Christmas 1979 Bentz Texaco. FIGURE 10.40 Photo courtesy Bentz family.

You can see the florescent lights under the canopy. They were outdoor "power–tube" lights made to operate in colder temperatures but would require early start up to facilitate a warm–up period. . .don't wait 'til dark to turn them on! The original 1928 lights were around the border in the slight arch on the edge of the canopy and there were ten 25–watt incandescent bulbs behind milk glass that would barely light the entrance to each stall. In about 1980, the florescent lights were replaced with six square boxes housing modern mercury vapor lights.

FIGURE 10.41 Photo courtesy Bentz family

Another forgotten piece of gas station history: these older style gas pumps would only register a price up to $0.999/gallon. When I opened in 1977 the price of gas was $0.599 which was about double the price from the pre–embargo prices of 1973–74. In 1987, the prevailing self–serve price was about 90 cents with full–service creeping over the dollar mark. So, what did we do when the price exceeded a dollar? We posted the price on the pump at half price and multiplied the final sale by 2.

Imagine the confusion in the beginning of this transition, when the street sign read $1.11; the pump price read $0.555; the sale of 10 gallons read $5.55; and you had to inform the customer that the correct sale was actually $11.10. Not only did we need to educate our customers, but we had to train our employees on how to multiply the sale. This was especially difficult for high schoolers working the evening shifts alone. They had to figure out the price of the sale and then explain it to customers, many of whom still didn't understand the concept. More often than not, most mistakes favored the customer and the cash register came up short. And now, every gas station in the country needed new gas pumps!

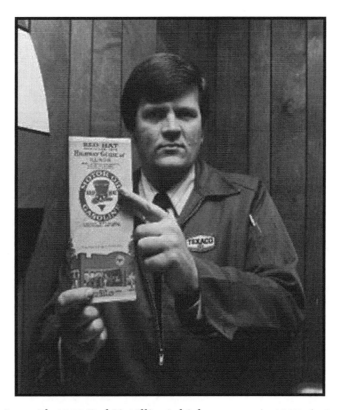

The author posing with 1928 Red Hat Illinois highway map in 1977. A standing joke was that a motorist needed to be certified in origami to re–fold a road map! FIGURE 10.42 Photo Courtesy Bentz Family & St. Charles History Museum.

I felt like I had found buried treasure in the attic of the gas station when I discovered one of the few remaining vestiges of the Independent Oil Company and Red Hat products. The map was unique in that the entire interior map of Illinois was stamped "SAMPLE" and at that point had survived in a filing cabinet for over fifty years before I found it.

We also felt privileged that Elmore McCornack entrusted us with the McCornack business photographs that pertained to our location, and likewise, with Mrs Frank Gray sharing her husband's original blueprints. In both cases the donors noted that their perception of us was that we were the historical custodians of the building.

During our unsuccessful battle to purchase this property, we recognized that Mobil Oil had no interest in the building and was planning to demolish this historically and architecturally significant landmark. My wife and I, with the help of McCornack descendants, immediately set about seeking an historic preservation recognition and the bronze plaque which effectively saved it.

During our tenure, we had gathered historical artifacts that included McCornack paraphernalia, original blueprints, photos and information, all of which we donated to the St. Charles Historic Society. Later, the very building that we saved would become the

St. Charles History Museum and ironically those artifacts returned home to the former "Super Service Station."

Archie & Linda Bentz with pump globe display from the oil companies the Bentz family had represented for past 45 years. FIGURE 10.43 Photo courtesy of St. Charles History Museum.

This photo was taken in January 1990 two weeks prior to our closing. I sold the globes, pump, and most of my sign collection to the *Filling Station Pub & Eatery in St. Charles* for an amount that would be about ten percent of the todays value. I have always been very proud of my business and personal relationships with my various suppliers who were under no legal obligation to buy back my extensive inventory. The most notable of those were Thompson Auto Supply and our B. F. Goodrich tire supplier, both of whom bought back all of my inventory. I credit my years of solid business relationships for being paid back with this generosity.

9 SOUTH 2ND AVENUE

- **1916–27: Judd Garage–Ford–**Ross O. Judd then moved to Hahn building on South Second street.

100 South 1st Avenue was constructed by L.J. Norris in 1933 to provide space for the *St. Charles Chronicle* and the southern portion of the building housed the Arcada Recreation facility featuring bowling lanes, billiards, and as the sign says: Blatz beer.
FIGURE 10.44 Photo courtesy St. Charles History Museum.

105 WALNUT AVENUE & 100 SOUTH 1ST AVENUE

North end of building, facing north and west

- **1933–50: The *St. Charles Chronicle***
- **1950–62: R.L. Wagner Plumbing & Heating**–Roscoe & Bob Wagner
- *With R.L. Wagner continuing as landlord:*
- **1965–67: Ron Hayward's Dodge**–John Mead Sales Manager, Don LeVine Service
- **1968–72: Fox Valley Dodge**
- **1973–75: Sports Car Emporium**–Edward English–specializing in custom Corvettes Ph 584–1456
- **1976: Harry's Village Motors**–Harry W. Weisschnur, formerly with Zimmerman and then his own business in Geneva, Ph 584–7707.
- **1977–79: Art's Body Shop**–Art Bolin
- **1978–88: Neri & Hochberg Law Office**–was located in the former showroom portion of the building (100 S. 1st Ave.). David G. Neri, David M. Hochberg, Charles H. Thorsen, John Biallis, and Ken Kaergard.

The era with Corvettes in the showroom and the Purple Carriage night club operating in the former bowling alley to the south. FIGURE 10.45 Courtesy Chronicle.

1980 announcement of my new daughter, Major Muffler, and Arcada Automotive Repair. FIGURE 10.46 Courtesy Bentz family.

- **1980–86: Archie's Arcada Automotive–105 Walnut Avenue–**Archie L. Bentz, Jr– An expansion of Bentz Texaco automotive repair service. As in the case of most service stations, there were space limitations which hampered growth, especially when you compared the available space of a typical 2 or 3–bay service station to that of car dealerships and big box stores. Obviously, a major repair could encumber 33–50% of the space of the smaller facility. Combine that with the need for an entire equipment room to house the tire mounting machine, wheel balancer, brake lathes, diagnostic analyzers, front end alignment equipment, tool boxes for each technician, along with cabinetry to house specialized tools that would not fit into the average tool box and space becomes critical. Fortunately, my Texaco station was blessed with both a basement and attic for storage of massive inventory needs when purchasing in volume was key to promote competitive pricing. However, large repair jobs such as valve jobs, camshaft replacements, engine and transmission rebuilding could take days, with components being sent out to the machine shops and rebuilders with even more specialized equipment. In a practical world, that meant pushing the disabled car out of the bay to free up space for other repairs and then pushing that vehicle back in to complete its repair on another day. There is not another former service station owner that can't relate to these constrictions of space as applied to a full–service repair facility.

  Desiring to expand my repair business and perform larger, more extensive repairs meant more space was required. That led to my expansion to a 3500 square foot, former dealership building with 2 lifts and 8 repair stalls. I then added two more Certified Technicians; a Major Muffler franchise with custom pipe–bending equipment; Hunter Alignment; AAMCO disc and drum brake lathes; more specialized tools and equipment; and full automotive repair to include engine and transmission rebuilding. Then in 1986, Texaco sold my gas station to Mobil Oil who saw this auxiliary business as a conflict to their interest and so I sold the repair operation to Master Automotive.

- **1986–95: Master Automotive–**Dennis Jamison, Steve Baumgartner, Berry Onterdorf, 3 former technicians from Town & Country Oldsmobile, (Berry left the business in 1989).

- **Danny's Side Pocket–Billiards and Pub** with the former office/showroom area as an open–air patio.

Currently being developed as "Flagship on the Fox" and "Pollyanna Brewing Co." by local Steve Mayer, Ryan Weidner, and Walter Payton's son, Jarrett Payton.
FIGURE 10.47 Current Google Earth view.

- **2019: Flagship on the Fox**–Steve Mayer & Jarrett Payton, son of Walter Payton
- **2019: Pollyanna Brewing**–Ryan Weidner

216 SOUTH RIVERSIDE

Former Riverview Dairy Building

- **1979–80: MPG Auto Performance**–Alan Erickson

McCornack Oil Co home office and Firestone Store, 114–116 East Main Street. FIGURE 10.48
Photo Courtesy McCornack Family & St. Charles History Museum.

114–116 EAST MAIN STREET

- **1924–40: St. Charles City Hospital**, note the medical symbols on the façade.
- **1940–47: Price's Economy Auto Supply–B. F. Goodrich Store**
- **November 1947–56: McCornack Firestone Ph 516**–Prior to this time McCornack had been the major supplier of Goodyear tires and at the same time dealt with the competition of Price's Economy Auto Supply, the B. F. Goodrich supplier across the street. With the Depression in the rear–view mirror many major companies entered the automotive product field; an early business philosophy that one might compare to the "Big Box" stores competing with our local retailers today. While they did not engage in the sale of gasoline, they targeted anything profitable which in turn would erode your local service station's product mix. As I often told customers, "Sears will not adjust your carburetor's choke, but they will sell you a whole new carburetor." Other early versions were Western Auto, Blue Star, Sears & Roebuck, and Montgomery Ward. Firestone, however, had apparently offered the proper incentives to McCornack to sign on with them, while B. F. Goodrich went to Geneva and the Goodyear franchise moved across the river to Hahn's.
- **1962: Western Auto Store**–Ned Zizzo, Ph 584–8795

Price's Economy Auto Supply / McCornack Firestone Grand Opening.
FIGURE 10.49 & 10.50 Courtesy *St. Charles Chronicle*.

While tires, batteries, and accessories were emphasized, the product line was expanded to include just about anything around the house: refrigerators, stoves, freezers, washers & dryers, lawn mowers, rakes, hoses, bicycles, dolls, play service stations for the boys, doll houses for the girls, radios, televisions, electric train sets, sporting goods, electric drills & saws, vacuum cleaners... and the list goes on.

The McCornack's were visionaries who embraced the future and this part of the business outlasted all other endeavors for the next 30 years and beyond as McCornack Firestone still exists today under different ownership on East Main Street.

C.M. Hanson's tow truck from East Side Garage, 512 South 1st Avenue.
FIGURE 10.51 Photo courtesy St. Charles Historical Museum.

512 SOUTH 1ST AVENUE

- **1917: William Brown Garage**
- **1919–25: East Side Garage–Oakland/Pontiac–**Frank Duerr & Daniels Ph 450. C.R. Spriet sells Twin City tractors here in 1920.
- **1926: East Side Garage–Hupmobile,** Frank H. Duerr, prop. Ph 283
- **1928–32: East Side Garage & Filling Station–Dodge Bros** in 1929. 1932 moved to 12 North 1st Avenue

12 NORTH 1ST AVENUE

- **1927–29: Oakland-Pontiac,** addressed as 12 East First Street, Ph 29
- **1932–35: East Side Garage–**Carl M. Hanson Ph 450. Became **Texaco** in 1934; Charles Hanson, a son, was added in 1935.

- **1935–41: East Side Garage–**Clare Miller–closed and went to war.

FIGURE 10.52 Courtesy *St. Charles Chronicle*

- **March 1946–53: East Side Garage Texaco–**Ph 455, Bud Yeomans & Al De Potter, Edwin Beeth, Ed Swanson. Chicago Motor Club in 1947; State Truck Inspection Station and Art's Radiator Shop when Art Henningson moved in. This was a 24–hour operation.
- **1953: Borman Hardware Annex** to the main store which faced Main Street.

FIGURE 10.53 Courtesy July 24, 1919 *St. Charles Chronicle*

2 EAST MAIN STREET

- **1919: L.F. Sinton–Overland** automobile, Ph 136

NORTH OF ST. CHARLES CITY LIMITS

ROUTE 25 AND COURIER AVENUE

NW corner in Valley View

- **1954–58: Stanton's Service Station**–Harry and James Stanton
- **1965: B & D Standard–** Possibly Adolph 'Bob' & Richard 'Dick the Termite' Carlson of B&D Cities Service at 210 S 2nd Street.
- **1970's Billy's Valley View Standard Oil**–Billy Jones, closed 1977

ROUTE 25 AND COURIER AVENUE

SW corner

- **1958–60: Cities Service**–Albert E. Hummel
- **1961: Dave's Cities Service**
- **Sinclair Station**–closed in the 1960's? Foreign car garage

FIGURE 11.53 Courtesy March 1954 *St. Charles Chronicle*

ROUTE 25 VALLEY VIEW

East side of road (formerly known as East Elgin Road)
- **1934–44: Hummel's Grocery & Gas**–Frank Hummel–McCornack supplied Texaco

ROUTE 25 NORTH OF COUNTRY CLUB ROAD

Little Woods, 2 miles north of St. Charles
- **1947–1954: Brauer's Royal Blue Store**
- **1954: Harm Brauer Texaco**
- **1970's–80's: The Country Store**–Mike Horton, had a single gas pump

32W252 ARMY TRAIL ROAD-WAYNE

- **1952–55: Steve's Garage** Ph 4023
- **1970's: Dewey's Mobil**–Dewey Sartos, later at West Main ARCO, St. Charles
- **1980–present: Village Mobil**–Bill Beebe & Sons, no longer selling gas.

ELEVEN

ST. CHARLES WEST SIDE

SOUTH 1ST STREET

- **77–79 West Main Street**–SE corner of South 1st & Main Street (Later site of The Log Cabin Restaurant and The Manor Restaurant. Was it by chance or design that the same architects utilized by Baker for the hotel, Wolf Sexton Harper & Treax Inc, designed The Log Cabin restaurant?)

This full page, multiple auto dealer advertisement in the 1920 Chronicle special edition emphasize a few of the automotive sales and service dealers located in the west side of downtown St. Charles. Over the next four decades this area becomes highly concentrated with about 13 service stations and 16 car dealerships. Today, only 1 gas station and 1 repair facility still exist in that same area. FIGURE 11.1 January 15, 1920 *St. Charles Chronicle*.

Corner of South First and Main Street.
FIGURE 11.2 Courtesy October 23, 1919 *St. Charles Chronicle.*

- **1919–21 Foley & Redmond Buick & Chevrolet**–Peter L. Foley & John N. Redmond.
- **1922: Foley & Hammond Buick**
- **1925–30: Foley Buick** Ph 74, moved to North 2nd Street about 1932

SOUTH 1ST STREET

Opposite North Western Depot
- **June 1940: Zale Motor Sales**–Used cars, wholesale & retail Ph 162

First Pure Grand Opening 1968, 201 Illinois Street. FIGURE 11.3 Photo courtesy Bentz family.

201 ILLINOIS STREET

SW corner Illinois and South 1st Street, now a part of Blue Goose. June 1966 building permit issued: Aug 66–July 67 advertised "available for lease"

- **September 1967–68: Woods' Pure Oil Service**–Edward Woods
- **1968–69: First Pure**–Jerry Drews & Tony Bilous Grand Opening Nov. 1968
- **1970: First Union 76**–Jerry Drews & Tony Bilous
- **1971–73: First Union 76**–Tony Bilous, Jerry left to manage West Main ENCO
- **Mid 70's–early 80's: Magic Oven Bakery**

12 INDIANA STREET

East of 1st Street

- **1960: Paul Ladewig Blacksmith,** and his son, Tim
- **1969: Howard's Garage**–Howard Maine, former mechanic at Boeman Chevrolet Garage in 1946.
- **1973–74: B & M Garage**–Waymon Brown & Howard Maine
- **1975: Howard's Garage**–Howard Maine, later joined by stepson Jerry Ford who eventually moved garage to Tri-City body shop building on Randall Rd.

115 INDIANA STREET

West of 1st Street

- **1960–62: Cunningham's Service Garage**–James Cunningham, J. Clemens Nober, manager. Cunningham also located at Sinclair on east Main street.
- **1964–66: Wilbur's Garage**–John Wilbur Ing Ph 584–3581
- **1969–70's: Tri City Auto Body:** Dale James & Mike Wetter, later located at 110 Randall Road.

116 INDIANA STREET

West of 1st Street

- **1946–48: Hendry's Weldery & Body Shop**–Ph 133
- **1948–50: Hendry Metal Products** (Iron railings)
- **1958–66: Orv's Body Shop**–Orvil A. Stegall
- **1969–71: Valley Towing**–Timothy R. Chalker

405 SOUTH 1ST STREET

- **1924–25: Henningson & Sills Garage**–Arthur Henningson & Joseph Sills
- **1966–68: St. Charles Chrysler Plymouth**–Marvin K. Miller & Edward J. Kenny, Ph 584–1390
- **1969: Fox Valley Dodge**–Robert Hanson

- **1973: Suburban Chrysler Plymouth** Ph 377–0700
- **1976: Gregg Chrysler/Plymouth**–Jack E. Guess
- **1980: St. Charles Dodge**–Maurice Johnson
- **1988: Torco Dodge**–Anthony Torerleo

100 PRAIRIE STREET

1st and Prairie Streets

- **1924–31: Kohlert Agency–Nash, Ajax, Willys/Overland (1929), & Ford–**Henry "Cap" Kohlert, Ph 181. Kohlert's earlier business venture was selling used cars at Hake's Tire Shop on Main Street. Henningson manages garage in 1924; Joe Sills was to manage garage starting in 1925.

  "Cap" Kohlert raced in the 1927 Indianapolis 500 as a climax to a long racing career that started on dirt tracks around the Midwest. June 3, 1927 *Geneva Republican*: "[Kohlert] originally was reported as fatally injured in the races at Indianapolis Monday, will recover! While first reported dead, he was still breathing when he reached the hospital had been involved in an accident striking a wall with veteran French driver, Cliff Bergère and their cars rolled together on the track…"
- **1931–40: Kohlert H. Motor Sales–Ford & Lincoln–Zephyr**–Henry "Cap" Kohlert Ph 425
- **1940–42: Kushler Ford & Lincoln–Zephyr**–William J. Kushler, A. Koch, & E. Cameron
- **1942–47: Spriet Motor Sales–Ford**–Alfred Spriet, Ph 3819
- **August 1947: Spriet Motor Sales–**Used cars and garage (The Ford Agency went to Boylan at Second & Cedar streets)
- **1951: Dooley Motor Sales–**Import and used cars Ph 5523
- **October 1955: Pleimling Motor Sales–Studebaker Packard**–George Pleimling, proprietor; Arthur Knutson, Service Manager, Ph 6521. Opened when he assumed the Hansen Studebaker franchise located in Geneva when Hansen switched to Chevrolet.
- **April 1956: American Gravure Inc.**–Louis Miller manufactures roto-gravure color printing plates.
- **1960–65: Brauer Bee-Line**–Front End Specialty, James Brauer, 104 Prairie, Ph JU 4–0411
- **1966–78: Kern Brake & Alignment**–Dick Kern (104)
- **1993: Suburban Tire**
- **1999: Discount Tire**

501 SOUTH 1ST STREET OR 602 GENEVA ROAD
The "Triangle" of 1st, Prairie, and 2nd Streets

Looking north at the triangle shaped property, Illinois Route 22, (now Route 31), on left with First street on the right. Wadhams Ethyl Gas/Blue Seal Products, Mobiloil, grease pit on right. The Prairie street extension through to First would later pass were the home sets behind the station. FIGURE 11.4 Courtesy St. Charles History Museum

- **1924–28: Blue Ribbon Filing Station–**Built by Henry Kohlert; C.L. Anderson, manager. The first service station entering St. Charles from the south on the west side of the river.
- **1928–33: Blue Ribbon Oil Co–**Lester Fisher, manager

Grand Re–Opening with new building, St. Charles Oil Co, Rasmussen Bros. FIGURE 11.5 Courtesy *St. Charles Chronicle.*

- **1933–35: St. Charles Oil Co.–White Rose Gas–**Eigel & Gerhart Rasmussen

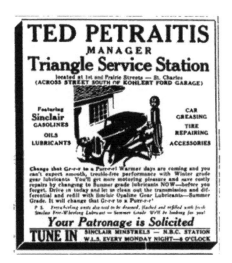

FIGURE 11.6 Courtesy *St. Charles Chronicle*

- **April 1935–39: Triangle Service Station, Sinclair–**Theodore "Ted" Petraitis
- **1940–42: Ted's Standard Service–**Theodore Petraitis
- **1943–49: Ted's Sinclair Service–**Theodore Petraitis

Change of Sinclair dealers in Nov. 10, 1949 Chronicle.
FIGURE 11.7 & 11.8 Courtesy *St. Charles Chronicle*.

- **1949–56: Bob's Sinclair Service** Ph 3551–Bob Olsen
- **1956–70: Olsen's Sinclair Service–** Bob Olsen, opened a 2nd location on East Main in 1966.
- **1970–74: Sinclair–**Stan Pakenas
- **1974 –77: PK's Tire Town–**Jim "PK" Pakenas, Stan's son, no gas, Ph 584–6200

- **Date unknown: Sally's Sub House**
- **Current: Jalapeno Grille**

GENEVA ROAD

South of the triangle, probably close to city limits
- **1932: Midway Service Station–**Orville Wells

NORTH 2ND STREET

On our way to North 2nd Street we need to first talk about Hotel Baker on

WEST MAIN STREET AND THE FOX RIVER

Hotel Baker circa 1928. FIGURE 11.9 Photo courtesy St. Charles History Museum.

At this point, I want to acknowledge the Hotel Baker. To many it would seem that this is a deviation from the history of service stations, auto dealers, and garages, but it is critical to understand the influence of the expansion created by the automobile and all of the businesses that spawned from that development. In 1920, Colonel E.J. Baker, one of the Texaco heirs, petitioned Springfield that the proposed State Route 64 should go through St. Charles, replacing what had been known as the Chicago–Iowa Roadway. Then in 1927 he built the Hotel Baker in an effort to make St. Charles a destination for people of northern Illinois. Col. Baker began construction of the hotel in 1926. The estimated cost to build it was $600,000 and two years later the "Spanish–Style Romantic Revival architecture with Baroque deco" hotel sported a final price tag of $1,250,000. In addition to fine dining in the Trophy Room and dancing to Tommy Dorsey, Guy Lombardo, Eddie Duchin, Lawrence Welk and Louis Armstrong in the Rainbow Ballroom, the hotel offered several shops: a women's clothing store, newspaper stand, barber shop and a beauty salon. The hotel was deemed, "The Beauty Spot of the Fox Valley."

Picture postcard from the 1930's depicting the garden gazebo at rear of hotel, the river–front observation platform, the Baker Garage on the right behind the trees and the boat house on the river. The hotel also housed hydro–electric generators in the basement. FIGURE 11.10

Airport Farm before Pheasant Run, note the gas pump between the buildings; no doubt that the product dispensed was Texaco. The right picture is a commemorative stamp sold in St. Charles in 1933 to support the World's Fair. FIGURE 11.11 &11.12 Courtesy St. Charles History Museum.

From the beginning the Hotel Baker thrived so well that an aircraft landing strip was built on one of Baker's farms to the east of town. That farm came to be known as 'Airport Farm' as noted by the sign on the barn. This was the predecessor to the DuPage Airport which at one time, was second only to the O'Hare Airport in total air traffic volume in Illinois. On the 1953 Silver Anniversary of the hotel, it was said, "the hotel had accommodated close to a half million–over–night guests, prepared seven course dinners for over three million diners and housed senators, governors, and other national figures."

Baker sold this farm in 1958 shortly before his demise on January 17, 1959. In 1963, Edward McArdle opened Pheasant Run here, later expanding from the original restaurant in the barn, to a full hotel/resort with multiple restaurants, bars, gift shops, golf course, and indoor/outdoor pools. This is ironic in the sense that Baker's former farm property later directly competed with his beloved Hotel Baker.

Leaving the rear of the Hotel Baker with a walk through the Baker Gardens
towards the rear view of the Baker Garage and Boat House.
FIGURE 11.13 Courtesy St. Charles History Museum.

The Hotel Baker Gardens extended north two blocks all the way to the railroad tracks, featured a boat house and docks on the river, an Art Deco garage, and even a miniature golf course. While traveling to the Hotel Baker all modes of transportation were encouraged including automobile, train, plane and boat. There was little doubt that the age of the automobile was here and many businesses sprang up to support those traveling the newly constructed highways.

Current Hotel Baker Gardens with salvaged terra–cotta from the Baker Garage façade.
FIGURE 11.14 & 11.15 Author's 2019 photographs.

Hotel Baker Garage under construction in 1929, North 2nd & Cedar Street. FIGURE 11.16
Photo courtesy St. Charles History Museum.

The hotel was constructed in 1927, but Baker's business model also included the Baker Garage which was built in 1929 in order to provide for the care of his guests' automobiles who had traveled many miles. Built on a grand scale, the two–story garage covered an entire city block north of the Hotel. The first floor was dedicated to the sale of multiple brands of autos such as Auburn–Cord–Duesenberg, Hudson, Essex–Terraplane, Plymouth, Chrysler, and Packard with grand showrooms sporting large windows for the passerby to be tempted by the latest models. The second story was the parking garage for the hotel and just to make sure the guest's every need were met, there was a full–service Texaco facility on the street that could tend to any needed repairs or service. The Texaco Service Station was one of the earliest in St. Charles which only stands to reason since it was the source of Baker's inherited wealth.

BAKER HOTEL GARAGE. FIGURE 11.17 1982 photograph Bentz family collection

Brass plaque on column between the two showrooms: "Hotel Baker Garage erected 1929 A.D. Edward J. Baker, Wolf Sexton Harper &Treax Inc–Engineers & Architects, C.A. Anderson– General Contractor." This plaque and a section of terra cotta now reside at the St. Charles History Museum. FIGURE 11.18 1982 photograph Bentz family collection.

The terra cotta in the museum's possession is just the section with the locomotive (located in the middle, bottom right). That one section measures about 24 inches wide by 20 inches tall, which will give the reader a scale for understanding the overall size of this entire section.
FIGURE 11.19 1982 photograph Bentz family collection.

Functional transoms w/leaded–glass windows above each of the showroom entrances.
FIGURE 11.20 1982 photograph Bentz family collection.

Formerly the North and South Baker Garage Automotive Showrooms, Photo 1982.
FIGURE 11.21 photograph Bentz family collection.

The center of the Hotel Baker Garage was split between two showrooms, north and south, with separate entrances featuring stained glass transoms and terra–cotta frieze spanning the entire showroom area. The terra–cotta represented all forms of transportation including dinosaurs, horses, boats, trains, airplanes, but centered on the automobile. One cannot over emphasize the other magnificent exterior details including the fine masonry work; the Art Deco lights at the entrances; and the lights along the roof–line that mimic the capitals of the columns framing the doorways. These photos were taken when the building was over 50 years old in 1982. The building was last used as an automobile dealer in 1974 and this photo shows how it became neglected and relegated to being a showroom and storage area for a swimming pool company.

In my possession, I had these 1982 exterior photographs which were taken the year before the building was razed. The photos have now been donated to the St. Charles Museum. To date, I am not aware of any quality early interior or exterior photographs of the Baker Garage or Texaco Gas Station there. In the 1960's, I visited the building interior only once when it was an Oldsmobile dealership and remember how much I appreciated the step back in time with its Art Deco features of either terrazzo or granite–tiled floors, wall sconces and overhead lighting in the showrooms.

The mobility brought on by the post–war automobile continued to influence our day–to–day landscape. Restaurants evolved to drive–ins; the downtown movie theatre was augmented by the drive–in movie, and the downtown hotels were gradually replaced with motels where you could drive your car right up to the door of your room.

Information sourced at the St. Charles Public Library tells us that Col. Baker had lived on the fifth floor of the hotel from 1940 until his death in 1959. Dellora Norris, Baker's niece, inherited the hotel. After she failed to find a buyer for the Hotel Baker, she donated it to Lutheran Social Services of Illinois in 1968. Following a remodeling of the hotel, Lutheran Social Services reopened it in 1971 as an interfaith, non–denominational residence for the elderly. Although the upper floors of the hotel were restricted to use by Hotel Baker residents, the first–floor areas remained open to the public. St. Charles businessmen Craig Frank and Neil Johnson bought the hotel in 1996 when Lutheran Social Services declared that the hotel building was too costly to operate and put the building up for sale. Following a $9 million renovation, Frank and Johnson celebrated the Hotel Baker's grand reopening as a luxury hotel with a festive 1997 New Year's Eve party. The hotel had regained its 1920s designation as the "Gem of the Fox Valley."

The Hotel Baker's elegant parking garage, however, was razed in early 1983 to make way for Carroll Tower, a senior citizen apartment complex that was managed by Lutheran Social Services. The contracted demolition company complained that they had under–bid the job as they had no idea that the floor of the upper area was constructed with a solid lead lining that no wrecking ball could penetrate. Salvaging the terra cotta involved a complex project of disassembling the brick wall from the interior; removing bars and pins; and finally chiseling the mortar away. It is difficult for me today to convey the mindset in making the decision for demolition of this historic building. It was seen as "just an old garage" that was obsolete and no longer needed for the hotel.

Edward Colvin of Emergency Demolition Contractors inspects the terra cotta panels which were made by American Terra Cotta & Ceramic Co., Chicago, in 1929. FIGURE 11.22 Courtesy of *Chicago Tribune* photographer George Thompson.

CHICAGO TRIBUNE, JANUARY 7, 1983, BY PATRICK REARDON:

"It was when the '20s were roaring and the dancing was fast that the garage was built for the Hotel Baker.

It was 1928, between two world wars, before the Great Crash and the Great Depression, when the two–story garage with its six fine sketched terra cotta panels showing the history of transportation was built on Ill. Hwy. 31 one block north of Ill. Hwy. 64 in downtown St. Charles.

Now, 55 years later, workers are readying the garage for demolition and laboring to save those six panels. Prominent on each panel is an auto, modern in 1928 but antique now, blanketed by two all–but–undressed women sporting pageboy haircuts that were to go in and out of fashion a number of times in the years following the creation of the panels. Also displayed on the panels, though much smaller, are other modes of trans-portation: an airplane, a railroad engine and a covered wagon. On the larger panels a horse–riding Indian and a somewhat fanciful log–pulling dinosaur are also featured.

The garage where tuxedoed partygoers and nervous honeymooners parked their cars on visits to the elegant Hotel Baker five decades ago is being razed this month so that Carroll Tower, a $2.5 million, rent–assisted, 106–unit, art deco, elderly housing project can be constructed on the site.

But the workers from Emergency Demolition Contractors, Chicago, are laboring to remove and save the terra cotta panels so the walls of the building can be knocked down.

Recovery of those panels, formed when liquid terra cotta was poured into a mold and hardened, is a requirement of the contract, said *Kim Schmitt, corporate secretary of Emergency Demolition.*

The labor is tedious because the terra cotta is brittle and the workers must first discover–by knocking out a brick wall behind one panel–how it was put into place before being able to reverse the process, Schmitt said.

He said the panels should be removed by the middle of next week and demolition completed a short time later.

Robert King, the developer of Carrol Tower, is donating the panels to the City of St. Charles, said James Urhausen, executive vice president of Westway Construction Corp, the project's general contractor.

However, Urhausen said, if possible, one large panel may be kept to display in the lobby of the new building as a reminder and tie with the garage that has stood on the site for half a century."

And the walls came tumbling down...the Hotel Baker Garage is gone. FIGURE 11.23 Courtesy of *Chicago Tribune* January 11, 1983 & photographer John Bartley.

I had the opportunity to visit the Auburn–Cord–Duesenberg Museum in Auburn, Indiana, which is the home for America's finest automobiles. It was constructed in the same era and reminiscent of the Baker Hotel Garage which was also home to an Auburn–Cord dealership. I beg your pardon for the detour to Auburn, but the significance of Baker's building and the loss of same, is emphasized with this sharing of photographs and quotations. Many comparisons can be made between these two architecturally significant art deco buildings from the same era.

Auburn Cord Duesenberg Museum, Auburn, Indiana.
FIGURE 11.24 Courtesy Auburn Automobile Museum website.

"The museum building, the museum's largest artifact, was constructed for the Auburn Automobile Company in 1929 after a design by A.M. Strauss of Fort Wayne. It is one of the finest examples of Art Deco architecture in the Midwest. The building is considered to be the museum's most significant artifact and it is listed on the National Register of Historic Places and was named a National Historic Landmark in 2005."

"During the Auburn Automobile Company's heyday, the Showroom was filled with the latest Auburns, Cords, and Duesenbergs. Milestones of automotive advancement. Each automobile is significant in at least one of four areas: luxury, design, performance, or ties to the Auburn Automobile Company. Technically the company was responsible for many patented innovations that are still on the cars driven today including hydraulic brakes, X–frame chassis construction, front wheel drive, and retractable headlights."

Notice the 1929 art deco architectural elements shared with the Baker Garage. FIGURE 11.25 Courtesy Auburn Automobile Museum website.

"Step back in time and enjoy the display of Auburns, Cords and Duesenbergs of the classic era (1925–1937) in their magnificent Art Deco Company Showroom!" FIGURE 11.26 Courtesy Auburn Automobile Museum website.

"After the demise of the Auburn company in 1937, the factory showroom and headquarters served as a parts and restoration center for the obsolete Auburn, Cord, and Duesenberg cars. Surprisingly, this activity lasted through the 1940s and 1950s, under the name Auburn–Cord–Duesenberg Company, directed by entrepreneur Dallas Winslow. When Winslow sold the business in 1960, the building fell into misuse and ill repair. Machine shops, garment manufacturers, auto and motorcycle lots and industrial warehousing ravaged the historic structure. By the early 1970s, the handsome art deco edifice was grimy, weather–beaten and modified beyond recognition inside."

The building was purchased in 1973 by the Auburn Automotive Heritage Inc. group with fundraising and restoration starting immediately. "By July 1974, Every remarkable characteristic of the main display room…had been revitalized: the elaborate, hand–painted ceiling friezes (breath–taking borders of ornamental plaster in colorful relief), ornate Italian three–tiered chandeliers, geometric terrazzo floor, 72 etched–glass side lights, gracefully curving central grand staircase, vertical wall panels, Philippine walnut woodwork, soaring plate glass windows carrying "Auburn," "Cord" and "Duesenberg" in blazing gold letters. The entire environment enjoyed by visitors in the 1930s was recreated with successful authenticity."

This author invites the reader to visit the museum and reminisce in the fine architectural elements that were also key to the beautiful Baker Hotel Garage which was also home to the Auburn–Cord and Duesenberg automobiles.

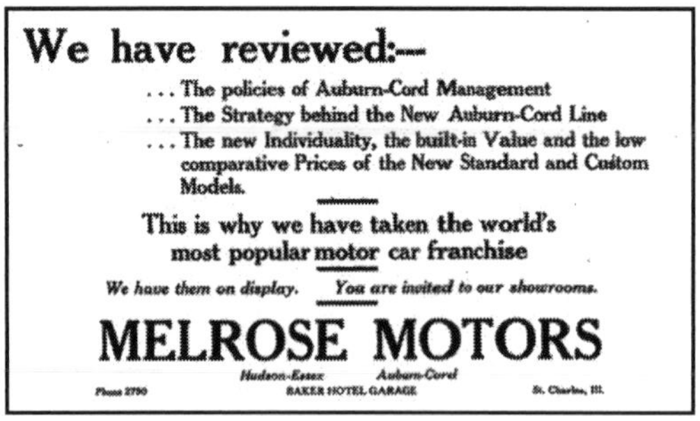

We have reviewed:—
. . . The policies of Auburn-Cord Management
. . . The Strategy behind the New Auburn-Cord Line
. . . The new Individuality, the built-in Value and the low comparative Prices of the New Standard and Custom Models.
This is why we have taken the world's most popular motor car franchise
We have them on display. You are invited to our showrooms.
MELROSE MOTORS
Hudson-Essex Auburn-Cord
Phone 2790 BAKER HOTEL GARAGE St. Charles, Ill.

Auburn–Cord Agency announcement for Melrose Motors, Baker Hotel Garage, St. Charles.
FIGURE 11.27 Courtesy September 24, 1931 *St. Charles Chronicle*.

ONE OF THE FINEST AND MOST MODERN GARAGE BUILDINGS IN KANE COUNTY, — ALSO TEXACO SERVICE STATION.
BEAUTIFUL MODERNISTIC SALES ROOMS, HUDSON, TERRAPLANE, CHRYSLER & PLYMOUTH SALES AND SERVICE.

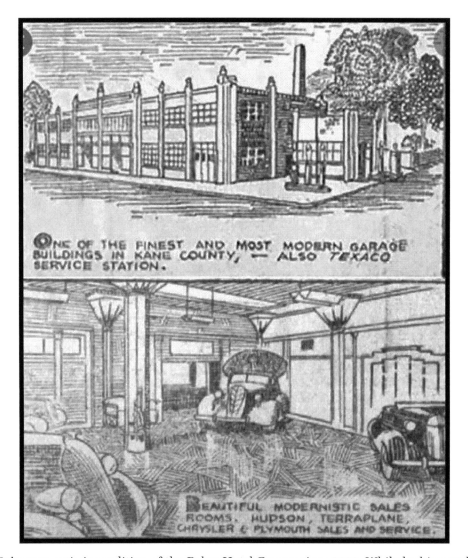

Unknown artist's rendition of the Baker Hotel Garage circa 1936. While lacking early photos of the Baker garage, this sketch gives a sense of the gas station and the magnificence of the interior of the building. The similarities between the Hotel Baker Garage and the Auburn Automobile Museum are quite striking.
FIGURE 11.28 Courtesy June 25, 1936 Elgin Courier–News.

In 1982, the ornate folding accordion–style wood garage doors framed by Art Deco lights stood as a testament to the grand days of the past when the Baker Garage was in its heyday. FIGURES 11.29 & 11.30 Courtesy author's collection & *Chicago Tribune.*

200 (25) NORTH 2ND STREET

Rt. 31 at Cedar Street

- **1929–44: Hotel Baker "All–night Garage & Gas Station"–Texaco–**Edward J. Baker, Owner; Alfred A. Cornelious, Manager; Ph 3120. Baker's business model was to provide services for the hotel guest's automobile and at the same time the building was large enough to accommodate two additional automobile dealers.

NORTH END OF BAKER GARAGE

- **1930–31: Kendall Motors Oakland–Pontiac**, T.A. Kendall, Ph 80, added **Studebaker** in May of 1931.
- **February 1931–32: Melrose Motors Hudson–Essex,** then added **Auburn– Cord–Duesenberg** in Sept 1931; **Essex–Terraplane** August 1932; Ph 2790. I.G. Melrose, owner and sales manager; August 1931 added servicemen: Cecil Stinson & Orvil Schroder. Mr. and Mrs. Lester J. Norris drove a Duesenberg in this era. Bill Zimmerman leaves the hotel as a bellman to work for Melrose and his $5 a day wages probably reflected that he was the general roust- about lot boy. During the Great Depression, Col. Baker took over operations

of the dealership and Bill worked his way up to salesman. At this time, Bill additionally worked outside the garage on repairing used cars, taking them to Chicago to sell, and then hitch–hiking back home. This information was sourced from his obituary.

SOUTH END OF BAKER GARAGE

- **October 1931–32: Peter Foley Oldsmobile Buick GMC Trucks**–South End Hotel Baker Garage. Ph 74. 1931 advertisement states that he had been selling Buick for 15 years.

- **1932–38: Hotel Baker Motors, Hudson–Essex–Terraplane/White and Indiana trucks,** E.J. Baker Owner; Albert Wolf, General Manager; L.G. Shrader, Garage Manager; Henry Sudduth & Wm. Zimmerman, Salesmen; Ph 2790. It is unclear at this point whether Baker took over control of some, or all, of both ends of the building. In 1934 he added **Studebaker & Rockne** then dropped this line in 1935 going to **Chrysler–Plymouth**. Added **Packard**, in 1936.

- **1935: Oldsmobile 6 & 8 Sales & Service**–a continuation of Peter Foley's operation in the south end, but proprietor unknown.

FIGURE 11.31 Courtesy *St. Charles Chronicle*

- *St. Charles Chronicle*, **March 31, 1938**: "Announcement! The Hotel Baker Garage has discontinued the sale of new and used cars. The [Texaco] Oil Station, Storage, Service and Repair Departments will continue in operation."

  Again, I will make some conjecture about the operation of the car dealership. While Baker could certainly afford to operate said business at minimal loss, (the hotel never made a profit in 30 years), there was apparently some dissatisfaction with the operations.

The same 1938 edition of the Chronicle: "W.P. Zimmerman Used Motors...for the last 7 years [he] has been employed as a salesman at the Hotel Baker Garage...he is opening his own used car business, being located at the used car lot, corner of North Second and Cedar street, directly across the street from the Hotel Baker Garage" Ph 479 or 2118. By November, Bill Zimmerman had secured his first new car dealership, a Pontiac franchise, and had relocated to 708 S. Third Street.

- **1938–44: Baker Hotel Garage/Texaco**–E.J. Baker–owner; Vernon F. Modine–Manager; John J. Smith, an automotive porter and night watchman, occupied living quarters in the parking garage where there were accommodations for 5–6 hotel/garage employees.

A rare photo of the Baker Garage with the Texaco Service Station taken after WWII when Zimmerman Pontiac is re-established here. FIGURE 11.32 Yellow Pages Advertisement.

- **September 1944–53: Hotel Baker Garage–Pontiac/GMC**–Bill Zimmerman, Inc; Vernon Modine, Service Manager; John Oksas, mechanic; with Fred Utroska, Jr in the Texaco station. Ph 3120. (Bill's fifth place of business as he is able to acquire new automobiles)

St. Charles Chronicle **November 25, 1945:** "Keeping in touch with the promotional interest in new cars and display rooms, the Hotel Baker Garage has been redecorated for the background of the two new Pontiacs which have arrived for show only. Stacey Nelson and his decorators have been in charge of the room which has been done in pastel green and trimmed with a darker green. The original Indian design of the pillars have been kept intact [remember the Pontiac logo was that of a Native American].

These 1946 Pontiacs, are the first new cars in the display room since 1938. Two GMC trucks are resting in the second display room. William Zimmerman, manager, announces two returned servicemen added to the business, Fred Utroska [Jr], who will assist at the gas station and John Oksas who will assist in the garage."

- **1954–55: Hames Motor Sales–Oldsmobile–**Anthony Hames from Chicago; brother Robert, Service Manager; and John Janozik in parts. Ph 6400 (the Oldsmobile franchise in Geneva had been given up when Fanning bought out Beal)
- **1955–62: Marquardt–Farrell Oldsmobile Inc–**August 1955; added **Nash–Rambler** 1958. Bob Marquardt and brother–in–law Don Farrell, prop; assisted by Jim Castner, Dave Hemming
- **1962–69: Don Farrell Oldsmobile Inc,** JU4–6400, Don Farrell relocated to East Main by Pheasant Run.
- **1970–74: Goettel Motors Renault BMW–**Daniel & Gerhard Helmut (Crystal Lake residents)

"THE LAKE AT AUTOMOBILE LANE"
FIGURE 11.33 Courtesy of St. Charles History Museum. Flood of October 13, 1954, standing in front of Baker Garage on 2nd Street looking south. We have history from the Chronicle Newspaper of the impact to the Colson's Department Store in the background, left, at about $30k; and the Baker Hotel at $100k! One can only imagine what it did to all of the inventory still present with all dealerships in that block. Powell had just finished painting his showroom for the release of the 1955 models at there were significant damages at Hames Oldsmobile, Powell Chevrolet, Davison Dodge, Pack Ford, and Feltgren Buick. Boats in the showroom of the Westside Boathouse were floating with the rest of the inventory. Cars were sitting in the water everywhere with early damage estimates totaling over $175k.

The flooded Baker Hotel Garage with the Texaco Service Station.
FIGURE 11.34 Courtesy of St. Charles History Museum

CONSTRUCTION on N. Second st., just off W. Main, caused the disruption of water service at the St. Charles National Bank, out of camera range to the left of this scene, shortly after noon Tuesday. R. W. Duntsman of Bensenville is the contractor for the relocation of Highway 31, of which the pictured improvement is a portion. City crews assisted in the repair of the break in the water main.

June 6, 1962 *St. Charles Chronicle* article about street closure for the relocation of State Hwy Rt. 31 under the bridge trestle along with improved storm drainage to avoid further flooding The Texaco station is now gone. FIGURE 11.35.

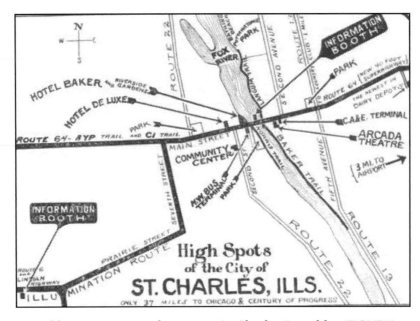

1933 World's Fair Century of Progress–St. Charles Pamphlet. FIGURE 11.36.

The old State Route 22 came from the south on 2nd street to Main Street, went 3 blocks west on Main to 5th Street, then turned north on 5th Street to travel through the only railroad underpass before 1960. Route 22 became identified as Route 31 before WWII, and the new railroad underpass was built to facilitate traffic from points south of Aurora to north of Elgin along the west side of the Fox River. Plans for this improvement had been on the books since 1945. Prior to this, what we know today as Rt. 25, the former "Fox River Valley Trail" (Route 13) had been the only major north–south Fox Valley highway from 1917 until 1962. During one of the roundtable discussions Lee Singer informed us that the first two stoplights in the Tri–Cities were at the intersections of old Illinois Route 13 (Rt. 25) and State Street in Geneva; and Route 13 (Rt. 25) and Main Street in St. Charles.

West Side Boathouse, note the Texaco Marine sign on the top railing of the white building and people standing in the area of the gas pump on the dock in front of white building. FIGURE 11.37 Photo courtesy Bill Schwab.

101 NORTH 2ND STREET

- **1953–1967: West Side Boathouse**–Fred VanLiersburg. Built north of Baker Garage on a portion of the former hotel gardens.

  From Bill Schwab: "This was 1955, the year my grandfather added the shop (white cinder block) to the building. He had just signed a contract with McCormack Oil in 1953 and sold Texaco marine gas. At that time most all of marine fuels were white gas, long before unleaded fuels started ruining valve train. The Texaco pump was moved out on a dock and the fuel moved through a rubber hose. The EPA would never allow that today." Bill's father was the subsequent owner. All that remains today are concrete steps leading to a landing in the river.

West Side Boat House. FIGURE 11.38 Photo Courtesy Bill Schwab

Bill Schwab's aerial view of his grandfather's marina located on North 2nd Street, approximately between modern–day Carroll Towers to the south and Salerno's to the north. All of that land was originally a part of the Baker Hotel Gardens. Note that the McCornack Oil distributorship is across the street in the upper right–hand corner of the photo. Til's Bait Shop was small white building top left–center off State Street.

5 NORTH 2ND STREET

NW corner Cedar Street

- **1912: Farm Implements & Gas Engines & Repair**–Harry L. Jones (later at service station on N Fifth St)–no relation to Jones in Brilliant Bronze.
- **1920: Joyce Motor Company–Nash and Marmon**–Tom Joyce, later the Ford dealer in Batavia. He is a part of the 1920 full page advertisement, Figure 11.1

The first of decades of Zimmerman automobile advertisements.
FIGURE 11.39 Courtesy *St. Charles Chronicle*.

NORTH 2ND STREET

NW corner 2nd & Cedar (first and fourth place of business)

- **March 1938: W.P. Zimmerman Used Motors**–Bill's first official business lasted just a few months here when he became a Pontiac agency in **November 1938** and moved to 708 South Third Street until WWII interrupted the sale of cars. In June 1943 he again started his used car lot at the Brilliant Bronze (Fred Utroska) location, but by **August, 1944** has moved back to this location. Then in **September, 1944**, Bill moves back to the Baker Garage with Fred Utroska as service manager.

25 NORTH 2ND STREET

SW corner–Roscoe L. Wagner built a new dealership building on the former blacksmith location, changing the address to **207 Cedar Street**, *then leasing to building to various dealers.*

- **August 1947–50: Lee Boylan, Inc–Ford–**In the recently completed Wagner building at the corner of Cedar and Second Streets. This site was so land-locked that a second car lot was located at 304 W Main, west of the Texaco. Employees: Oscar Christensen, Russ Messer, Ken Johnson, Harry McMillion & Larry Kerry. Mr. Boylan died of self–inflicted carbon monoxide poisoning January 1, 1950. Roscoe Wagner, the landlord, oversaw the continued operations to assist the widow with disposal of the dealership. Ph 3945
- **May 1950–54: Pack Ford Sales–**Thomas & Harry Pack, Ph 3944. Sales staff in 1954: Don Uphoff, Darrell Olsen, Bob Haas, and Bud Froh.
- **March 1955–56: Rabb Motors–**Carlton A. Rabb, prop; Oscar Christiansen Service Manager, had served both Pack and Rabb; Paul McMahon Sales Manager. Rabb attempted a 2nd location by the railroad station in Geneva.

FIGURE 11.40 Courtesy *St. Charles Chronicle*

- **October 1956–57: John Norris Ford–**Ph 6860. John Baker Norris, son of Lester and Delora Norris, loved cars and desired to be in the business. He also acquired the rights to the Ford franchise in Geneva and operated at the 415 West State Street address. He died after a tragic automobile accident on Dunham Road while on his way home. He had worked late at the Fox Valley Livestock Center (Kane County Fairgrounds) helping to prepare for an auto show conducted by the Tri–City Automobile Association and the Geneva Jaycees. He had apparently dozed off at the wheel after the long day and left the road. His participation in the show was a reflection of his love for cars and community involvement, and unfortunately the Texaco heir passed on Christmas day, 1957 at the age of 23.

- **1958–60: Mills Automotive–**Hayden R. Mills, Ph 8888
- **1961–80: Davison Buick–Pontiac** added this space to their existing building.

Post WWI advertisement emphasizing short supply of automobiles.
FIGURE 11.41 Courtesy July 17, 1918 *St. Charles Chronicle*

17 NORTH 2ND STREET & CEDAR

This was the former site of a blacksmith turned machine shop.

- **1917: Eastman Garage–**Charles P. Eastman
- **1918–21: Ross Motor Sales Ford, Sales and Service–**Ross O. Judd Ph 191. Showroom at 56 W Main, garage at 2nd and Cedar. C. Eastman became garage manager in 1919.

FIGURE 11.42 March 28, 1940 *St. Charles Chronicle*

- **1922–41: Spriet Motor Sales–Chevrolet–**Celest R. Spriet Ph 438, he added the **Hupmobile to** the line for a short while and completely rebuilt the building in 1925.

17 North 2nd Street, Boeman Chevrolet w/Texaco visible gas pump and yet this had to be a relic from the 1920's still in use in 1947. One would tend to draw the conclusion that the visible hand–pump had been there for decades along with the Mobiloil Gargoyle sign.
FIGURE 11.43 Photo courtesy St. Charles History Museum.

- **1941–50: Boeman Chevrolet Sales, Texaco–**S. Leroy "Roy" Boeman (Elgin) Ph 438. *St. Charles Chronicle*, September of 1949: "Boeman supplies the first student driver auto to St. Charles High School to instruct students who are approaching the legal driving age of 15 with Harold Wilkinson as instructor. The program was instituted under the sponsorship of the Chicago Motor Club and car use was donated by Boeman Chevrolet. The program states that only 3% of school trained drivers have had accident compared to 14% to those who did not take the course."
- **March 16, 1950–56: Powell Chevrolet Sales–**William A. Powell, Ph 6800

SOUTH 2ND STREET

SW CORNER 2ND STREET NEAR MAIN STREET

- **1912: Auto Livery**–Adolph F. Luscher

10 SOUTH 2ND STREET

- **1932: Judd & Christensen Garage**–Donald Judd & Oscar Christensen

13 SOUTH 2ND STREET

- **1926–29: Mosedale Hudson–Essex Auto/Tire Service**–Fred M. Mosedale, Ph 10. Also takes over **Chrysler** at 105 (205) Main St (southside of the street) in December 1927.
- **1948–61: Lloyd's Auto Service**, Lloyd E. Drury, rear of building Ph 464. Lloyd moved to D–X on west Main street.
- **1962: Earl's Auto Repair** "Automatic Transmissions Our Specialty" Ph 584–4114
- **1981: Jim's Garage**–Jim Swain Ph 584–6262

49 (17–23) SOUTH 2ND STREET

NW corner 2nd and Walnut Streets

- **1930–31: Blue Ribbon Service Station**–Ross and Elmer Judd

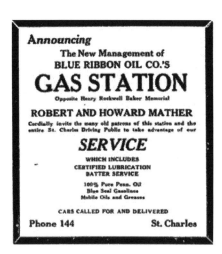

FIGURE 11.44 Photo courtesy *St. Charles Chronicle.*

- **March 1932: Blue Ribbon Service**–Robert & Howard Mather, Ph 144, evolved to Diamond gasoline, then D–X logo was in a diamond. Mid–Continent Petroleum Corp was the supplier.

Temple D–X. FIGURE 11.45 Photo courtesy *St. Charles Chronicle*.

1933–40: W.H. Temple D–X–William "Bill" Temple, Ph 3581

Smith D–X. FIGURE 11.46 Photo courtesy *St. Charles Chronicle*

- **April 1941–46: Smith D–X Service Station–**Richard "Dick" A. Smith Ph 3581

Smith D–X. FIGURE 11.47 Photo courtesy *St. Charles Chronicle*

Stan's and Vern's D–X, "Opposite Post Office."
FIGURE 11.48 Photo courtesy *St. Charles Chronicle*.

- **1946–68: Stan's D–X**– Stan Pakenas; **1949–50 Stan & Vern's**, Ph 2144
- **1968–69: CITGO**–Adolph Shuls
- **Current:** a parking lot across the street from the Baker Community Center

SOUTH 2ND AND WALNUT STREET

SW corner, now the site of the Baker Community Center

- **1915–16: Kramford's Garage–Chandler automobile–**Frank Kramford. A brief venture in the automotive business before operating an ice cream shop at 222 (87) West Main in 1919 and later succeeding Gartner Bakery for another 20 years.

13 SOUTH 2ND STREET

East side of the street just north of the Hahn Garage

- **1916: Lambert Garage**

+*+*+*+*+*+*+*+*+*+*+*+*+*+

E. J. HAHN,

HOT WATER, STEAM & GAS
FITTING,
PLUMBING & GENERAL REPAIRING.
Bicycles for Sale or Rent ; also
a full line of Bicycle Sundries.

Gas Stoves for sale. Work guaranteed
Telephone 212

West Second st .   St Charles, Ill.

+*+*+*+*+*+*+*+*+*+*+*+*+*+

St. Charles Chronicle February 23, 1903: "E.J. Hahn has purchased the plumbing and tinware business of G.A. Lawson. Mr Hahn has been employed for the past six years by the Crown Electrical Manufacturing company as a die and tool maker." FIGURE 11.49.

E.J. Hahn's Repair Shop. Emil Jacob "E.J" Hahn, a former tool and die maker has evolved to automotive repair. He started in business in 1903 and it has been suggested this photo was at a shop on North 1st Avenue in St. Charles. We know he was in Geneva on State street in 1915. By 1918, his son, Walter, had grown to take over the business on 2nd Street, St. Charles. Photo left to right: R. Roehlk, Tarmenson, E.J. Hahn, his son Walter, and unknown.
FIGURE 11.50 Courtesy St. Charles History Museum.

15–17 SOUTH 2ND STREET

Hahn's Garage, Michelin Tires, agent for Chevrolet, and taxi service. FIGURE 11.51 & 11.52
Courtesy July 1916 *St. Charles Chronicle* 1/15/20.

- **1916–18: Hahn's Garage**–Emil J. Hahn with Adolph Lusscher. I am unsure of the duration of Hahn's operation in Geneva, but it would appear that Adolph was a key manager or partner in St. Charles.

- **August 1, 1918:** Emil's son, Walter Hahn, has taken over the E. J. Hahn Garage, 17 West 2nd Street. Having seven years of experience in Detroit Auto Shops and one–year experience with Doble Steamer he has now rejoined his father.

E.J. Hahn with granddaughter, Nora Hahn, mother of John & Jim DeBates of Auto Machine.
FIGURE 11.53 Photo Courtesy of St. Charles History Museum.

- **1925–29: E.J. Hahn Garage–Overland dealer–**Walter Hahn, the business still retains his father's name, but is many times just referred to as the Hahn Garage.

Hahn Garage, ticket agent for the electric trolley system.
FIGURE 11.54 February 1919 *St. Charles Chronicle.*

- **1920–30: Hahn's Garage–Checker Cab–**Walter Hahn, Ph 78. He was also the ticket agent for the Chicago–Aurora–Elgin electric trolley car system.
- **1930:** New brick addition wrapped around to face Walnut St, making the building "L" shaped. Now addressed as 114–116 Walnut Street, Ph 79. There had been a prior 50x75 addition in 1920 facing 2nd Street.

Hahn's (Walter) Garage & Cab Company on South 2nd Street.
FIGURE 11.55 Courtesy of St. Charles History Museum.

1928 Walter Hahn and Valdemar in front of Hahn's garage with hand–crank visible glass gasoline pumps dispensing Sinclair gas. Hahn switched to Phillips 66 in 1934.
FIGURE 11.56 Courtesy of St. Charles History Museum.

- **Judd Motors Sales is now located in a part of Hahn building.**
- **1927–31: Judd Motor Sales–Ford**–Ross O. Judd–January 1930, the new Fords were introduced and Judd reported to the *Geneva Republican*, "470 people visited my showroom on Tuesday and Wednesday to view the new cars." Judd dropped Ford and Lincoln in 1931.

FIGURE 11.57 Courtesy *St. Charles Chronicle*

- **1934–35: Buick–Pontiac–Oldsmobile & Plymouth–DeSoto–**Ross O. Judd, "On display at Hahn's garage, 114 Walnut Street." Ph 79

FIGURE 11.58 Courtesy *St. Charles Chronicle*

- **1934: INTERNATIONAL COMMERCIAL VEHICLES–**Ross Judd at Hahn's Garage.

FIGURE 11.59 Courtesy *St. Charles Chronicle*

- **1936–43: St. Charles Motor Sales–Pontiac–**James Cunningham & Walter A. Hahn have taken over Judd's operations, Ph 79. Cunningham, a former Judd salesman, was later in Standard and then Sinclair stations on East Main.

1958 International Harvester foresight of what we really wanted in 2000 and the 1961
International Scout is credited with being the precursor of the SUV!
FIGURE 11.60 Courtesy *St. Charles Chronicle*.

- **1945–75: Hahn Implement–International Harvester,** Phone 79. Walter Hahn followed by Bob Hahn, with a combined 30 years with **International**. Operated Goodyear Tire Store with full line including home appliances. In 1975, Bob constructed a new facility on Randall Road with a full truck, farm, construction, and implement line.
- **1947–64: Randall Tire & Supply Co.–Goodyear (**116 Walnut, a division of Hahn Implement**),** Ph JU4–0655. Randall Tire division sold to Fox River Tire in 1964.
- **1960's–80's: St. Charles Radiator**–Dick and Bill Vogel
- **1974–86: Auto Machine Inc.–**Jim & John DeBates, Hahn descendants, w/Kim Ramont. Moved to 310 North 6th Street in the late 1980's and still conduct the machine shop business there.

WALNUT STREET BETWEEN 1ST AND 2ND
- **1940: Ken's Garage–Hudson**

201 SOUTH 2ND STREET
SW corner 2nd (Route 22 in 1932) and Illinois Street
- **1932–34: Phillips 66**–Joesph G. Hanlon, Manager, Proctor Scott, partner
- **1935: Lile's "66" Service Station**
- **1938: Lovelette's "66"–**James S. Lovelette
- **1939–43: Myers Phillips 66 & DeSoto/Chrysler**–Clarence C. Myers

• **Oct 44: Pure Oil Service**–Gilbert Nelson

FIGURE 12.61 Courtesy *St. Charles Chronicle*

• **September 1945–47: Bill's Texaco**–William L. Meier Ph 584
• **March 1947–49: Vern's Cities Service**–Vern Metz Ph 584, went on to partner with Stan Pakenas in 1949.
• **September 1949–50: Boyer's Cities Service**–Clarence Boyer after Geneva Brilliant Bronze.
• **September 1951–53: Jack's Cities Service**–Jack Wait, Ph 3182
• **1953–60: Bob's Cities Service**–Robert M. Mortimore

FIGURE 11.62 Courtesy *St. Charles Chronicle*

- **1960–62: Don Reese Cities Service**
- **August 1962: Bob & Elwin's Cities Service** Ph JU 4–0716
- **1964–65: B & D Cities** Service–Adolph "Bob" Shuls & Richard "Termite" Carlson
- **1966: CITGO–**Adolph Shuls & Richard A. Carlson (later at Arnie's Texaco)
- **October 1966: Bud's CITGO**
- **1968: CITGO–**John W. Kruse, graduate of Allied Motor Mechanic School.
- **1974–77: Stan and Morgan's CITGO–**Stan Pakenas & Morgan Davis
- **1977–79: Stan and Morgan's Texaco** Stan would retire November 1, after 34 years.
- **1980–85: Morgan's Texaco–**Morgan Davis. With his son, Kevin, in 1979
- **1985–89: Morgan's Phillips 66**
- **1989–93: Kevin's Phillips 66**
- **Present: Kevin's–**Kevin Davis, stopped selling gas, but still operating a repair garage reflecting the 87–year history of auto service at this location. Steve Baumgartner has been working here since closing his business, Master Automotive.

202 SOUTH 2ND STREET

SE corner 2nd and Illinois, the old address was "61 West Second" meaning West side of the river. The genealogy of this site is very confusing due to the combination of a service station and a garage that started as two separate businesses, but were sometimes combined.

- **1922: Standard Oil Service–**William Larson

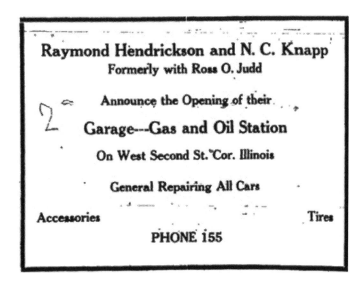

FIGURE 11.63 Courtesy September 7, 1922 *St. Charles Chronicle*

- **1922–24: Hendrickson & Knapp**–Raymond Hendrickson & N.C. Knapp, Ph 155. Garage and service station.

ANNOUNCEMENT!

. We wish to announce that we are in good condition to do expert repairing on your car.

Bring your car to this garage and we will take care of the rest.

Have your car greased and washed here. Satisfactory work guaranteed.

Free Crank Case Service

DAY AND NIGHT SERVICE OUR SPECIALITY

Walter Hahn's New Garage
West Second Street

Building formerly occupied by Hendrickson & Knapp

TEXACO SERVICE STATION

Located at Hendrickson & Knapp's old place
IS NOW OPEN FOR BUSINESS

Washing - Simonizing Polishing, Oiling and Greasing

General Automobile Repair Work

S. G. EDWARDS

61 West 2nd St.   ·   St. Charles, Ill.
QUALITY AND SERVICE IS OUR MOTTO

FIGURES 11.64 & 11.65 Courtesy February 14 & May 1, 1924 *St. Charles Chronicle.*

- **1924–25: Hahn's New Garage** followed quickly by **S.G. Edwards**, with the **Paige–Jewett** automobiles, in two short–lived ventures.
- **1925–27: Dodge Sales & Service**–A.H. Landmark, Ph 284
- **1928–29: St. Charles Motors, Hudson Agency w/Essex & Plymouth**–F.M. Mosedale, Ph 404. He also operated the Standard Service station here and the Chrysler dealership on Main street.
- **October 1931–32: Standard Oil Company Service Station**–Ralph C. Nippert, Standard Oil Agent
- **1930–32: "Service" Garage**–Harry LaFoon & K.L. Carruth, Ph 31. Dec 1932, LaFoon moved on to 212 West Main.
- **1935: Standard Oil Co**–1935 Manager, Charles Star

FIGURE 11.66 Courtesy *St. Charles Chronicle*

- **1934–35: Al's Garage–International trucks–**Al DeWolf, Ph 439. He had worked for Spriet Chevrolet, now operates next to Standard Station, facing Illinois Street.
- **1936–37: Al's Garage Phillips 66 & Oldsmobile & Willys–**Al DeWolf
- **October 1937: Hahn's Cities Service–**Earl Hahn Ph 2734
- **1939–46: Swanson Cities Service–**Emil F. Swanson
- **August 1946: McKamey Bros. Standard Service–**Harry & Paul, Phone 417
- **1940–55: Al's Motor Sales–DeSoto & Plymouth–**Al DeWolf, proprietor; Henry Sudduth, sales manager; R.P. "Van" Van Treuren, sales. Mr. DeWolf died of a heart attack December 31, 1955.
- **1956: McDonald–Johnson Motor Sales–DeSoto & Plymouth–**LaVerne E. McDonald & Evald L. Johnson Ph 439
- **October 1957–58**: **McDonald–Dynes DeSoto–Plymouth–**Marvin W. Dynes bought out Johnson.
- **September 1958: Classic Cleaners–**garment cleaning, E.R. Thusius, Prop.
- **1964–80: Fox River Tire–***St. Charles Chronicle* June 3, 1964: "Don Novak of Aurora, Peter Pratt of Wayne, and Jim Penning of Elgin have purchased the Fox River Tire and Supply, Inc. from Hahn Implement [Randall Tire & Supply Co.] and are now open for business at 115 Illinois St. The purchase

was completed last week. Prior to the new partnership, Pratt was with Hahn in charge of the Goodyear tire franchise, Novak was also with Hahn as a salesman for TBA [Tires, Batteries and Accessories]. Penning had been with Bunge Goodyear of Elgin for the past three years." The side of the building faced Illinois street, hence the 115 address. Ph 584–0655 (same phone as Randall Tire & Supply)

- **1975–80: Fox River Tire**–Don Novak & Tom Sipos. Tom had been the outside salesman calling on gas stations & garages for TBA and then he bought out Pratt. In 1975, Archie Bentz, Jr had left Bentz Bros and took the outside sales position with Fox River until 1977 when he left to open Bentz Texaco. Fox River Tire later moved to Randall & Main in the remodeled Phillips 66 building.
- **155 West Illinois Street**–same building as above, new address
- **1983: Rocky & Bullwinkle's Pub** Ph 377–7171
- **Rio Charlies**
- **Current: Francesca's By the River**–now addressed as 200 South 2nd Street

423 SOUTH 2ND STREET

NW corner of Prairie

- **1925–27: Overland Sales Co**–J.R. Winzey Prop, also sold **Whippet, Willys-Knight.** Ph 80 & 81
- **1928–35: Reidy Bros Service**–Bernard W. & M.J. Reidy Ph 539
- **1936–40: Reidy Bernard**

FIGURE 11.67 Courtesy *St. Charles Chronicle*

- **1951–54: Zimmerman Used Car Annex**–(Bill's sixth place of business) Fred Utroska, Used Car Manager in 1951, then he was at Bob & Len's Texaco in 1952. The used car lot supplemented first the Baker Garage location, then the adjoining new dealership building at 3rd & Prairie.
- **Date unknown: Fox River Title**

510 (426) SOUTH 2ND STREET
NE corner of Prairie

- **1917: Motor Service Co**–Joseph R. Winzey Ph282, moved to North 3rd Street
- **1923: Spriet C. R. Motor Sales–Chevrolet** 510–512, moved to North 2nd Street

Herb's Texaco. FIGURE 11.68 Courtesy *St. Charles Chronicle*.

- **1938–41: Herb's Texaco**–Herb Grossklag (next to Kohlert garage)

NORTH 3RD STREET

12-24 (109) NORTH 3RD STREET

FIGURE 11.69 Courtesy May 1918 *St. Charles Chronicle*

- **1918–29: Motor Service Co–Overland Sales Co–Sinclair Gasoline–**Agents for **Overland, Willys–Knight, and Federal & White Truck–**J.R. Winsey and I.F. Sinton, Ph 282. In 1919, Sinton is selling his surplus Overland inventory on East Main.
- **1928: Pottawatomie Garage–Willys–Knight–**J.R. Winsey
- **1929–30: Red Arrow Garage–**Petrosky and Ray Van de Kamp. They defaulted on their rent, and Claire Miller bought the tools from the landlord in August 1930.

Clare Austin Miller at the Red Arrow Garage with tow truck declaring it as an Official Garage of the Illinois Automotive Club. Note the Red Crown Gas sign and pump in background. He later operated the East Side Garage until enlisting in WWII. FIGURE 11.70 Courtesy of granddaughter, Susan Davis-Gren.

- **1930–37: Red Arrow Garage–Standard Oil–**Clare A. Miller, formerly employed at Anderson Dairy, Ph 2970. **1930: Miller Motor Sales** featuring the "**Oakland 8,**" Ph 442.
- **1940–41: Judd's Motor Sales–Buick–**Ross O. Judd, Ph 3505
- **1941–45: Operadio WWII storage warehouse.**

FIGURE 12.71 Courtesy *St. Charles Chronicle*

- **November 23, 1945–June 1956: Feltgren Buick Co–**Henry A. Feltgren, Ph 2774. Ross Judd, sales; and Tony Tomasovich in service dept.
- **June 1956**: **Skate–N–Fun–**Roller Skating Rink–William J. Birtwistle
- **1966: Voss Furniture**
- **1982: Antique Market–**Terry Grove

SOUTH 3RD STREET

201 SOUTH 3RD STREET

SW corner Illinois Street

FIGURE 11.72 Courtesy *St. Charles Chronicle*

- **1951–56: Used Car Court–Al DeWolf Motor Sales**, one block west from main showroom.
- **1956–66: McCornack Firestone** Robert C McCornack, Pres; Richard V. Weagley, V–Pres; Warren Kammerer Sec–Treas. 201 S 3rd St. crew in 1963: Bill Menees, Warren Kammerer, Wally McCornack, Norm Anderson, Bob Hawkins, Don Jines and Dick Weagley. McCornack later sold to Firestone Tire Inc and Warren Kammerer the business moved to 1645 E Main.
- **1972–2000: NAPA Auto Parts**–Branch of Aurora Automotive, Elden Madden early Manager.
- **Current**: **West Valley Graphics**

440 SOUTH 3RD STREET

NE corner of Prairie Street, Bill Zimmerman's seventh place of business

January 1954 Zimmerman Pontiac Grand Opening–*St. Charles Chronicle*.
FIGURE 11.73 Courtesy *St. Charles Chronicle*.

Zimmerman Ford car lot north of 3rd Street building.
FIGURE 11.74 Photo courtesy St. Charles History Museum.

- **1954–56: Zimmerman Motor Sales–Pontiac/GMC–**Bill Zimmerman

  St. Charles Chronicle, 1954: "Zimmerman moved here from the Baker Garage to a new building he constructed at an approximate cost of $50,000. His first employee, Perry Snyder is still with him. Harry Weisschnur is a recent addition to the sales staff."

FIGURE 12.7 Courtesy *St. Charles Chronicle*

- **October 1957: Zimmerman Pontiac–Rambler** was added for just 3 months.
- **January 1957–September 1964: Zimmerman Ford Inc–** During Bill's tenure here on 3rd Street as a Pontiac dealer, John Baker Norris, son of Lester and Delora Norris, was the Ford dealer in St. Charles as well as Geneva. John Norris' untimely death in a car accident on Dunham Road in 1957 was an unfortunate circumstance that occurred about the same time Bill Zimmerman was acquiring the Ford franchise. He operated as Ford here on 3rd street from 1957–64. Zimmerman later relocated to Rt. 64 & Dunham Rd., apparently a site also chosen by Norris for his future enterprise. The Pontiac dealership was reacquired at a later date and moved next door to Ford on that same corner.

   The Pontiac franchise went to Davison Buick, Rambler went to Marquardt–Farrell Oldsmobile. Oscar Christensen Service Manager came here from Norris Ford. Harry Weisschnur, Fred Utroska, John Schrieber were longtime employees with Top Salesmen in 1962: Phillip Keene, John Schreiber and Jerry Dupuis.
- **1970's–90's: R. L. Wagner & Sons Plumbing**
- **Date unknown: Westway Construction & Westway Carpentry**

(624) SOUTH 3RD STREET

- **1928–29: East Side Auto Sales–Oakland/Pontiac–**a branch of Elgin Fox Valley Motors, Ph 29. Later renamed Fox Valley Motors, Inc.
- **January–May 1930: Hallburg Hudson–Essex Co–**Ph 479

- **January 1932: Fox Valley Body & Fender Shop** Ph 3120 Joe Sills, formerly at the H. Kohlert Garage 'performing first class Nash service.'

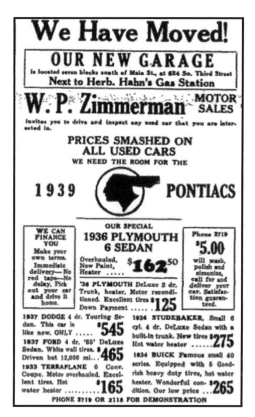

Zimmerman's first new car dealership "Next to Herb Hahn's Gas Station."
FIGURE 11.76 Courtesy November 17, 1938 *St. Charles Chronicle.*

708 (624) SOUTH THIRD STREET

Zimmerman's second place of business

- **1938–42: W.P. Zimmerman Motor Sales–Pontiac** Ph 2719, William "Bill" Zimmerman's first new car dealership opened in September1938. In 1936–43 a Pontiac dealership is also listed with Cunningham and Hahn on south Second Street? Unusual, in that agencies were generally granted an exclusive territory.
- **August 27, 1942–**Bill Zimmerman announced the closing of this business. New car sales stopped in early 1941 and he has survived selling used cars to this point. He was compelled to close due to the lack of new or used autos and war rationing. Over the previous eleven years Bill estimated that he had sold around 2500 cars and trucks. He was confident that employment would be found in war work given his mechanical knowledge.

FIGURE 11.77 Courtesy June 26, 1941 *St. Charles Chronicle.*

- **June 3, 1943**–By the Spring of 1943 Bill has set up a used car lot at Fred's Brilliant Bronze on West Main.
- **1943: Hahn's Storage** (708) This building was destroyed by fire in 1944.

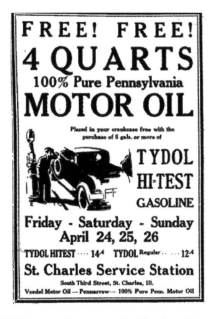

FIGURE 11.78 Courtesy *St. Charles Chronicle.*

710 SOUTH THIRD STREET

- **1928–29: Texaco Gas Station** (706)–P.G. Larson
- **September 1931–TYDOL–**R.J. Starman, Manager
- **1933: TYDOL Service Station–**John Paulus, Manager
- **1934–45: Hahn's Service Station–Standard Oil, Firestone–**Herbert J. Hahn, Ph 502, Closed September 29. 1945.
- **1970's: 7–Eleven–**No gas pumps
- **Current: St. Charles Mini–Mart**

Gerhart Rasmussen and Igel Rasmussen at St. Charles Oil bulk plant in 1935. I believe the bulk plant was located on the river side of south Geneva Road more commonly known today as Rt. 31. FIGURE 11.79 Courtesy St. Charles History Museum.

1232 SOUTH 3RD STREET

- **1923–46: St. Charles Oil–** Gerhart N. Rasmussen with his brother, Igel, as an early partner; they operated out of their home/office. Igel's son, Don, was a historical contributor to this manuscript with memories of St. Charles.

  Later known as **Rasmussen Oil Co** (Cities Service, CITGO, Marathon)–JU 4–2186. Gerhart Rasmussen, prop; Howard Rasmussen, driver; John Rasmussen, driver.

306 OAK STREET

- **1973–74: Petrolane Gas Service**

WEST MAIN STREET

(56) WEST MAIN STREET

NW corner 2nd Street, later the St. Charles National Bank

- **1912: Overland Sales**–Karl C. Wettstein & Co
- **1919: Ross O. Judd** Ford accessory store & Ford showroom.

(114) WEST MAIN STREET

- **August 1932: E. L. Morse Tire, Battery and Ignition Service Station**
- **September 1937–42: Montgomery Ward**–Ph171. Riverside tires, batteries, automotive parts and accessories. Closed 2/14/42. Most of us can remember them later on Randall Road in the 1960's–80's.

Corner of West Main and 2nd Street looking west: Bank, Hotel sign and then Tanner Garage sign about the middle of the block in 1926. The traffic signal centered in the intersection was a gift of Col Baker and when the city council was entertaining the thought of establishing a cycle–mounted patrolman, Baker instructed them to "purchase the finest motorcycle and send him the bill." FIGURE 11.80 Courtesy St. Charles History Museum.

212 (79) WEST MAIN STREET

North side of street, early days was known as the Tanner building.

- **1890: Ward's Livery**–John Ward, sold to Tanner
- **September1891: Tanner's Livery**–George K. Tanner from Marengo, IL

- **January 1892: Ward & Tanner Livery–**Tanner & John Ward bought out Frank Clark's livery and "are doing a good business selling carriages."

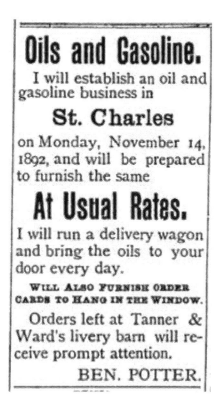

Ben Potter of Marengo, 1892 start–up of oil and gas delivery, orders taken at Tanner & Ward Livery. W.H. Streeter had similar ads for Standard Oil & Gas in 1890. FIGURE 11.81 Courtesy November 11, 1892 *St. Charles Chronicle.*

- **1900–17: Tanner & Modine Livery–**Bert Tanner & Frank Modine, Ph 243. From carriages to automobiles, with St. Charles' last livery, "all livery and livestock up for auction in February, 1917."

FIGURE 11.82 Courtesy April 11, 1918 *St. Charles Chronicle*

- **1917–19: Tanner & Modine Motor Livery–Buick & Chevrolet**–George K. Tanner & Frank A. Modine. The **Saxon** and **Oakland** automobiles were also sold here.
- **1919–31: Foley & Redmond Garage–Buick, Chevrolet & Oakland**–Peter D. Foley & John N. Redmond, Ph 74. In October 1931, Foley moved to the Baker Hotel Garage.
- **December 1932–33: The Service Garage–Dodge & Plymouth** Ph 31, moved here from 2nd and Illinois street.
- **1932–33: Main St Garage–Pontiac**–J.A. Miller
- **1933–37: LaFoon Service Garage–Dodge & Plymouth**–A.H. LaFoon
- **1938–39: LaFoon/Davison Motor Sales**–A.H. LaFoon & Martin R. Davison partnership; Ph 31. Henry Sudduth salesman who was formerly at Baker Garage.
- **1939–56: Davison Motor Sales–Dodge & Plymouth**–Martin R. & Phillip L. Davison; 1956 Service Manager, Donald Judd. 1948 they operated a second location at 216 Prairie St, Elgin. Arthur "Smash" Anderson worked as salesman in 1943.
- **1956–1977: Davison Motor Sales–Buick & Pontiac**– Davison acquires Buick dealership of Feltgen Buick. St. Charles Chronicle April 18, 1956: "Due to ill health, Henry A. Feltgen has been forced to release the operation of the Feltgen Buick Co and the Buick franchise. The assets of the company, formerly located at 12 North Third Street, have been purchased by Davison Motor Sales, 212 West Main, owned by M. R. Davison of St. Charles. Davison began the sale of Buicks Monday at his Main St. agency; he is releasing his Dodge and Plymouth franchise. The acquisition of the Buick dealership by Davison returns Buicks to the same building where Peter S. Foley sold them from 1918 to 1933."

Davison continued warranty and parts support to his former Dodge and Plymouth customers of 20 years. When Zimmerman drops Pontiac in favor of Ford, Davison picks up the Pontiac franchise for the next twenty years until the dealership is sold to Richard Masserelli. In 1958 Opel was also added.

Davison eventually took over all of the former dealer locations on the block between 2nd and 3rd Streets. While primarily located on Main Street, this is the former home of Pack Ford Sales, 25 North 2nd, on the corner with Cedar Street. The building on the left was the former C.R. Spriet Chevrolet dealership shown in an earlier photo. I took delivery of a new 1975 Pontiac Gran Ville and a new 1980 Buick Park Avenue in this showroom, both sold by Bob Junkins of Geneva. Art De La Cruz of Batavia ran the Body Shop.
FIGURE 11.83 Courtesy St. Charles History Museum.

- **1977–80: Richard Buick–**Richard Masserelli, In May 1980, they moved to 1845 East Main Street.

(217) WEST MAIN STREET

- **June–Sept 1931: Sears Allstate Tire & Accessory Store**

105 (205) WEST MAIN STREET

South side of street

- **1927: St. Charles Motor Sales–Chrysler,** Ph 10
- **December 1927–30: F.M. Mosedale–**successor to St. Charles Motor Sales
- **1937–40: Davison Motors Sales–Packard, Dodge & Plymouth**

FIGURE 11.84 Klink's Wagon 3rd Street & Main.
Lithograph courtesy St. Charles History Museum.

3RD & MAIN STREETS

SW corner

- **1848–51: David Browne–**blacksmith, retired farming near Canada Corners
- **1850: Klink's Wagon & Carriage Shop–**Louis "Dutch John" Klink, a documented link in the anti–slavery "Underground Railroad".
- **1888: Poole Bros–**blacksmiths, moved to 1st and State Avenues
- **Trumbull & O'Brien–**blacksmiths
- **1920–21: Morton Garage & Auto Livery**

300 (91) WEST MAIN STREET

McCornack Independent Oil, 300 West Main, occupied this building from 1920–36. FIGURE 11.85 Photos courtesy of St. Charles History Museum and McCornack Family.

- **1920–34: McCornack Oil Co.** –C.S. McCornack's first retail establishment was also St. Charles' first purpose–built service station. Constructed 1920 as the first retail location for the independent oil company. Martin Hanson–Manager 1928–37, Ph 2766. Alan Case was an attendant and victim of armed robbery April 1932; later he was a Batavia Texaco dealer.

McCornack Texaco in newly remodeled building, circa 1936. An outside lift and tire machine are to the right of the building. After Texaco Oil purchased the property and the home pictured to the right, an enclosed service bay was added to the right side of building. Walter Teague was the architect of the new porcelain oblong box design that was released and approved by the Texaco Oil Company Board in 1937. Yet, that very design is used by McCornack in 1936 leaving one wondering if board member Lester Norris may have helped with the design to McCornack. FIGURE 11.86 Photos courtesy of St. Charles History Museum and McCornack Family.

- **1934–62: McCornack Texaco**–remodeled as Texaco in 1936. There is an incomplete history of the managers: Gearrad Spittael, 1947 manager.
- **1962–70: Del's Texaco Service**–Delbert Mullenburg, Texaco Oil Co lease, with Texaco constructing a new building in 1970 with the acquisition of more land to the north.
- **1971–77: Arnie's Texaco**–Arnie & Richard "Termite" Carlson, June Carlson owner
- **Texaco ceased operations as a service station here in December 1977.**
- **1979: St. Charles Township Building**
- **1980–86: Cooking Craft**–Jean Becker, gourmet shop and cooking school.
- **1988–Current: The Filling Station**–Casey Milligan. Eatery and bar decorated with gas station memorabilia that celebrated a 30th Anniversary in 2018. Some of the memorabilia came from the author's collection seen in Figure 10.43.

300 East Main Street, circa 1936. Looking towards the street, Fire Chief and Sky Chief available w/electric Tokeim pumps. Texaco had also purchased the Indian Oil Co and the second pump had Indian Gas. FIGURE 11.87 Courtesy McCornack family & St. Chas History Museum.

304 WEST MAIN STREET
- **August 1947–50: Lee Boylan, Inc–Ford**–used car overflow lot for dealership.
- **1950's: Alfred Spriet,** who formerly had the Ford agency, was continuing as a used car and garage business next door to the Texaco.

(119) WEST MAIN STREET
- **1921: G & H Tire & Vulcanizing Co**–Arthur A. Grote & Clyde H. Hakes
- **1921–23: Hakes Tire**–Clyde Hakes Ph 403. H. Kohlert starts his career selling used cars from this shop. Hakes sold out inventory and equipment in January 1923.

307–315 WEST MAIN AND 4TH STREET

Brilliant Bronze, constructed by Johnson Oil Co in 1941. This photo circa 1950's (Ethyl = $.0279). FIGURE 11.88 Photo courtesy of St. Charles History Museum.

- **1941–42: Brilliant Bronze–E.A. Phillips, lessee.** Opened by Johnson Oil Co of Chicago. A history of the company tells of the sale to Gaseteria of Indiana in 1956 which sold the **'Bonded'** brand; then sold to Standard Oil of Oklahoma, the **'OK Oklahoma'** brand; and then Standard of New Jersey in 1957 as **ENCO**.

1941 Brilliant Bronze Grand Opening. FIGURE 11.89 Courtesy *St. Charles Chronicle*.

- **1942–44: Fred's Brilliant Bronze**–Fred Utroska, formerly with the Kushler Motors sales force took over management in February 1942 and **Zimmerman's Used Cars** joined him in 1943.

- **August 1944:** Because the Brilliant Bronze is closed at this time, I speculate that the Johnson Oil Company may not have been happy to see their station converted to a used car lot and eliminated that operation by closing. The gas station resumes operation in September with a new lessee.

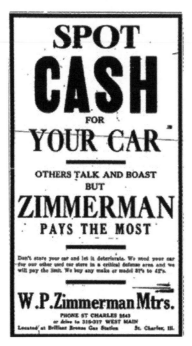

Zimmerman Motors' Third New Location c.1943–At Fred's Brilliant Bronze Station.
Bill had good cash flow from a number of rental properties.
FIGURE 11.90 Courtesy *St. Charles Chronicle*.

September 7. 1944. FIGURE 11.91 Courtesy *St. Charles Chronicle*.

September 1944–Harry Jones' wife, Grace and son Bayard, pictured (Ethyl = $ .177).
FIGURE 11.92 Courtesy Jones family.

- **September 1944–51: Harry's Brilliant Bronze**–Harry E. Jones, Ph 3597.
  Jones had a successful Johnson Oil station in Morris, Illinois and was asked
  to take this over this location.

Grace Jones in the office. Note the Armed Forces Service Flag w/3 stars in window for her 3
sons serving in WWII: Bayard, Dale, and Harry, Jr. It was reported that Moline Malleable had
a flag with over 30 employee stars for those serving. FIGURE 11.93 Courtesy Jones family.

- **1946: Brilliant Bronze–Harry E. Jones and Sons**

Road map and, Bayard Jones home on leave. "Jonesy" married my aunt, Betty Clever, and was later a proprietor of this station and then at the J & L on corner of Riverside and South 5th Avenue in 1956. FIGURE 11.94 Courtesy Jones family.

Bayard Jones at Brilliant Bronze with Texaco in background.
FIGURE 11.95 Courtesy Jones family.

- **July 1951–Mar 1952: Brilliant Bronze–**Bayard P. Jones
- **1952–57: Johnson & Roos Brilliant Bronze–** Harold Johnson & Rinse Roos
- **1957: 'Bonded' Service–**Harold Johnson & Rinse Roos
- **Aug 1957–58: Roo's Bonded Service–**Rinse Roos
- **1958–1960: OK Oklahoma–**Rinse Roos
- **1960–64: Jerry & Ray's Service Station–ENCO–**Jerry Olson & Raymond A. Heath
- **1965–68: Ray's ENCO–**Raymond E. Heath
- **1969: West Main ENCO–**Lloyd G. Jones, Manager (no relation to Harry)
- **1970–72: West Main ENCO–**Jerry Drews, Manager (from First Union 76)
- **1977–80: Buy–Rite Gas–**Jack Gervase (also 801 East State, Geneva)
- **1981–82: Ye Olde Gas Pump–**Jack Gervase
- **1983–84: Buy Rite Gas for Less–**Jack Gervase
- **1985–91: Union 76**
- **2020: Shell–**the only gas station remaining in downtown St. Charles.

Brilliant Bronze was always advertising with a different weekly "promotional giveaway."
FIGURE 11.96 Courtesy *St. Charles Chronicle*.

FIGURE 11.97 Courtesy *St. Charles Chronicle.*

321 WEST MAIN STREET

- **1944–45: Fox Tire Service "Specialists in re-capping"**–Hugh E. McConville, Ph 403. A popular tire recapping service offered during the rationing of WWII.

313 NORTH 5TH STREET

–Before 1960 this was the primary route heading North under the railroad tracks on the West side of town.

- **1931: Lyman Filling Station (301)**–C. Lyman, Ph 3149
- **1931–35: Wheeler's Shell Oil Station**–Roy Wheeler, and son Irving.
- **1939–42: Harry's Conoco**–Harry L. Jones, no relation to Harry E. Jones at Brilliant Bronze.
- **1945–56: Myers Phillips 66**–Clarence C. Myers, formerly at 201 S 2nd Phillips 66; Elmer Thompson, partner in 1949; Ph 3595 (same Myers at 611 E State Geneva)
- **1958–62: Schulz Phillips 66 and used cars**–Harry Schulz
- **1970's: Schulz Body Shop**–Mike Schulz
- **1980's: Body Shop and Towing Service**–Don Cinkus
- **1996–Present: Boyle Body Shop**–Denny Boyle

312 NORTH 5TH STREET

- **1958–71: Sills Garage**–Joseph A. Sills

418 SOUTH 6TH STREET

- **1928: Nichols Garage–**John B. Nichols

840 WEST MAIN STREET

NE corner 9th Street

1930 Texaco "Clean, Clear, Golden" curb sign on left. Firestone Tires on right. At that time, this would have been the western outskirts of town. FIGURES 11.98 Courtesy Cyril DePoorter family, Regina Krahenbuhl, and St. Charles Museum.

- Each of the Tri–Cities had at least one Texaco prior to McCornack signing on with the company in 1934. In Batavia there was a Texaco on Batavia Avenue in 1929 and another on River Street in 1928. In Geneva there was Clark's 1928 Texaco on the SW corner of Fourth and State. In St. Charles there was the Baker Garage Texaco in 1929; Harold Morter's Texas Service Station in 1931 at E. Main St. at 13th; Larson Texaco on S. Third St. in 1928; and we now have circa 1930 photos for the NE corner of 9th and Main St. in St. Charles.

FIGURE 12.99 Courtesy *St. Charles Chronicle*

- **1931: Kinst Service Station**–Cornelius Kinst Ph SC 3121
- **1932–33: West Side Texaco Station**–Vernon Haygreen, Manager, Ph 3121
- **1934: Modde Texaco Service Station**–Thomas Wilcox? Converted from being Texaco company supplied to McCornack supplied in 1934.
- **1935–41: Smith's Standard Service Station**–Harold Smith; J.R. Benson, Attendant; Ph 2764
- **1942: Herbert Hahn Standard**
- **1943: Johnson Bros Standard Service**–H.T. & G.L. Johnson
- **1944: Car–Youth Standard Service**
- **1946: Arthur Geldmeyer Service**
- **1947–50: Tierney & Kribs Standard Service Station**–Gilbert W. Tierney & Howard Kribs, Ph 184
- **1950: Knott's Standard Service**–here just a couple of months
- **1950–51: Tierney's Standard Service**–Gilbert Tierney. He became a St. Charles policeman in January 1951. His son, Gary operated J&L and ARCO.
- **1952–53: Hainer's Standard Service**–George Hainer, Ph 3565. Moved to Sinclair across the street.
- **July 1953–May 54: Fred's Standard Service**–Fred and George Knowles, Ph 3543 (Standard leased property from Mrs. Rachel Geldmeyer)
- **1955–56: Stanton's Standard Service**–James Stanton
- **1957: Bill's Standard Service**–Bill Nielson, note conflict in dates.
- **1956–62: Howard's Standard Service**–Howard A. Glissendorf
- **1965: St. Charles Motorcycle Sales**–repairs in lower level accessed from rear.
- **1966–68: Champion Motorcycle**–Bumgarner's
- **1981: Prime Time Beef Market**
- **1983: Cada Pools & Spas**–Al Cada, had previously been in Baker Garage.

FIGURE 11.100 Courtesy *St. Charles Chronicle*

900 WEST MAIN STREET

NW corner 9th Street

- **April 1951–53: Ruby's Sinclair–**William Ruby, Ph 3581. Jake Heyob
- **July 1952: Ruby's Dairy Dream–**opened next door to the west.
- **1955–66: Hainer's Sinclair Service–**George A. Hainer
- **1966–68: Hainer–Christenson Service Sinclair–**George Hainer, Earl Christenson
- **1969–79: Tierney Sinclair/ARCO–**Gary Tierney, formerly at J&L
- **1979–80: Dewey's ARCO–**Dewey Sartos, previously at Wayne Mobil.
- **1981: Dewey's Automotive Clinic–**no gas, Dewey left here to start a garage on East State, Geneva, then moved to 14th Avenue, St. Charles.
- **Current: Dairy Queen–** had continued for many years under Ruby ownership.

1023 WEST MAIN STREET
SE corner 10th Street

- **1930–40: Johnson Bros Service Station:** one brother identified as Ray.

FIGURE 11.101 & 11.102 Courtesy *St. Charles Chronicle.*

- **March 1940: "Sox" Santus Cities Service**–Alex "Sox" Santus
- **August 1940: Walt's Cities Service**–Walter Thurnau, prop, worked out of another location for 18 months before this.
- **1941–44: Johnson Bros Cities Service**–H.T. & G.L. Johnson, also operated Standard Oil on East Main in 1943.

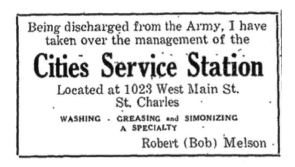

FIGURE 11.103 Courtesy August 31. 1944 *St. Charles Chronicle.*

- **1944–46: Melson's Cities Service**–Robert "Bob" Melson, Geneva
- **1946–62: Swanson's Cities Service**–Emil F. Swanson, Ph 3386, formerly at South Second street.

- **1964–66: Bob's Cities Service**–Robert L. Davidson
- **1968–85: Go-Tane Gas for Less**–Ace Silveri, Ph 584–9468. 1973–77 manager Art Butcher.
- **1985–2010: Mobil Gas N Go**–Contrary to Mobil's written policy, this was branded as a Mobil Wholesale Jobber in direct conflict with new Bentz Mobil retail dealer less than one mile away. Gas price disparity was 10–20 cents below the dealer's cost over the next 5 years. By now, the 1981 AMOCO protest in Geneva that objected to wholesale/retail price intervention by the oil companies had directly impacted the author's business.
- **Current: Clark Oil**–closed in late 2019

1008 DEAN STREET

- **1930's–40's: Dean Street Store**–Robert Madsen, there has been some conjecture that when this early store was outside city limits that there was a gas pump here. The store came under the operation of Edward Verachert in 1957.

1315 WEST MAIN STREET

SE corner 14th Street

- **1961–62: Lloyd's D–X**–Lloyd Drury, formerly on South 2nd street.
- **Jan 1962–64: Stuart & Lorenz D–X Service**–Charles E. Stuart & Howard J. Lorenz, assisted by Batavia mechanic, Al Schmidt, Ph JU 4–9415
- **1966–69: Bob's D–X –**Robert Lee Swagger
- **1970–72: Bob's Sunoco–** Robert Swagger
- **1980: Valley Auto Repair**
- **1981–85: Prime Time Beef & Rug Doctor**–Cliff and Linda Hughes
- **Current: Lundeen's Liquor**

1625 WEST MAIN STREET

SE corner South 17th Street

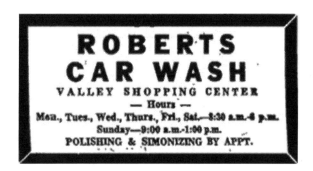

FIGURE 11.104 Courtesy *St. Charles Chronicle.*

- **1958–69: Robert's Car Wash–**George Roberts

Burt Roper, owner Valley Mobil Service. FIGURE 11.105 Courtesy *St. Charles Chronicle*

- **1961–62: Valley Mobil Service–**Burt Roper JU 4–9592

Fairview Mobil Service, 1625 West Main Street.
FIGURE 11.106 Courtesy August 1962 *St. Charles Chronicle.*

- **1962–69: Fairview Mobil–**Richard Fitzsimmons & Harold Fisher
- **Sep 1969–80: Fairview Mobil & Car Wash–**combined Richard 'Bud' Fitzsimmons & Robert 'Bob' Szweistis. Located in front of Valley Shopping Center
- **1980–86: St. Charles Enterprises–**Robert 'Bob' Szweistis

20 NORTH 17TH STREET

- **2004–2012: Fox River Tire**–moved here from Randall & Main to 17th Street, Wally Gazdzick owner; Chris Griffin, manager; Merle Korlaske, tire manager.
- **2013–present: Fox River Tire & Auto**–Kevin Bickford, owner; Joe Garity, manager; and Merle Korlaske, tire manager.

FIGURE 11.107 Courtesy *St. Charles Chronicle*.

1660 WEST MAIN STREET

NE corner North 17th Street

- **Dec 65–69: Cook's Super One Hundred–Clark Gas**–Bill Cook
- **1970–77: Cook's Super One Hundred**–Jeff Cook
- **1978–84: Clark's Super One Hundred–** Damian Toledo, manager
- **1985–1991: Clark's Super One Hundred**–Clark Oil Company operated. 1991 Ernie Retiz, manager.
- **1715 West Main Street**–SW corner South 17th Street
- **1970: Les' Gulf Station**–Les Palmer, Jr
- **1971: Cliff's Gulf Station**–Cliff Shuman
- **1977–89: E–Z–GO GAS**–William Dolan, Manager. Address now is 1705 W Main.
- **1989–91: Gas Stop Inc**–1991 manager Suzanne Leonard.
- **Current: White Hen Pantry, 7–11**–no gasoline.

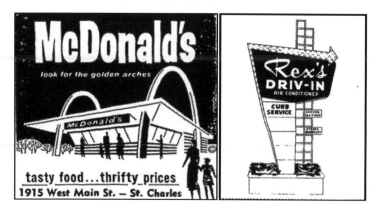

Cruising down Main St, St. Charles from one drive–in to another.
FIGURE 11.108 & 11.109 Courtesy *St. Charles Chronicle.*

2009 WEST MAIN STREET

SE Corner Main Street & Randall Road

Ron's Standard, SE corner Main & Randall circa 1962.
FIGURE 11.110 Courtesy Joe Jakubaitis.

FIGURE 11.111 Courtesy *St. Charles Chronicle.*

- **1962–72: Ron's Standard–**Ron Scheitlin, assisted by James Sutton, Melvin Garrett, and Paul Eby. The original opening date of October 1961 was delayed by prolonged denial of zoning until Standard Oil threatened suit with a newspaper campaign showing how the zoning could not be denied based on Federal Court decisions. The station opened in February 1962.
- **June 1973–99: Way's Standard–**Wayland Wilson Enterprises. Way had a successful career with full–service, repairs, and towing services. In 1993 he petitioned the city to convert his station to a convenience store, following the trend of the company–owned stations. Way did attend the first gas station roundtable that we hosted at the Batavia Library and later passed in 2019 during the writing of this manuscript.
- **Current: TitleMax**

Phillips 66 distinctive design had the desired effect of making the brand identifiable from long distances. The sharp angled 'V' design canopies sometimes gave way to being incorrectly identified as the architectural style as that of Frank Lloyd Wright, but it did reflect his influence. See figure 12.83. FIGURE 11.112 Courtesy Phillips 66 stock photo.

2010 WEST MAIN STREET

NE corner Main & Randall

- **1962: Phillips 66–Merit Petroleum Co–**Aurora based
- **1964: Phillips 66–**George Salter

FIGURE 11.113 Courtesy *Geneva Republican*

- **August 1965–68: Rudy's Phillips 66,** Rudy Kunzelman
- **1969–70: Randall 66**–Clifford L. Johnson, Ph 584–9432
- **1972: Scot's Gas**–Wes P. Young Ph 584–9432, 1973 manager John Ward
- **1976: Sheahan's 66**–Mike Sheahan
- **1977–79: Fox Union 76**–Fox River Tire owners: Don Novak & Tom Sipos with Merle Korlaske as manager.
- **1980–2004: Fox River Tire**–pumps were eliminated & building remodeled with the removal of the sweeping canopies.
- **Current: Pep Boys**

The only Phillips 66 designed and built by Frank L. Wright was in Cloquet, MN. FIGURE 11.114 Photo from post card and text courtesy of Cloquet Chamber of Commerce.

Cloquet Chamber of Commerce: "Wright had designed station owner R.W. Lindholm's house in 1952, and, knowing Lindholm worked in the oil business, presented him with a proposal to design the gas station envisioned as part of Broadacre City Plan. Lindholm seized the opportunity to beautify gas station design with Wright completing his design in 1956. The station ultimately opened in 1958 at a cost of $20,000, roughly four times the cost of the average filling station at the time."

"Commonplace the Lindholm station is not. Stepped cement blocks support a copper canopy that extends approximately thirty–two feet. A glass–walled observation lounge anchors the signature cantilever while a slender towering pylon reaches from the polygonal roof to a height of sixty feet. Wright originally envisioned eliminating standing pumps and placing fuel lines in the cantilevered roof, thereby offering motorists uninhibited access to the station. This was never carried out due to fire code standards and the traditional ground fuel pumps were utilized instead. The three service bays are fitted with skylights to help facilitate the work of mechanics. Cypress wood is found throughout the structure, from the shelving for auto accessories located in the garage and diamond shaped sales office, to the decorative cut elements in the restrooms."

"This design was only a partial success for Wright, as his vision of the gas station as a social center never took hold. However, Phillips 66 did incorporate several of the gas station's design elements, particularly the triangular cantilevered canopy, in later gas stations."

I later discovered that in 1927, Frank Lloyd Wright had already designed a unique fuel filling station intended for the corner of Michigan Avenue and Cherry Street, downtown Buffalo, NY. That station was never built.

James T. Sandoro, founder of the Buffalo Transportation Pierce Arrow Museum in Buffalo, New York, "began planning in 2002 to construct the filling station as a one–of–a–kind installation to supplement the automobiles, motorcycles, and bicycles on display at the existing museum. Sandoro and architect, Patrick Mahoney, traveled to Scottsdale, Arizona to the Frank Lloyd Wright archives to locate the drawings related to the Buffalo design. Rights to build from the drawings were secured."

"Frank Lloyd Wright called his design "an ornament to the pavement." It was ahead of its time, featuring a second story observation room with fireplace, restrooms, copper roof, two 45–foot poles (Wright called "totems") overhead gravity–fed gas distribution system, and attendant quarters with a second fireplace. The second story observation room provided patrons a comfortable place to wait as their vehicle was serviced." Ironically, the station is located inside the museum just down the street from the originally proposed location. Most of the features were included in the 1956 Cloquet design with the main exception being the omission of fireplaces burning under the overhead gas tanks!

Gleaming copper roof and three gas hoses hanging from overhead tanks.
FIGURE 11.115 Courtesy Pierce Arrow Museum & Patrick J. Mahoney.

Buffalo's first neon sign was planned between the 45–foot totems touting TYDOL gasoline.
FIGURE 11.116 Courtesy Pierce Arrow Museum & Patrick J. Mahoney.

2101 WEST MAIN STREET

SW corner Main & Randall

- **October 58–61: Dave's Cities Service**–David E. Bunker, was the first service station to open on the brand–new section of Randall Road, the former "Cut–Off" road between Route 64 and Alternate 30.
- **1961–62: B & G Cities Service**–Robert Mortimore, formerly on South 2nd

Street, Joe Petraitis and Joseph Detloff, mechanics.

- **July 1962: Olsen's Cities Service**–Harold Olsen, owner; Joe Petraitis, mechanic.
- **April 1965: Clement's Cities Service**
- **August 1965:** For Lease
- **1966–74: Earl's Citgo Service**–Earl Mustard, Jr, moved to East Main Phillips 66.
- **1977–91: Citgo Quick Mart**–Tom Uthe, 1977 manager.
- **1992–98: 7–Eleven**–Gloria Hughes, manager.
- **Current: 7–Eleven Mobil**–The highway intersection was reconfigured necessitating the elimination of the Half–Moon bar/restaurant plus the Long John Silver's restaurant on the NW corner. The demolition of the Dog 'n Suds (1952) and former 7–Eleven on the SW corner made way for a new 7–Eleven convenience store and gas station built on the combined properties.

540 SOUTH RANDALL ROAD

- **1960's–80's: Montgomery Ward** operated for over two decades.

110 NORTH RANDALL ROAD

- **1967–79: Wilbur's Garage**–John Wilbur Ing
- **Howard's Garage**–Jerry Ford
- **Tri City Auto Body:** Dale James & Mike Wetter

FIGURE 11.117 Courtesy *St. Charles Chronicle*

225 NORTH RANDALL ROAD

- **1975: Hahn Truck Center–International–**Bob Hahn, Ph 584–3079
- **1976–79: Payline West–International Harvester–**Williams, Ph 584–8700. In 1979 they moved to Kirk road in Batavia.
- **Current: Mercedes Benz of St. Charles**

37W599 RT. 64

- **1983–89: A & A Tire–**Alex Poppel Ph 377–2920
- **1990–present: St. Charles Motor Sports–**Alex Poppel

TWELVE

WASCO & LILY LAKE

When traveling further west on Route 64 today a stranger would need the help of signage to distinguish between leaving St. Charles and entering Wasco, but back in the 1800's it was a trip of 5 miles to the very rural village. Wasco then became a stop for the Minnesota & Northwestern Railroad for the shipment of agricultural products, primarily milk, to Chicago.

I had knowledge of three places to purchase gasoline in Wasco and about the same number of garages along with what was one of the few blacksmith shops in operation nearly to the end of the twentieth century: The Wasco Blacksmith Shop and Melvin Peterson.

Dan Ryan secured a phone number so I could call the former blacksmith's son, Tom Peterson, and was told that Melvin still had a pretty sharp memory for a fellow in advanced years. Through Tom's help, I was able to write Melvin and I asked him for information about his blacksmith business and others before him, along with any information he might remember about the garages and gas stations. While quite helpful with his answers at the age of 97, he also told me about a new book, *Wasco, Illinois: A*

History and I contacted the author, Adam D. Gibbons in Geneva. The *italicized quotes* in this chapter will be duly noted as from this publication.

Since contacting Gibbons, I have received permission to share both text and photos from his book so you can enjoy what is germane to the service station business in Wasco. Some may feel that I have spent a disproportionate amount of time on the little unincorporated berg, but I feel that it represents a microcosm of very small communities that sprang up all across the country. Whether the reasons were railroads, mining, agriculture, water, or hydro–power, these little bergs were the life–blood of the country's growth and history. The Minnesota & Northwestern Railroad which came westward through St. Charles on its way to Sycamore and points beyond, was not only responsible for Wasco's beginnings, but also for the beginnings of Canada Corners (now known as Lily Lake) and Franklin (now known as Virgil) which were also designated railroad station stops. Locally this train was referred to as the 'Great Western Milk Train' and in later years transported Wasco youth to St. Charles for High School.

The only known photograph showing the blacksmith shop in Wasco on its original site
on the west side of LaFox Road. The photo dates to the early 1890's and the large doors on the
first floor of the building (below the sign) are just visible. The Bergland General Store is
to our left in this photo and note the milk cans in the wagons.
FIGURE 12.1 Courtesy *Wasco, Illinois: A History.*

WEST SIDE OF LAFOX ROAD
North of the Bergland Store
- **1889–1904: Will Ruddock, Blacksmith**

Erickson blacksmith shop about 1920 on the east side of LaFox Road after the building had been moved. FIGURE 12.2 Courtesy *Wasco, Illinois: A History*.

EAST SIDE OF LAFOX ROAD

This is the same building that had previously been on the west side of the road, but was turned and moved across the street to the east side.

- **1905–08: Ben R. Kayner, Blacksmith**
- **1908–48: Andrew J. Erickson, Wasco Blacksmith** for 40 years. In August 1948, Erickson sold the building to Philo and Carolyn Plummer and the business itself to Dan Rediger. Erickson went to work at Burgess–Norton

ROUTE 64 WEST OF BERGLAND STORE

- **1890–1910: William A. Hiser, blacksmith.** In *Wasco, Illinois: A History*, Gibbons makes a conjecture that Hiser preceded Erickson at the LaFox Rd location which leads to some confusion with overlapping dates. According to the 1904 *St. Charles Chronicle*, Hiser does run a smithy in Wasco, but it is my contention that it was a separate location from that of Erickson and located west of the Bergland Store. Hiser was later employed as a blacksmith at the St. Charles School for Boys.

Wasco Blacksmith Shop–late 1950's. FIGURE 12.3 Courtesy *Wasco, Illinois: A History*.

EAST SIDE OF LAFOX ROAD CONTINUED

- **1948–52: Dan Rediger Blacksmith**–replaced the smithy coal forge with an electric welder. He had been involved with shoeing race horses and worked for Col. Baker for five years at Twin Pines Farm.

- **1952–1970: Wasco Blacksmith Shop**–Melvin Peterson. On July 30, 1954 the property was transferred to Roy and Ellen Peterson, Melvin's parents.

- "[Melvin] had learned blacksmithing while working on Colonel Baker's farms in St. Charles in the late 1930's." Frank Hiser, unknown if there was a relationship to William Hiser, was listed as a blacksmith in St. Charles from at least 1912–1925 and later became employed by Col Baker's Twin Pines Farm. From Melvin Peterson's own statement "I knew (Frank Hiser) when he worked for Col. Baker," it is my belief that Hiser may have been responsible for teaching Peterson some, if not all, of his blacksmithing skills. Mr. Peterson also shared that "He (Hiser) caught on fire and died from shock in 1940."

- **1971–77: Charlie's Garage**– Charlie Foulkes, held title to the building and property with his parents, Walter C. and Mary Foulkes. I called on Charlie in 1976 for auto parts and supplies and marveled at the decades–old wide–plank wooden floors, often wondering what that floor had experienced and who had crossed that floor before me.

- **2002:** The building was demolished that summer.

4N969 OLD LAFOX ROAD

- **1970–1992: Wasco Blacksmith Shop**–Melvin Peterson and son, Tom, had 40 years in the two locations combined. The longevity of the Petersons was only exceeded by Needham in Kaneville who is still in business with what may be a national record of five generations spanning almost 150 years.
- **May 1992: Wasco Blacksmith Inc**–Ted Frerichs & Dan Arand Ph 584–WELD
- **1992: Wasco Lawn & Power**–separate business from blacksmith

40W514 STATE ROUTE 64

NW corner Route 64 & LaFox Road

The oldest extant photograph of the original Bergland store in the early 1890's with a partial view of the blacksmith shop on the right. FIGURE 12.4 Courtesy *Wasco, Illinois: A History*.

- **1888–1914: Bergland's Store**–George C. Bergland is of record doing business in this store as early as 1888 in a building probably constructed by J.V. Millen on a lot that sold for $50 in 1887. The Wasco map of 1892 listed the building as the site of a "Store & P.O."

The old and new Bergland stores side–by–side, still with hitching rail, c.1912–13.
FIGURE 13.5 Courtesy *Wasco, Illinois: A History*.

- The old store was moved to the west lot and a new brick building built in its place in 1912–13. The older building was later demolished prior to 1918. The ground floor in the new building was split into two halves with the grocery and meat market on the west side of the building, and a hardware store and post office on the east side.
- **1914–1937: Bergland & Company**–Upon George's demise in 1914 the business was bequeathed to Louise Bergland, widow; Floyd H. Bergland, son; and daughter, Florence (Bergland) Peterson. Floyd managed the company, but when Floyd was away at college and the U. S. Army, his sister handled the affairs.
- The estimated date for the gas pumps on the front sidewalk was in the late teens or early twenties. In 1928, the former *Chicago–Iowa Trail* was recognized as Illinois State Route 64, which in 1930 ended just west of Sycamore. It was a common practice for the state to widen roads with ditches and make provisions for utility easements. In about 1930, in order to avoid exposure to the traffic lanes of the new state highway, Mather's Service Station relocated their pumps and I will speculate that it was about that same time when Bergland moved their pumps to the lot on the west side of the building for the same reason.
- A 1935 advertisement read "Campton's Oldest Business House–We Sold to Your Grandfather, We Sold to Your Father, We Want to Sell to You"

The Bergland Store, in the early 1920's, two gas pumps on the front sidewalk, with Red Hat and Independent logos on the globes which would mean they were McCornack Oil supplied and later converted to Texaco in 1934. Hitching rail still available for horses on right.
FIGURE 12.6 Courtesy *Wasco, Illinois: A History.*

- **1937–1946: Bergland & Company–**Floyd Bergland, sole proprietor, having bought out the family interests. Under Floyd's ownership the company continued with rapid expansion including a full lumber yard with building supplies, hardware, coal and feed.

- **1947–1980: Hummel & Company–**Fred Hummel, purchased from Floyd's heirs after his passing in May 1946, Ph St. Charles 100. Fred Hummel, Jr joined his father in the business upon his return from serving in Korea. The grocery store portion of the building had been operated by Frances and Mayme Anderson from the early years until they sold out to Wesley A. Johnson in February 1948. The grocery transitioned through a number of owners that you can read about in *Wasco Illinois: A History.*

- **1980–2001: Collin's General Store–**Patrick Henry Collins and his wife Julie, operated a general store, but the days of the lumber yard, hardware store, and gasoline sales were long gone. The U. S. Post Office has continued in the same location, but in two different buildings, since 1888.

  In 1984, a visible hand–pump, gravity–fed Texaco gas pump was still present on the west side of the building having been supplied gasoline by McCornack Oil for 40–50 years.

- **2001: The Corner Store–**Cathy Munyon

Current view General Store & Post Office with former Mather's Standard in background.
FIGURE 12.7 Courtesy Dan Ryan.

STATE ROUTE 64 & LAFOX ROAD

NE corner

Early photo c.1910 of general store that would later become Mather's gas station.
FIGURE 13.8 Courtesy *Wasco, Illinois: A History*.

- **1897–1901: Johnson's Store**–Oscar M. Johnson operated as a General Store
  in direct competition with Bergland. In 1898, Oscar sold to Andrew Johnson
  who in turn sold to John W. Larson (Geneva). Larson apparently fell on hard

times and foreclosure proceedings followed in 1901, resulting in Bergland's purchase of the property.

- **1904–1920: Peterson's Store**–Elmer T. Peterson now operated the store out of the building owned by George Bergland. He also sold automobiles and farm implements. July 1904 *St. Charles Chronicle* stating that Elmer Peterson had "for some time run the store opposite Mr. Bergland's, and with such a degree of aggressiveness that at last he possesses as his wife, the daughter and bookkeeper of his competitor." Peterson had just married Florence Bergland, George's daughter.

The Larson Garage with building addition c. 1921 the sign above the door indicates he is apparently selling Fords and/or Fordson tractors. Goodrich tires, no gas pumps are present and horses are still accommodated with the horse–hitch rail on the left. FIGURE 12.9 Courtesy *Wasco, Illinois: A History.*

- **1920–1924: Larson's Garage**–Albert V. Larson. Peterson had retired and the Bergland Company heirs sold the property for considerably less than valued but conveyed the property with an important stipulation, "until January 1940, no building on the property shall be used to sell "the goods and chattels commonly sold in a general country store, such as staple groceries, meats, hardware, dry goods, and clothing, boots, and shoes." Bergland had just effectively restricted his competition. There were, however, no restrictions on its continued use as a garage, gas station, or sales of automobile accessories.
- **1924–1929: Larson's Garage**–John Larson of Sycamore had probably added the sale of Standard Oil gasoline during his tenure.

Rare photo showing 2 gas pumps on stoop just prior to building modifications brought on by lease with Standard Oil. Signage in addition to Red Crown Standard shows, ISO VIS Standard Oil, Mobiloil, Quaker State, Firestone & Chicago Motor club; note tow truck behind building and utility pole on the corner. Circa 1920's. F IGURE 12.10 Courtesy *Wasco, Illinois: A History*.

Mather's tow truck, note the windshield is open for visibility because there were no effective heaters or defrosters in this era truck. FIGURE 12.11 Courtesy *Wasco, Illinois: A History*.

•   **1929–1992: Mather's Wasco Garage**–Arnold and Grace Mather purchased

on November 1, 1929. Arnold had previously been the dealer for Titan Tractors in 1920. By the Spring of 1930 they had entered a contract with Standard Oil of Indiana which brought about the modifications to the south-west corner allowing vehicles to pull off the highway to 3 gas pumps on an angle under the cover of a canopy. Apparently the 4-year lease may have had a provision with Standard participating in the remodel costs which were estimated at $1500.

Mather's Garage, now with Red, White, and Blue Crown gasolines, Chicago Motor Club & Goodrich signage along with International Harvester. Circa 1930.
FIGURE 12.12 Courtesy *Wasco, Illinois: A History.*

- "In 1930, Howard and Robert Mather, the two oldest sons worked in the garage as 'machinists' but by 1940 they had moved on and the census listed Grace Mather as "Store Keeper" with youngest son, Lee, still living in the household and working as an attendant in the gas station." During the war years, while Lee was serving, Grace continued to pump gas and operate the store until his return when he became the primary operator from that point on until a week before his death in 1992. Phone St. Charles 4071-R-2

Mather's Standard Circa 1950. FIGURE 12.13 Courtesy *Wasco, Illinois: A History*.

Lee Mather's Standard Service circa 1960, crowns now gone from pumps.
FIGURE 12.14 Courtesy *Wasco, Illinois: A History*.

40W331 ROUTE 64

East end of town on south side of the State highway

- **1924–1929: Wasco Garage**–Harry Travis & Lawrence McGowan purchased the garage in 1924 from a 'Mr. Larson' who had operated before them. Harry and Marjorie Travis took up residence above the garage.
- **1929–1945: Travis Garage**–Harry Travis entered into a lease with Shell Petroleum Corp and on his property, he agreed to operate *"in a business–like*

manner and will at all times endeavor to promote and increase the sale of gasoline at said station." Travis agreed to pay consideration of one–half cent per gallon for all gasoline sold over a two–year period. He also agreed to the painting of all buildings on the property *"in Shell colors",* namely yellow, white, and red. Author's note: it was customary that the oil company, Shell, would foot the bill for "branding" a location with painting, signage, tanks, and pumps, hence the practice of paying 'rent' on your own property. In 1931, Travis entered into a new lease with Texaco, which would now provide for the installation of a second tank and two gas pumps. McCornack Oil became the supplier in 1934 after converting to Texaco.

- **1945–1948: Raasch's Garage–**Clarence W. Raasch, Ph 4061, his home being east of the Bohr's Tavern (Wasco Inn). In 1948 he sold some of his land to Peter Bohr and sold the garage building/filling station to Victor Thomas. The Denny family also bought more land from Raasch in 1952.
- **1948–49: Victor Thomas** bought the garage from Raasch and was apparently responsible for the remodel of the building into a home. Sold in 1949 to Harvey and Alma Cole.

40W301 ROUTE 64

East of Wasco Garage

- **1930's–45: Travis Sandwich Shop–**Marjorie Travis operated a sandwich shop on land Harry Travis had purchased in the late 1920's just to the east of his garage. The restaurant had a long single bar for customers and at times was operated as a tavern. Another example of meeting the traveler's needs where they could go to the restaurant while their auto was being serviced at the garage.
- **1945–1950: Bohr's Tavern–**Peter Bohr was a former Greyhound bus driver and hired Louise Swanson who prepared the fish for the very popular Friday night fish fry tradition at the tavern.
- **1950–1973: Denny's Den–**Peter & Della Denny. Peter had experience in the tavern business and grew this business by continuing the Friday night fish fry and adding a full menu specializing in spaghetti, Italian beef, and fried chicken. They enlarged and remodeled the restaurant in 1958. I remember the Friday Fish Fry where you had to park out on the highway and stand in line outside waiting for a table. All this started with a housewife turned entrepreneur who opened a sandwich shop next to her husband's gas station.
- **1973–1999: Wasco Inn–**John & Athina Karametsos, with daughters Georgia, Vicki and Margie operated, remodeled, and expanded the menu over 26

years, closing in 1999. Margie continues to own the property and operate other businesses such as a Dairy Queen and Taylor Street Pizza.

40W299 ROUTE 64

East of Wasco Inn

- **1945–79: Raasch Home**–Clarence & Elaine Raasch had purchased the land from Harry & Marjorie Travis
- **1979–85: Wasco Inn Pizza**–the Karametsos family (Wasco Inn) bought the Raasch home and ran a pizza parlor from that building until a 1985 fire.
- **2012–present: Marathon Gas Station**–Western Trail Outpost of Hinckley

ROUTE 64 & SCHOOL ROAD, OFFICE: 4N793 SCHOOL ROAD

White Bros. Trucking formerly had gas pumps in the left foreground area of this current photo when Joe White had plans to build a truck–stop and garage. Their land had included where the fire station stands today. Those pumps remained for company use well into the 1980's. The sign above the right door still designates the Illinois State Truck Safety Lane that has operated for decades. FIGURE 12.15 Courtesy Google Earth.

Two of the early Joe White trucks that started the business back on the Deerpath Road farm.
FIGURES 12.16 & 12.17 Courtesy Bob White.

- **1939–2016: White Bros. Trucking & Test Lane–**Joseph & Charles 'Chuck' White. Joe started the business of hauling produce from his father's farm on Deerpath Road in Batavia to a fruit and vegetable stand in Aurora while taking other side jobs of hauling. His brother, Bob, still operates the farm today. When Joe went into the Air Force in WWII, he asked his brother Chuck to keep the business going and this resulted in the business name of White Bros. Trucking. In 1947 the brothers purchased 6 acres east of the school in Wasco. Joe died of leukemia in 1957, but Chuck and his son, Jim, have grown from this unassuming building as their home base, to the specialized heavy– carrier business serving all of North America for 80 years.

41W379 ROUTE 64

The original Farm Vegetable Stand in 1930 also offered gasoline from a hand pump, gravity–flow dispenser and motor oil was available in the hand–carrier sitting on the ground. The gable sign: The Farm, Sandwiches and Refreshment. The post reads: Fresh Eggs–For Sale.
FIGURE 13.18 Courtesy *Wasco, Illinois: A History*.

- **1925–45: Farm Vegetable Stand–**Bert & Zilpha Brown. McCornack Oil supplied. It is unknown how many years the Brown's dispensed gasoline, but it had to be a popular commodity as the nearby grove evolved over the next couple decades to a picnic grove, baseball diamond, swimming pool, and race track. The vegetable stand evolved to a food stand serving sandwiches, chicken, and a steak plate, all of which eventually evolved into a premier restaurant of the area. There were literally thousands of visitors attending company picnics and special events including live bands in the 1930s and 40s. The onset of WWII brought about rationing and a natural decline in participation in many of the special events as people's focus was to support the war effort and the attractions slowly faded away.

The Farm Race Track and Picnic Grove. Half–mile dirt race track was utilized by drivers from far and wide on Sunday afternoons. The Start/Finish Line is in front of Starter's platform with vehicle–mounted loudspeakers. In the background Rt 64 is lined with parked autos.
FIGURE 12.19 Courtesy *Wasco, Illinois: A History.*

A busy week in 1935; Memorial Day Races on Thursday, Fish Fry and Dance on Friday.
FIGURE 12.20 & 12.21 Courtesy *St. Charles Chronicle.*

- "The Farm" also hosted the Republican Barbecue on October 24, 1936. In anticipation of a crowd of 20,000 Republicans from northern Illinois, the feast was to include 50 beef steers, 50 hogs, 100 head of sheep, thousands of dozens of buns and an undetermined quantity of coffee. The previous Republican Barbeque was held four years prior at Col. E.J. Baker's Twin Pines farms and the roads leading to the farm were clogged with traffic to the point that resupply of foodstuffs and beer would take hours. When the food was free during the depression there was no doubt that the turnout would be large.
- **1945: The Farm–**E.J. Sanetra, prop. "Dine & Dance–Orchestra every Saturday," Ph 4063
- **May 47: The Farm–**William Frohling, prop.

The Farm run by Joe & Ruth Garaghty, circa 1960. FIGURE 12.22 post card photograph

- **1948–1977: The Farm–**John Gerald 'Jerry' & Ruth Daum, formerly of The Ranch in Plano. In 1955 Ruth had re-married Joseph Garaghty and they worked together, though she was the driving force running the popular restaurant for almost thirty years even suffering through a 1971 fire that gutted the interior, until her declining health forced retirement. Phone–JUno 4–9534
- **1983–1985: The Farm Inn–**Donald R. Thompson of Batavia. The restaurant had become a popular night club venue with entertainment, but in February 1985 it was raided and closed in connection with a money laundering

scheme designed to hide the drug profits from "an elaborate Florida smuggling operation" of Don's brother, Raymond. In 1988, Don was convicted for his part in those charges.

- **1989: The Olde Farm Inn**–Bruce & Valerie Jablonski
- **1991: The Silverado Grill**–Dave Walradt
- **2006: Niko's Lodge**
- **The Lodge Bar & Grill**
- **2012–current: The Lodge**–Aaron & Kristie Perez

LILY LAKE, ILLINOIS

STATE ROUTE 47, LILY LAKE

1916 EMPIRE automobile with an 18–volt battery, demonstrated by E.M. Abrahamson.
FIGURE 12.23 Courtesy *Elburn Herald*.

- **1902–1949: E.M. ABRAHAMSON**–Eric Marcus Abrahamson. General Store and implement dealer, with a front porch gas pump converted in 1934 to Texaco gas, McCornack Oil supplied

ROUTE 47 AND EMPIRE ROAD

NE corner, this store was built in the late 1870s when Lily Lake was known as Canada Corners, named for the original settlers' country of origin.

The Reed Grocery had been vacant for years at the time of this photograph.
FIGURE 12.24 Courtesy *Kane County Chronicle*

- **1898: Reed's Grocery**–Frank Reed
- **1919–1968: Reed's Grocery**–Ray Reed. May 10, 1923, *Elburn Herald*, there was the announcement for the addition of a service station. The McCornack Oil supplied gasoline was converted to **Texaco** in 1934 and was about the same era that Reed announced that the last portion of the horse hitching rail would be taken down.
- **1968: Lily Lake Grocery**–Lawrence and Florence Beier.
- **1995:** A 1993 *Elburn Herald* article about trying save the building states that it sat empty for 25 years. In 1995 the 1840 building sold to Keith and Robin Reed, no relation to Reed's Grocery, who had plans to move it approximately one–quarter mile away and undergo a yearlong restoration.

ROUTES 64 & 47

NE Corner

- **1930: Lily Lake Texaco**–William Harding Llalta
- **1931–44: Nelson's Service Station–Phillips 66**–Carl A. Nelson, Ph 155R3, operated livestock trucking as his primary business. In 1937, Carl's brother, Clarence A. Nelson, built the **Phillips 66** in Elburn.

    From the 1998 *Elburn Herald* obituary of Carl's widow, Ethyl A. Nelson: "Carl operated a trucking company and gas station, and Ethel kept the books, raised the [4] boys and managed the barnyard livestock. On December 10, 1944, Cart died tragically of tuberculosis of the kidneys, just five months after the death of his brother, Clarence. That year, Ethel squared her shoulders, leaned on her faith and faced the responsibilities of running both her husband's business and her brother–in–law's gas station, as well as the family household. The following year, she sold the trucking company to Earl Johnson and Lyman Thomas and continued to manage the gas stations in Lily Lake and Elbum. To her credit, she continued to operate those enterprises through many challenging years until 1973 when she retired."

- **1944–73: Nelson's Lily Lake Texaco**–Ethyl A. Nelson, Ph 2081, while Ethyl retained ownership of the property, I do not have much recorded as to whom she may have leased the property during this time period, but there were several leases at the Elburn station.
- **1963: Vogel's Service Station**–Gordon Vogel, operator, leased from Nelson.
- **1977: John's Texaco**
- **1980: Lily Lake Texaco**–Bob Gerhke who also operated the Texaco distributorship bulk plant in St. Charles. Ph 365–2205
- **1980–87: Pride Gas**–Tom Hughes, St. Charles resident, former Texaco Representative, with multiple locations in Batavia, Lily Lake and Aurora that were all later sold to Phillips 66.
- **1988*: Phillips 66**–Mike Hughes manager, Tom's son.
- **2008–2012: Closed**
- **2012–Present: Marathon**–Syed Irfan of Geneva based Gasco Inc

ROUTES 64 & 47

SW Corner

- **1933: Rowe's Corner Garage**–Ph Elburn 140

FIGURE 12.25 Courtesy *Elburn Herald*

- **1958–1964: A & H Cities Service–**Archie L. Peterson and Harvey Hoback, Ph EMerson 5–5001. Peterson, formerly with G.R. Johnson Ford and later worked at Elburn Co–Op until retirement. He was a brother to "Pike" Peterson of Batavia. Partnership with Harvey dissolved April 18, 1964.
- **August 1964–69: Pete's Cities Service–**Archie Peterson, Ph 365–5001
- **Gas tanks removed in 1972**
- **Current: Pete's Hot Dog Stand**

ROUTE 64, ¼ MILE WEST OF ROUTE 47

FIGURE 12.26 Courtesy *Elburn Herald*

- **July 1950: Standard Oil Service Station–**G.L. Martin

NOW OPEN
UNDER THE MANAGEMENT
OF LEO AND CATHERINE PARKS

Standard Oil Service Station
Route 64, ¼ mile West of Route 47, Lily Lake

Auto Repairs - Cafe
Open Daily—7:30 A.M. to 11:30 P.M.   Phone: Elburn 2081

FIGURE 12.27 Courtesy *Elburn Herald*

- **October 1952: Standard Oil Service Station–**Leo & Catherine Parks

THIRTEEN

Elburn and Rural Kane County

In addition to my own research with the Elburn Library and *Elburn Herald*, this chapter has been greatly complimented utilizing Marilyn Robinson's *The Sidewalks of Elburn* and the help of the *Lawrence J. Martin Heritage Center.*

ROUTES 38 & 47

SW corner

- *Elburn Herald*–**August 25, 1921:** "A spacious garage erected on a portion of the G.L. Sharp farm by J.B. Nix, Lloyd Warber, and Arthur Anderson to accommodate motorists traveling the Lincoln Highway and accessibility for Chicago Motor Club members."

The Elburn Garage, Routes 38 & 47. Per the Sidewalks of Elburn, "it was built in Queen Anne Style, red shingle siding w/white trim, green roof. The intersection of Rt 47 and the Lincoln Highway (Rt 38) was known early on as Blackberry Corners when the town of Elburn had previously been called Blackberry Station. It was the only gas station between Geneva and DeKalb on the Lincoln Highway and sold gas for 5 cents per gallon. Nix and Anderson names were spelled out in the shingles on the siding."
FIGURE 13.1 Courtesy Lawrence J. Martin Heritage Center.

The Sidewalks of Elburn: "John Nix had formerly operated the Elburn Garage in town where he did automotive and blacksmith work. Legend says that the building was built by the mob as a pick–up point for corn mash from area farmers during prohibition. Supposedly, the large doors provided a quick entrance for the farmers, and the balcony provided a view for 30 miles, lessening the dangers of a bust by police officers."

Research of newspapers supported by 1988 statements from Charles Nix, John's son, dispelled those rumors. That's not to say there may, or may not have been, a vehicle or two hauling "hooch" passing through.

- **1921–33: Nix & Anderson Garage, Red Crown Gasoline/Standard–**John Nix, G.M. Holbrook, and Arthur Anderson (not Batavia Anderson) built the garage. Warber is no longer listed as part of this venture, but Holbrook is now included. Did Holbrook take the place of Geneva's Warber in the building construction? They also sold home appliances. The second floor was a dance hall, which was eventually closed by order of the Fire Marshall for having just one exit. The second story 2,000 sq. ft. dance hall was converted to living quarters and most of the subsequent operators lived and raised families there. Apparently, rooms were available to travelers based upon the words "Motor Club Inn" on the balcony above the pumps in the above photograph.

FIGURE 13.02 Courtesy *Elburn Herald*

- **1923–24: Elburn Garage–**agent for Studebaker

Nix & Anderson Elburn Garage with Standard Oil & Gas. Photo: L to R, Arthur Anderson, two unidentified employees, possibly Michael Paul Szula, Archie Wickwire, & John Nix. FIGURE 13.03 Courtesy Mildred Fink, *Elburn Herald*, and Lawrence J. Martin Heritage Center.

- **1924–25: Elburn Garage–Willys–Overland**
- **1926: Elburn Garage–Dodge**
- **1927: Elburn Garage–Dodge added Graham Brothers Trucks–**Holbrook had sold out to his partners and just prior to his passing, Nix sold to Anderson in 1933.
- **1933–35: Elburn Garage–Dodge–**Arthur "Art" Anderson, proprietor, with Jesse Gum assisting at the "four corners."
- **1935: Elburn Garage–**R.C. Carr & Ed Yarnell, Ph Elburn 111
- **1936–48: Jackson Corner–CONOCO–**Allen J. Jackson, closed in the fall of 1942 when Jackson went to work at a World War II defense plant in Aurora and then re–opened in 1946. About that same time in 1946, a 4–way stop was introduced due to the number of accidents at "Death Corner".

The original Lincoln Highway was routed west of Geneva on Kaneville road to what is now known as Keslinger road. That was until the concrete highway was poured between Geneva and Dekalb along State Route 30, thus bypassing Elburn. In 1921, it was announced that the Lincoln Highway from Chicago to Fulton was 95 percent complete which was a good reason for the Elburn Garage to be constructed on this corner that same year.

FIGURE 13.4 Courtesy Lawrence J. Martin Heritage Center.

- **1948–1954: Anderson Service Garage–Standard Oil–**Harold Anderson, later joined by his brother Leonard in 1952.

"CORNER OF ROUTES 47 AND 330"

FIGURE 13.05 Courtesy *Elburn Herald*.

FIGURE 13.06 Courtesy 1960 *Elburn Herald.*

- **1954–1976: Swift's Service–Cities Service/ARCO/Standard Oil–** Fred and Grace Swift, parents of mechanic Fred Swift, who worked for the Chevrolet dealership for 36 years.

FIGURE 13.07 Courtesy 1961 *Elburn Herald.*

FIGURE 13.8 Courtesy Lawrence J. Martin Heritage Center.

- **1976–83: Albert's Corner–Standard Oil–**Mike Albert, owner, with Tom "Tiny" Fesser. When it came time for Mike's father to retire, local banks would not finance Albert in the purchase of the property from his parents as the 27–acre site was deemed "not a viable business location."
- **January–March 1984: Larry's Gas Station** at Albert's Corner **Marathon** gas.

Albert's Corner during demolition in 1990, side view shows the formerly screened porch as a canopy over the gas pump area. FIGURE 13.09 Courtesy *Kane County Chronicle* Nov. 1990 and Lawrence J. Martin Heritage Center.

- UNDER THE TITLE OF "YOU CAN'T MAKE THIS UP!" **Truck wedges under Canopy at Albert's Corner by Ros Mcintosh of the** *Elburn Herald*. On the afternoon of December 7, [1976] the anniversary of the attack on Pearl Harbor, the Albert family thought they were being bombarded by sneak attack. It all began innocently enough around 3:30 p.m. when a large *Chicago Tribune* delivery truck stopped at Albert's Corner to ask directions on how to get back to Chicago. Albert's Comer is the landmark service station at the corner of Routes 38 and 47 which until recently was known as Swift's Service Station. Mike Albert answered the driver's questions, warning him not to try to drive under the station's canopy, to turn around, and went inside. Then it happened! There was a crash outside, the whole building shook.

   That was when the Albert said, "We are being bombarded! " When Mike and Tom Fesser, the other operator of the station, rushed out they saw what had happened. The driver of the Tribune truck had tried to wedge his way under the station's canopy. He struck a steel supporting post and then slid into a gas pump and toppled it over. The canopy collapsed onto the truck and there it was stuck. Even so, according to Mrs. Albert (Mike's mother), when Mike went out the driver was trying to back out of his predicament. The Elburn Fire Department was called because of the danger of fire from the leaking gas pump. The Elburn police answered the police call. According to Mrs. Albert, Tom Fesser got the canopy braced up and freed the truck. Then, she said, everyone went inside to write up the accident report but before the report was finished the two men who were the drivers of the truck took off before the report was finished. They were later picked up in Geneva by the Kane County Sheriff's deputy.

- **1991–Current: BP Pumper–** The "not a viable business location" is prospering today.

FIGURE 13.10 Courtesy McCornack family and St. Charles History Museum.

As previously mentioned in Chapter 9 on the history of McCornack gas stations, I am unsure of the location of the building shown above. In my research of telephone directories, there was a listing for Allen Faucett with Texaco gas in the 1930's and a possible address of 233 South First Street, Elburn. That current address is in a residential neighborhood off Main street, but this would not be the first time that a pre–war address has since changed. A location on the corner of First St. and Main St. would make sense. I have researched the *Elburn Herald* using multiple ways of spelling and worked with Laura Chaplin Lawrence of the J. Martin Heritage Center to locate either Allen and/or this building. Please contact this author if you have any further information at tricitygas@gmail.com.

MAIN STREET, ELBURN

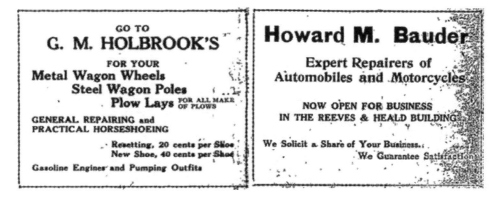

Holbrook operating in 1912, Bauder in 1913.
FIGURES 13.11 & 13.12 Courtesy *Elburn Herald*.

- **1912–15: Elburn Garage**–G.M. Holbrook, blacksmithing, shoeing, and expert work on gasoline engines. Auto Livery, Ph 133, Res Ph 130. 1913 agent for high grade **Excelsior** motor cycle. Mr Holbrook (1860–1931) came to Elburn in 1889 and was associated with Stevenson blacksmithing business for some time.

FIGURE 13.13 Courtesy *Elburn Herald*

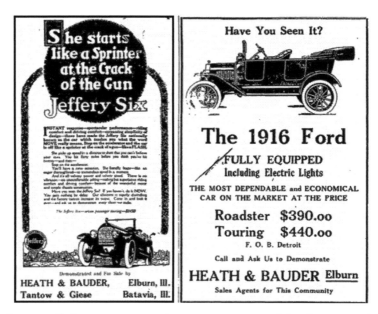

Ernst Heath gives all the appearance of an entrepreneur of the day. He and his partner, Bauder, are agents for both the Ford and Jeffery Six automobiles. Then a year later he has a different partner and a different automobile. By 1918, Holbrook, the landlord, is now the partner and eventually Heath is replaced with a different partner. I had no record of a "Jeffery Six" agent in Batavia, but here it is with the names Tantow & Giese as partners in May of 1916. FIGURES 13.14 & 13.15 Courtesy *Elburn Herald*.

- **1916: Elburn Garage**–Ernst Heath & Bauder, Ph 133
- **1916–17: Elburn Garage– Elcar** motorcar–Ernst Heath & William Morrell

As was the case in most small towns, there are no business addresses listed in the *Elburn Herald* as it was assumed that the reader should already be familiar with the location of every business in town. FIGURE 13.16 Courtesy *Elburn Herald*.

- **1918–20: Elburn Garage**–G.M. Holbrook & Ernest Heath, Fisk Tires Ph 133
- **May 1920: Elburn Garage–Goodrich Tires**–G.M. Holbrook & D. Brelsford, a short–lived venture when Brelsford left for a job in Rochelle IL.
- **December 1920: Elburn Garage–Ford**–John B. Nix, former Virgil blacksmith, had sold his Virgil shop to Frank Reiche. In 1921, with partners, he constructed the service station at the four corners while maintaining this as a second location for a short period afterwards.
- **On the site of the former Hoyt feed mill.** *Elburn Herald* **Pioneer section:** Sometime in the late 1880s Clark's mill burned again (date unknown). Mill history from the Centennial Herald also mentioned that Clark had been joined by G. S. Beam and that Clark sold to Barker. In the fall of 1894 R.C. Hoyt bought the mill from Barker & Son. On November 1, 1894 Hoyt

combined business with Morris Bros., an implement firm. James Spalding bought the mill in 1902 and owned it until 1905 when it was sold to J.L. Meredith. Meredith's ownership was short–lived; in 1906 he sold the mill to N.A. Haile. The most recent operators of the mill in Elburn were Leo and Nona Nichols of Countryside Feed & Supply. Author's note: The 1906 date of sale was in error; the advertisement below is dated 1908.

FIGURE 13.17 Courtesy of the April 3, 1908 *Elburn Herald*

- **1908: J.L. Meredith**–The Maxwell automobile will continue to be a favorite of Elburn motorists with multiple dealers subsequent to Meredith.

136 NORTH MAIN STREET

FIGURE 13.18 Courtesy *Elburn Herald*.

- **1914–15: Anderson & Warne–**Agents for **Maxwell** automobiles
- **1920: Maxwell & Chalmers Automobiles & Service Station–**Ambrose Griffith

FIGURE 13.19 Courtesy *Elburn Herald.*

- **1921: Griffith & Dobson–**Agents for **Maxwell** and **Chalmers**, Ph 25
- **1923–25: Griffith Garage–**Mayor Ambrose Griffith; A.C. Parker manager; official **AAA Garage** listed in the motor club.

FIGURE 13.20 Courtesy 1925 *Elburn Herald.*

- **1925–28: Ambrose Griffith–**Agent for **Chrysler & Maxwell**, **REO,** Ph Elburn 25
- **1928: Chrysler–**Griffith sold to Martin Prailes, who then sold to Orman.

FIGURE 13.21 Courtesy 1925 *Elburn Herald*

- **May 30, 1929: Griffith Chrysler–**Harry Orman from Chicago with S. Sorenson, service manager, from Elburn.

FIGURE 13.22 Courtesy October 31, 1929 *Elburn Herald*.

- **November 1929: Elburn Chrysler**–Lester Hapner moved here from Crystal Lake and installed new Texaco tanks prior to opening. Two weeks later, he suffered painful facial burns from an explosion when working on the furnace. He resumed work through February and then sold the business.

March 13, 1930–Public announcement of sale of Chrysler Garage.
FIGURE 13.23 Courtesy *Elburn Herald*.

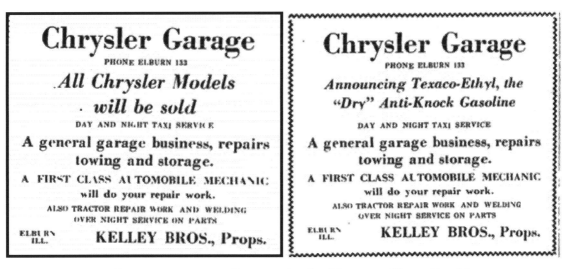

FIGURE 13.24 & 13.25 Courtesy April & May 1930 *Elburn Herald*.

- **March 1930: Chrysler Garage**–Kelly Bros.–May1930 started sale of Texaco–Ethyl
- **August 28, 1930 announcement:** Clarence Malliet has taken over the complete management of the Chrysler Garage. The owners, Kelley Bros., have other interests which they wish to devote their time to, and have rented

the garage to Clarence and the business is now under his control. It is well known that Mr. Malliet has had charge of the mechanical department of this garage for some time and his friends will wish him well in taking full responsibility for the success of this garage business.

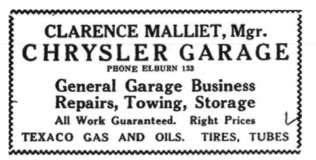

Advertised in this manner for less than one month. FIGURE 13.26 Courtesy *Elburn Herald*.

- **September 25, 1930**: Clarence Malliet, who managed the Chrysler garage for Kelley Bros, the past month, has gone to DeKalb and Peter Leuer is now in charge. Mr Leuer is well known in this community where he was raised. For five years he has been working at the Geneva Garage and should be well qualified to take the responsibilities of operating the Chrysler garage here.

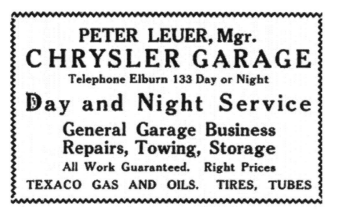

Peter Leuer was manager for Kelly Bros for almost a year and we did not find their name on the business again. Leuer then purchased the equipment and quickly makes the improvements to the business to distinguish himself from all the predecessors.
FIGURE 13.27 Courtesy *Elburn Herald*.

- *Elburn Herald*, **August 13, 1931**: "PETER LEUER BUYS CHRYSLER GARAGE MACHINE EQUIPMENT: Recently, Peter Leuer purchased the tools and wrecking car truck from former owners of the Chrysler garage. The truck has been painted white and Pete has made many improvements in the business office and other parts of the garage."

- *Elburn Herald*, **1932: "Roby Speedway will Have Chance to See Elburn's Entry Burn Up the Track:** Sunday racing fans and interested spectators kept their eyes on the Chrysler Garage for signs of the Hudson 6 racer of 1919 vintage, which Pete Leuer is entering in the "Ash Can Derby" at Roby–Speedway track, Chicago, this coming Sunday. They were not disappointed when a great Whirr! bang! bang! soon emitted from the back of the garage and outshot the "racer" with Ture Paulson and "Red" Bartlett, crouched behind the wheel. A few trial spins south and then north, soon convinced everyone that Elburn's entry would not be the last one on the one–mile track oval. It is said that one of the requirements of the race is that after going around the track once, all cars are required to repeat – in reverse. With this in mind, the boys "gave it the works," on the new Lily Lake road north of town." Author's note: Ture Paulson was later employed by Ted Larson Phillips 66 in St. Charles and then opened his own Pure Oil station in Batavia in the 1960's.
- **August 1931–34: Leuer Chrysler–**Peter Leuer–**Texaco** and converted to **Chevrolet** in 1934. Peter had previously worked in Geneva with his brother, Jack Leuer, and for Anderson & Nix at the four corners.

Leuer Chevrolet, a close examination reveals two pumps, one gravity flow and one electric, flanking the garage door entrance which is directly under the Chevrolet sign. This location is currently used as storefronts. FIGURE 13.28 Courtesy Lawrence J. Martin Heritage Center.

- **1934–45: Leuer Chevrolet–Texaco–**Peter Leuer, Ph 133. Chevrolet Guest of Honor in 1940 with a record sales year exceeding 44 other area dealerships. In 1945, after 15 years in automotive, Peter decided to concentrate his efforts on his farm. He leased the Chevrolet dealership to Ed Thompson who had experience with Buick and Chevrolet in both Batavia and West Chicago.

FIGURE 13.29 Courtesy *Elburn Herald*

- **1945–47: Thompson Chevrolet:** Ed Thompson, Ph 2531. He succumbed to injuries incurred from an automobile accident on Christmas Eve, 1947. Peter Leuer assisted with continued operations until a buyer could be found.
- **January 27, 1948–93: Harms Chevrolet–**Fred Harms purchased the dealership, coming from Aurora with 5 years in a service station operation and 13 years with Felz Motor Service. Harms brought Harold Hanson from Aurora, with Virgil Stonecipher continuing in the garage. Harms' son, Dean, joined the firm in 1949.
- **1955: Harms Chevrolet–**a building permit was issued for new building just south of Dari–Ripple (Alice's Place) on South Main. No gasoline sold at this location.
- **1969: Harms Chevrolet–**Fred had retired in 1969 and Dean built a new building at the corner of South Main and Kansas streets, just to the south of the 1955 location which is currently occupied by Ream's Meat Market. 1988 saw the addition of a new associate, Bob Jass, a ten–year veteran of Chevrolet Motor Division. This was actually the beginning for a transfer of ownership.
- **1993–Current: Bob Jass Chevrolet–**Robert "Bob" Jass, owner. As of 2008, mechanic Fred Swift had worked for the dealership for 36 years, having

started with Harms. He had "grown up in the business" at the gas station operated by his father at the four corners.

NORTH AND MAIN STREETS

G.R. Johnson Company, North and Main St, Elburn. FIGURE 13.30 Courtesy "The Sidewalks of Elburn" and Lawrence J. Martin Heritage Center.

Banner above left window with wringer–type washing machine reads "A New Ford V–8 for 1934," the gas pumps feature Cities Service with "Koolmotor" gasoline.
FIGURE 13.31 Courtesy Lawrence J. Martin Heritage Center.

- **1918–1920: G.R. Johnson Co-Emerson-Brantingham** autos of Rockford, IL. Johnson had bought out early 1917 partner, John Kindberg.
- **1921–64: G.R. Johnson Co-Ford, New Idea, Minneapolis Moline, EB Newton (Batavia) Wagons.** G.R, Johnson & C.A. Sorenson (1920); C.A. Cowan (1922); Ph 3351.

  In 1946, as a Ford Dealer celebrating 25 years of selling Fords, Johnson recognized long time employees: Charles Boyer (1919), Ernest Heath (1920), Martin Johnson (1921), Harold Anderson (1929), and Charles Roster (1935). A 1935 map shows the company location on the west side of Main street just north of the tracks. The company has moved directly across the street to the east side of Main. In 1960 a celebration for the completion of a new service wing east of the Ford showroom and **Cities Service Station** marked the 40th anniversary.
- **1964–80: Swan Ford-**Charles "Chuck" Swan, having worked here for two years, bought the Ford dealership and with his sons, Allen working as service manager and Craig operating the **Cities Service** gas station.
- **1980–81: Enck Ford-**Delores and Bernie Enck, closed after one year.

WEST OF MAIN STREET BY THE CO-OP

- **1940: Westlake Hatchery-**Gilbert and Leslie Westlake **Allis-Chalmers** and **All-Crop** harvesters.
- **1946: Westlake Hatchery-**Jerry Baier expanded the **Allis-Chalmers** tractor line to include the **Kaiser-Frazer** automobile. Chuck Swan worked here until it sold to Geneva Farm Equipment in 1952.

Nelson Phillips 66, Main & Kansas streets.
FIGURE 13.32 Courtesy "The Sidewalks of Elburn"–Marilyn Robinson.

MAIN & KANSAS STREETS

- **1937–42: Nelson Phillips 66**–Clarence A. Nelson, brother to Carl A, Nelson, built this service station.
- **December 1938: Nelson & Barnett Phillips 66**–announcement of Barnett as manager and the building was sporting a new addition.

FIGURE 13.33 Courtesy *Elburn Herald*.

- **1942–51: Paulson Service Station–Phillips 66**, Carl A. Paulson, a former mechanic with Leuer Chevrolet for 7 years. Paulson had a partner, Julius Matthys, for a time ending December 1947.
- **1944: Ethyl A. Nelson** became property owner.
- **1952: Swan's Phillips 66**–Charles Swan, formerly employed at G.A. Westlake, and Harms Chevrolet.
- **1956–60: Chuck and Dick's Phillips 66**–Charles "Chuck" Swan and Richard "Dick" Williams, Ph Elburn 4361
- **1960–62: Chuck's Phillips 66**–Charles Swan, went on to be proprietor of Swan Ford.
- **1963: New Shell Station constructed**
- **1963: Oasis Shell Service Station & Edna's Restaurant**–Mr and Mrs Lawrence Kamp; Edna Doane, restaurateur.
- **1964–68: Oasis Shell**–Virgil Stonecipher (previously at the Sinclair station).

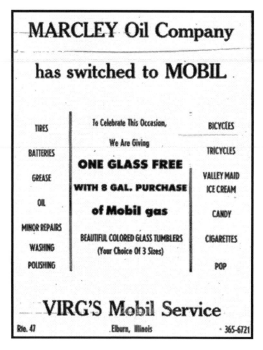

April 11, 1968 Marcley Oil announcement of switch from Shell to Mobil.
FIGURE 13.34 Courtesy *Elburn Herald*.

- **1968: Virg's Mobil Service–** Virgil Stonecipher with Cecil Ostrom and Don Grenniger.
- **1969: Cec's Mobil Service Station–**Cecil Ostrom and wife, Barbara, who operated the restaurant next door, "until the lack of morning help for the restaurant; changed the business to a pool hall with pin ball machines in 1973."
- **1980: Village Mobil–** Charles Fitzmaurice, former Standard dealer in Geneva.
- **1990: Gas tanks removed. Architecture of Shell station still remains.**

MAIN & NEBRASKA STREETS

"South of the tracks"

- **September 1954–56: Hawk Sinclair Service–**William Hawk, per *The Sidewalks of Elburn;* "*was the victim of an armed robbery on January 26, 1955*".

FIGURE 13.35 Courtesy *Elburn Herald*.

- **February 1956–64: Virg's Sinclair Service**–Virgil Stonecipher, former Service Manager at Harm's, while Mr Hawk went to work at G.R. Johnson service station in 1956.

  In 1964, Virgil Stonecipher, "after 8 years at the Sinclair station, moved next door to the **Shell Station** built earlier that year." Ph EM 5–2051

- **1972: J & L Gas & Oil Co.** Vernon Hills, Illinois based independent oil company.

- **J & L Union 76**– they took on major brand gasoline.

- **1998: J & L Mobil**–changed brands because Union 76 ceased operations east of the Mississippi River.

4 EAST NORTH STREET

- **1984: Valley West Automotive**–Allen Swan, Chuck Poust, & Jim Sandberg.
  Ph 365–5541. Allen's career paralleled his fathers from the Phillips 66 and Swan Ford. Chuck Swan worked here with his son until shortly before his demise in 1988. Allen's wife, Dorothy, was the daughter of Ture Paulson, Pure Oil dealer in Batavia. Valley West moved to 8 South Dempsey about 1997 and Allen worked until cancer took him in 2014.There were a number of wholesale jobbers, competing to supply gas and diesel to the area farmers, most with Elburn bulk plants in the area of the railroad siding.

McCornack and G.R. Johnson in Elburn were associated with Phillips 66 starting October, 1929. They used the Globe Ethyl product in all markets in 1932 before switching to Texaco in 1934. FIGURE 13.36 & 13.37 Courtesy *Elburn Herald.*

WEST NORTH STREET

Two bulk plant locations on the North street railroad siding.
- **1920's–70's: McCornack Oil**–Richmond R. Read & Stafford Meek, Jr were agents of record. Ph 29
- **1935: Standard Oil**–R.C. Wriedt and Clyde Wells were agents of record Ph 33

WEST MAIN STREET

With railroad siding access
- **1921–2016: Elburn Co–Operative**–Jim Gillett manager 1968–2004, sold Co–Op gasoline at the pumps and delivered gas to farms. **2016** Elburn Cooperative merged with CHS Inc, the nation's largest farmer–owned cooperative, and becomes **CHS Elburn**.

EAST NORTH STREET

On a railroad siding access.
- **1935–60: Northern Farm Service (FS)** Ph 365–3251

BATAVIA BULK PLANT

- **1934–Current: Feece Oil Co.**–still supplies farmers from their Batavia and Mendota Bulk Plants.

1956 magazine ad with Dale Feece, of Batavia's Feece Oil, showing Elburn's Les Meredith "With up to 1,000 head of cattle to be fed on his 450–acre farm at Elburn, Ill...Meredith farms have been dealing with Feece Oil Co., since 1931, when Leroy Feece joined Deep Rock." Dale was still in high school. FIGURE 13.38 Courtesy Feece Oil Company.

MORE RURAL KANE COUNTY

ANNOUNCING

McCornack Oil Company's

Association with

TEXACO *Petroleum Products*

We are pleased to announce that we have been given a franchise for the wholesale distribution of TEXACO products throughout the territory covered by our trucks from our bulk plants at St. Charles and Elburn.

Recognizing the unquestioned quality and nation wide acceptance of TEXACO products, (The TEXAS COMPANY is the Worlds largest independent Refining and Marketing Organization), we

chose them and their products after months of careful consideration of several other brands.

This acquisition of TEXACO products will in no way change the present ownership, management or personnel of the McCornack Oil Company.

TEXACO products will be delivered from our tank trucks and also may be purchased in this vicinity from the following dealers:

LEUER'S CHEVROLET SALES	ELBURN
SNYDER SERVICE STATION	MAPLE PARK
RAY READ	LILY LAKE
E M. ABRAHAMSON	LILY LAKE
POTTER & CO.	LA FOX
W. C. MASTERSON	BALD MOUND
H. E. TRAVIS	WASCO
BERGLAND & CO.	WASCO

USE TEXACO FIRE - CHIEF GASOLINE

Developed for Fire Engines   —   Yours At No Extra Cost

McCORNACK OIL COMPANY

Established 1904

ELBURN HERALD, March 15, 1934 advertisement, McCornack Oil announcement of rural locations to procure Texaco Products: There were other ads also announcing: The Farm–Rt. 64, County–Line Tavern–Maple Park, D.D. Meek–Kaneville, LaFox Corners–Rt. 330 LaFox, and Vern Kibling–Bald Mound. FIGURE 13.39 Courtesy March 15, 1934 *Elburn Herald.*

ROUTE 64 & MEREDITH ROAD, VIRGIL

- **April 1, 1960–92: Norm's D–X**–Norman "Norm" C. Tischnauser

Potter's of LaFox used this photo in their advertisements, gas pump at left end of porch.
FIGURE 13.40 Courtesy *St. Charles Chronicle.*

1N279 LAFOX ROAD, LAFOX

- **1863–2004: Potter's General Store–**Store, Post Office and gasoline sales. McCornack supplied and converted to Texaco in 1934. The family's 5th generation closed the store in 2004.

LAFOX ROAD AND ROUTE 330 (ALT. 30/RT. 38), LAFOX

- **1938: LaFox Corners–Texaco**

MAIN STREET & BLISS ROAD, BALD MOUND–BLACKBERRY TOWNSHIP

- **1870: Bald Mound General Store, Post Office, and Cheese Factory**
- **1904: Henry Brummel, manager, fatally injured in grist mill**
- **1934: W.C. Masterson General Store–**McCornack Oil converted to Texaco.
- **1938: Vern Kibling General Store–Texaco**

KANEVILLE ROAD & ROUTE 47

- **1933: Howard Gas Station–**William H. & Ray Howard

MAIN STREET & HARKER ROAD, KANEVILLE

- **1938: Kane County Grocery Store–**S.D. Meek, Ph 4491, later proprietors still had gas in the 1960's.

MERRILL & LOVELL ROAD, KANEVILLE

- **Kaneville Grain & Feed–**Flanders family, hardware store and gas pump

ADDRESS UNKNOWN, KANEVILLE

Figure 13.41 Courtesy *Elburn Herald*

- **1950–1962: Square Deal Garage–Mobil Gas & Oil.** Ralph Bohn, Ph 4934

221 MAIN STREET, SUGAR GROVE

Keck's Store–Hardware, Grocery, Post Office, and Gas, Sugar Grove Ph 6341. Three generations of the Keck family were in this business from 1893 to 1980. Note the original stepping–stone which served to help folks in and out of horse–drawn wagons could now assist the attendant fill large farm trucks with gasoline.
FIGURE 13.42 Courtesy Sugar Grove Historical Society website.

The photo above of Keck's Store in Sugar Grove again exemplifies the early distribution of Red Crown gas through rural general stores and is just one more example of a multi–generational operation.

ROUTE 47 & CROSS STREET, SUGAR GROVE

- **1963–64: James McGraf Texaco**
- **1966–84: Rich's Texaco**–Richard Wendling
- **Current: BP Convenience/Gas**

ROUTE 47 & ROUTE 30 (GALENA), SUGAR GROVE

- **1941: W.S. Cornell Standard Oil, Sugar Grove** Ph 602
- **1954–74: Theis Standard Service**–Walter J. and Alma Theis
- **Current: Shell Convenience/Gas**

SUGAR GROVE

Lacking addresses, these were advertisements in 1941 Sugar Grove High School yearbook, The Ember:

- **1941: P.Y. Bliss General Store & Gas**
- **1941: A.G. Perschnick, Standard Oil Agent/Jobber,** Ph 6441
- **1941: Will A. Johnson & Son**–real estate, farm implements, gas & oils, automobiles, livestock, hay & grain, Crosley Refrigerators Washing Machines and Radios, Assessor for Sugar Grove, & Notary Public.

FOURTEEN

WHERE DID FULL–SERVICE GO?

The gimmicks of gasoline retailing, free steak knives, china, potholders and such were driven by massive advertising campaigns and it was estimated that in 1955 $42 million had been spent on driveway premiums to boost sales. By the late 1960's it was estimated that cost of trading stamps was about $150 million annually.

By 1969, the market expansion included some 2000 "Truckstops" based on serving the interstate system. Pure Oil had set the example, sometimes purchasing entire interchanges, partnering with Travelodge and Aunt Jemima restaurants and leasing adjacent tracts to serve the traveling needs of the motorist and large trucking company fleets. Massive truck stops would often have an adverse effect on any local business in close proximity.

The Tenneco Corporation was the first petroleum company to link grocery and gasoline sales in outlets across the southeast. Southland Corporation's 7–11 stores had

grown to 1400–units, the largest convenience store chain. This style of station was the model for self–service. The irony is that "gasolene" which was first sold at some general stores has now came full circle.

The Supreme Court ordered the dissolution of Standard Oil Company in 1911; the company was in violation of the Sherman Antitrust Act. It was determined that the actual retail sale of gasoline would be performed by independent retailers to foster competition, hence the establishment of your local neighborhood gas station dealer who was supplied product either by the oil company itself, or local jobbers/wholesalers in smaller rural markets.

The rules changed again in 1981 when Congress deregulated the oil industry and other industries such as telephone and banking. For the oil companies, this meant that they could now sell gasoline directly at retail locations. They then became both wholesaler and retailer and were in direct conflict with the existing dealer network. There had been another law passed as an afterthought that was supposed to protect the existing dealers and the businesses they had established. The Petroleum Marketing Practices Act, PMPA, was passed in 1978 to protect dealers from the aggressive actions of the oil companies designed to eliminate the dealers who had represented their brand for years. A part of the act was the guarantee reasonable supply of gas at competitive prices; however, the law was weak and fraught with loopholes favoring the oil companies. The end of the "Mom 'n Pop Era" was on the horizon, as the companies would build large–volume stations and eliminate many low–volume locations. Reduced staffing was a natural evolution of fewer locations and since the oil companies did not want the burden of a large uniformed and trained staff, they promoted self–serve.

The first example of the introduction of wholesalers competing in the Fox Valley market was met with picket lines:

Geneva Republican, **November 19, 1981:** "About 20 service station dealers from throughout the Fox Valley walked a picket line for about three hours Monday morning around the newly remodeled Geneva Amoco station at 206 E State St. The dealers, members of the Illinois Gasoline Dealer Association, were attempting to discourage motorists from entering the new self–service station because of what they charge are unfairly low prices being charged [versus} the station's owners [cost] for gasoline from Standard Oil Co. This, they said, allows the station to charge wholesale–level prices to retail customers and takes away from other gasoline dealers. They were conducting an orderly protest to attempt to educate the consumer that the oil company was directly "price undercutting" the very dealers that were already established in the neighborhoods and paying to lease the company's other stations. Randy Marcellis, is listed as the station operator and the owner was Pete Spina."

To clarify, Pete Spina had a history with the wholesale jobber KANCO and later owned the Parent Petroleum Company site located on Route 38 east of Geneva. Randy Marcellis had a history of being a Standard Oil Company Field Supervisor who also operated the 102 West State Street station for Standard Oil.

Robert Jacobs, president of the Illinois Gasoline Dealer group, was on hand throughout the morning to plead the dealer's case to reporters or anyone else that would listen. Jacobs heatedly called Standard's price undercutting "immoral, and we think illegal" in that the stations status as a "jobber" disguised as an independent dealer enabled the station to buy gasoline at five cents per gallon lower than the price paid by Amoco dealers whose stations are owned by the company.

The company was allowing the wholesaler to enter the retail market with an unfair price advantage, and as we now know, to facilitate the effort to undermine the dealer network to the point of extinction and replace them with company-run self-serve facilities. As time progressed and more stations were eliminated or came under company control, the nation witnessed the pricing collusion that would take the market to $4 per gallon.

Looking back at how this article was formed by the reporter almost 40 years ago, I can see the reporter's lack of comprehension of the true message the dealers were attempting to communicate: unfair pricing will lead to the elimination of the dealer down the street from you; that loss will reinstate company-owned monopolies which the Anti-trust laws were designed to protect you from. It is ironic that this jobber-operated station is now closed and surrounded by stations operated directly by the oil companies today.

My personal experience showed that Texaco Oil, the only oil company represented under one brand name in all 48 contiguous states, now withdrew from less profitable markets, starting in the Northwest Territory and across the Midwest. The one exception to the withdrawal in Illinois was the Chicago market, which was deemed profitable, but some said it was saved due to the influence of Texaco board member and St. Charles citizen, Lester Norris and his wife, Delora, who insisted on continued availability of the family-owned product.

This influence became more apparent with the passing of Norris and his wife. The abandonment of Texaco in the Chicago market came shortly after in 1986. The remaining 81 locations in Chicago were traded or sold to Mobil, while Mobil, in turn, handed over their holdings in the southwest markets of Oklahoma, Arizona, and New Mexico to Texaco. Actions like these on the part of oil companies spurred the outcry of local dealer organizations like The Illinois-Indiana Gasoline Dealers Association who stated that this was just a ruse to disguise the establishment of regional monopolies. Less than a decade later we witnessed the merger of ExxonMobil and Chevron-Texaco.

I had been an award-winning 'Shining Star' within the Texaco dealer organization, and I continued the same pattern with Mobil, being recognized in the top ten dealers in a seven–state district evaluation/award. It was my personal observation that being a good dealer marked you as a priority target for elimination by Mobil; in short, they did not want you to survive as a potential competitor in the future.

Mobil adopted a very aggressive elimination of their dealer network, going so far as to build shiny new locations directly across the street from some existing dealer locations while retailing gas at the dealer's cost. At the same time increasing that dealer's rent and forcing 24–hour operation with higher overhead. Over the course of the next 4 years, Mobil became so aggressive in their elimination of dealers, that when I sought legal counsel, the determination was made that I could win on 5 different counts. Despite the merit of a lawsuit on my behalf, the reality was that the cost of pursuing what was then the fourth largest corporation in the country through the legal system would have been prohibitive. I learned that the PMPA, Petroleum Marketing Protection Act, which was intended for dealer protection, was a very weak barrier against the oil company.

Having been frustrated with the lack of legal recourse against Mobil, I attended the Mobil Dealer Convention in 1989, where I spoke in an open microphone session to over 5000 dealers regarding how Mobil unfairly priced products to its retailers and the company's lack of support with the environmental issues surrounding the disposal of used waste oil. It was after this that Mobil offered to sell me the property, if I would "go away" and cease agitating other dealers. We agreed upon a purchase price and I had secured financing. Then Mobil dropped the bomb. I would be responsible for any and all contaminations from both the past and the future. All the gas tanks had been replaced in 1981 and the property had been tested in 1986 when Texaco transferred the site to Mobil. The results of those tests were good–there was NO contamination found. In 1989, in order to protect myself in the purchase of the property I had to insist on a new test to cover the past 4 years. The prior borings 13 feet down to bedrock had reflected a clean site and these new borings down to bedrock also reflected a clean site. However, the EPA had since enhanced the rules and came back to us saying they now required an additional boring that was to go through the limestone bedrock and into the ground–water level.

It is at this point that I want to dispel the rumors over issues involving our contamination of the location. The soil, 13 feet down to bedrock was clean, but the testing of the groundwater beneath that bedrock revealed contamination of toluene and benzene running towards the Fox River in an underground stream. Further testing confirmed that we were NOT the source, but since we had discovered it, we were responsible for the clean–up. We could not move forward with the purchase. The EPA worked on the deep–pockets basis and held Mobil responsible for the remediation that closed the station on January 31, 1990 even though we were vindicated as the source.

I have in my collection three different publications, *Fill'er Up* by Jim Draeger &

Mark Speitz, *Pump and Circumstance* by John Margolies, and the aforementioned, *The American Gas Station* by Michael Karl Witzel; all recreating the nostalgic era of the neighborhood service station. They tend to summarize the demise of this icon of Americana as the natural attrition associated with the smaller operations inability to compete. I disagree based on my personal experience and conversations with my contemporaries of the era. We experienced the extreme prejudice of the oil companies and their immoral and downright illegal intimidations brought upon us by their representatives.

There are examples evidenced in this journal, having been chronicled by the newspapers, of Shell Oil building a competing company-owned station about two miles from Parillo Shell in 1987. Shell representatives argued that it was not direct competition since their target market differed from Parillo's in that it was a self-serve convenience store vs. a full-service neighborhood station. Another example is when ARCO sold off about 2,000 stations east of the Mississippi to other oil companies and Jim Gorecki's ARCO station in St. Charles was sold in 1986 to Standard Oil; the company removed all the pumps and tanks insuring the elimination of competition. Jim joined other ARCO dealers in lawsuits that demanded that existing dealers had the right to purchase their stations under the guidelines of the PMPA. However, having lost his station, Jim went on to operate a garage in Geneva.

Let's talk about Self-Service from the perspective of your local dealer. Most consumers perceived that service station operators were resistant to change from full-service to self-service due to anticipated lower profits. True, we were expected to sell for less, but doesn't it stand to reason that you should sell for less if you were no longer required to staff multiple uniformed attendants? However, in spite of potentially lower employee overhead, the oil company expected more rent every year and the formula was to sell more gas through competitive pricing called Weighted Average Margin (WAM). The pricing policies introduced with self-service expected dealers to sell self-service regular unleaded *below cost*. How were we to survive? The solution was to charge a disproportionately higher price for the premium lines and even more for full-service; WAM. So, the preferred loyal full-service customer was to bear the burden of the self-serve price shopper. When the oil company then started to add a 4% credit card surcharge on all sales, the full-service customer was again punished since they were paying 4% on top of an already inflated price.

I once had a customer say to me, "I use my car in my business and fill up my tank 2–3 times per week and because I use the credit card as the tool to track my purchases, which is what your oil company offered, I now have to pay a surcharge while some kid comes in here and buys just a few bucks of self service, pays cash, and gets a discount! Which one of us does the company really value?"

Now let's take the WAM and apply it to present times. When I was in business the mid–grade gas cost to the dealer was 4 cents more than regular and another 4 cents was added for premium. I recently had a dealer tell me his cost difference averaged in the 5–cent range, but customers had become accustomed to paying a much higher price for premium gas which offset the below–cost sale of regular. Even though there are more cars today that require premium gas, the oil company run establishments have taken prices to an extreme with 25 and 50 cent markups.

When visiting River Falls, Wisconsin in 2012, I went to my former choice of stations that I had patronized and found an interesting scenario in how the different grades were priced. The regular was priced higher than most of the other stations in town, but at the same time, the mid–grade was only 5 cents more and premium another 5 cents. I sought out the owner and had my suspicions confirmed that the difference in cost between grades of gasoline had changed very little since the 1980's. This dealer's marketing plan was to drop the company doctrine of pricing regular at cost and making up the loss in inflating the prices of the higher grades. He was now the price leader of mid–grade and premium gasolines. His sales of regular had only suffered from the persons passing through town, but the locals remained loyal in understanding that he wasn't gouging premium customers.

Now is a good time to quote Witzel, "Small yellow machines installed at today's convenience stores for the purchase of air would have been considered ludicrous by yesterday's service station standards." The update to this 20–year–old quote now is that the machines are expensive, slow, often not well maintained, or not even available; windshield squeegees are worn out and the water in the buckets is filthy.

Remember the prior mention of the gimmicks for gasoline retailing? Free steak knives, china, glasses and such, were driven by massive advertising campaigns. It was estimated that in 1955, $42 million ($400 million today) had been spent on driveway premiums to boost sales. By the late 1960's, it was estimated that annual costs of trading stamps were about $150 million annually. Those costs were born by the dealer, not the oil company. The overhead costs associated with maintaining the large uniformed staff for full–service, cleaning restrooms, helping with directions, along with sometimes forced 24–hour operation, even when not profitable, were all the dealers' burden. The one thing the companies did furnish at their expense were road maps, which they had initiated decades earlier to create brand loyalty when traveling. That 50–year program of providing free maps ended in 1984 with the oil companies plans to take over all dealer–run gas stations. To not appear to be the "bad–guy" who stopped the free map program, the oil companies started charging dealers for maps, which meant dealers had to start charging their customers.

Oil companies sold the public on the concept of self–service with the initial idea that you would save money pumping your own gas, but with that transition you are now subject to speculative oil price increases, reduced services, and windshield squeegees with the rubber falling off. Have you experienced standing in line at the register behind Lottery ticket buyers to ask for directions? Have you taken notice that the company-owned station charges a higher price where there is less competition down the road? Why? Because they can! In the past, if the price of gas went up on Monday, the dealer was not allowed to change his price until he purchased his next load on Thursday, yet when the price went down, dealers were expected to suffer the loss and lower our price to stay competitive. Today, if a hurricane is headed to the Gulf of Mexico, fueling speculation that one or more offshore oil platforms might need to shut down results in the price being driven up at every level, especially at the pump. Self-Service was simply a tool used by the oil companies to reduce their overhead, lure the public into a perceived savings, and once the dealer network was eliminated, raise prices and profits.

So, I take exception to statements made that the "dealers fell from grace as the dinosaurs that and could no longer compete in the industry." It was my personal experience that there always a natural attrition process by which some weak dealers would be eliminated but the 1980's ushered in a very deliberate process of elimination of all dealers by the oil companies. When was the last time an oil company either advertised a "Clean Restroom" program, provided a free map, came out to the pumps to give you a promotional gift, or got under your hood to check your oil?

The intimidation by company representatives ran the gambit of forced pricing policies, gross increases in rent, forced 24-hour operation, and the withholding of normal contracted maintenance of the property. The dealers who did not own their property were eliminated; those who did own their property were free to seek out different suppliers for competitive terms and pricing, but that became problematic. As time went on those competitive wholesale suppliers were either intimidated with restrictive supply and pricing, or outright elimination by the monopolistic oil companies. There are many examples in the Fox Valley of those dealers who owned their property ceasing gasoline sales and yet surviving as repair service facilities. In the 1980's, some Mobil dealers attempted the transition to convenience stores in the lobby area, while the service bays were rented to customers on an hourly basis for do-it-yourself auto repairs. The problem with that convenience store business model was that Mobil required the "franchise dealer" to purchase Mobil equipment and supplies from approved purveyors at exorbitant pricing. The franchise model was heavily weighted in the oil company's favor and I witnessed more than one established dealer end up in financial difficulty. In his own words, one West Chicago dealer told me he was, "driven to bankruptcy by the lopsided franchise contract with Mobil.

With the advent of the automobile age, garages and service stations lined Tri-City thoroughfares. It is hard to imagine this because only a handful remain today in each city. When looking at the area of the Tri–Cities in 1960 with a combined population of about 23,800, we had 51 choices on where to purchase gasoline, in 1970 we had 49. Now in 2018, with a combined population of about 72,373, we have approximately 21 choices, with residents driving further from home in heavy traffic and with less competitive pricing. We had in fact, more choices during WWII when gasoline was rationed, and 25 percent of the stations were closed.

FIFTEEN

THE "BLACK EYE" ON THE INDUSTRY

No different than the wagon peddler that would hawk his cure–all elixir and the shyster that would promise to make it rain for a fee, there were opportunists at the ready to take advantage of the motorist traveling through his town.

It most likely started with the short measurement of gasoline when dispensed into buckets before accurate measurements of distribution were implemented. How did the customer really know the actual capacity of the 5–gallon bucket being used to fill his gas tank? Even later, the sale of gas through early pumps could be modified and I recall a story my father told me about the early visible pumps. Gas was hand pumped into the glass cylinder on the top of the pump which then allowed gas to be gravity fed into the car. Gas was stored in the ground at 54 degrees and unscrupulous dealers would pre–pump about 9 ½ gallons into the cylinder allowing it to sit in the sun and expand to about 10 gallons. People eventually were made aware of the scam in that you never bought gas from one of those pumps where the gas had already been pumped into the glass cylinder. This is the same reason why you should not "top-off" your tank today because the gas will expand on a hot day.

The early electric gas pumps were equipped with in-line sight glasses that would allow the customer to see the flow of gas through the pump. Even as the electric pumps evolved into the 1960's, the following National pump face, FIGURE 17.1, stands testament that the public still needed to be reassured about the pump accuracy. The glass at the top of the photo would show the flow of gasoline as the internal plastic blade would spin as the gas was dispensed. It was also called out that *"GLASS MUST BE FULL BEFORE AND AFTER DELIVERY"* to avoid possible shenanigans. Then to be certain that a prior purchase total could not be added to your bill it was posted that, *"GALLON AND SALE INDICATIONS MUST BE AT ZERO WHEN DELIVERY IS BEGUN–UNDER PENALTY OF LAW"* and it also clarified that the price on the pump had *"TAX INCLUDED."* The final assurance concerned the accuracy of the dispensing pump, *"MAXIMUM ACCURACY AT ANY RATE OF DELIVERY AT ANY PRESSURE"*.

When I was in business, the State of Illinois came through town unannounced to check the calibration of the pumps at least once a year to inspect for any tampering. We would pay the inspector for the license and pumps were then validated by official inspection labels. In recent years I have seen many outdated or missing inspection labels on the company-owned gas pumps. Even today, the modern pump calibration can be short-changing the customer on the sale and calibration checks will vary by state, but usually every two years.

RESTORED NATIONAL BRAND GAS PUMP FACE.
FIGURE 15.1 Author's photograph

You may not recall, but in Illinois, before 1980, the price of gas posted on street signs did not include the sales tax. In the early days of 10 cent gas plus 4 cents in tax the average motorist could do the math and thereby expected the price on the pump to read 14 cents. The math became more of a mental challenge as the price of gas advanced and the calculation of sales tax became more complex. Most customers did not understand that the state sales tax was to be computed on a number that did not include the Federal Tax, which would have resulted in a tax on a tax. So, what should the pump price be if the street sign advertised $1.079 and the state sales tax rate was .0725? Now imagine the difficulty for service station owners to calculate the correct tax on 3 self–service and 3 full–service products when the cost of gas fluctuated often with price changes reflected in tenths of a cent. Before the advent of the computer many dealers just estimated sales tax to the best of their abilities. So now put yourself in the role of customer who in one week, filled their tank at two different gas stations, both advertising the same price on the street, but reflecting different prices at the pumps.

It was common knowledge among dealers that there was also a certain predominately ethnic group, largely representing the same oil company, that intentionally overcharged by misrepresenting the price including tax and pocketed the overcharged difference. The net result of this was that the State Legislature, after many complaints about overcharges, passed a new law stating that the price of gas on the street must include the sales tax and match the pump price. This was totally unprecedented; imagine if all businesses had to advertise prices including the sales tax!

The same group of unethical opportunists were notorious for not submitting some or all of the sales tax collected to the state. Some even purchased a tanker of gas at a lower price from an independent brand and then resold the product as a higher priced major brand. This bootleg purchase could be slid through with no record of the buy and the payment of sales tax could be avoided. The result of such fraudulent maneuvers was the passing of another new law where gas stations were singled out as the only retail point of sales tax collection business required to pre–pay 50% of the tax upon the tanker truck delivery to the place of business. The rationale behind this approach was that the entire tax could not be charged due to not knowing if the product was sold at either the self or full–serve retail price, but the State was now guaranteed receipt of at least 50% of the sales tax. They also now had a traceable record of ALL gas deliveries and a way of tracking who was responsible for paying the second half of the tax.

The early days of dispensing oil were also subject to unscrupulous devices that came under some controls requiring a clear glass container to demonstrate that the oil was clean and unused; and a "fill–line" showed the measure of a full quart. Even with that, there we individuals who were adept at checking your oil while holding their finger on the side of the dipstick thereby artificially preventing the stick from touching the oil.

This was called "short–sticking" in order to sell an unneeded quart of oil.

The following cartoon from *Geneva Republican* in the 1930's was an informative editorial showing how a lower grade of oil was mislabeled to represent that it was a high grade which was then sold at the higher price. This was done at "GYP" gas stations where low–grade bulk oil was pumped into the clear glass quart oil containers labeled at the higher grade.

FIGURE 15.2 Courtesy *Geneva Republican.*

This cartoon demonstrates that the American Automobile Association survey of motor oil purchases revealed, "79% short measurements, 63% substitutions, and 40% lower grade oils that cost the American public $80 million annually." I believe that it may have actually shown support for the larger oil companies use of "tamper–proof" canned oil to avoid unlabeled bulk oil dispensed with hand pumps into the old–fashioned glass bottles with spouts. Isn't it ironic that today, the 10–minute Oil Change industry has gone back to the use of bulk oil. . .another historic example of coming full circle?

Every community across the country had civic leaders advocating a city beautification movement and more often than not, the local service station was targeted as an example of urban blight. Stations were often looked upon as dirty, noisy hostels for undesirables that should be relegated to some location outside of town. Granted, the constant ringing of the driveway bell, hammering of metal, air tool operation, junk parts piled outside and non–running cars littering the landscape were less than desirable. Then there was the issue of young "gearheads" loitering around at night, arriving and leaving the property with load exhaust and squealing tires.

There were numerous historic examples in our local newspapers of both the citizenry and city councils resisting any additions to the number of gas stations in town. The *Geneva Republican* had articles against the West State Street Standard station (1928) and again resisted zoning changes to allow the Hilltop Sinclair on East State Street (1950). The *St. Charles Chronicle* had many articles resisting Bill Zimmerman building a station at Routes 25 and 64 (1955); the Martin station on East Main (1956); the Pure Oil on Illinois and First (1966); and the Standard at the corner of Randall Road (1961). The St. Charles City Council went on record in 1954 and passed the most restrictive zoning ordinances disallowing service stations, and while popular with many locally, the ordinances would eventually not stand up in federal court.

AUGUST 10, 1966 CHRONICLE EDITORIAL AND CARTOON

"Filling A Need...Chances began to look a bit better recently for St. Charles to get that other gas station it needs so desperately on West Main street...As everyone knows, all Main street intersections...need a minimum of four gas stations, except where the streets are not through streets, and there, three stations will suffice. Of course, this has not been completely achieved, because we have a few Main street intersections where drug stores, and banks and hardware stores and churches...and even a library and a high school have gotten there first.

Incidentally, we were interested to note at 8 a.m. Friday as we drove through town from the west that all three stations at Randall road, both stations at 17th street, the station at 14th street, the station at 11th street, the one at Ninth, and the two near Third, did not have a single cash customer at the pumps.

Imagine our delight at the possible advent of the BULKO station at 17th street is exceeded by the delight of the present West Main street gas station owners at having another few pumps added to gasoline alley."

FIGURE 15.3 Courtesy *St. Charles Chronicle.*

"Ya know, I made a pretty good living here until they opened the 117th gas station just down the street."

There were also certain stereotypes and stigmas associated with being in the service station industry with first and foremost of being just a "grease–monkey" lacking any formal training. With that also came the reputation of being a slovenly sort whom you did not want to sit on your car's fine leather upholstery; track oil on the carpeted flooring; or even touch the steering wheel to leave evidence of a hard day's work. Then there was a period in the 1960's that oil companies advocated having driveway attendants on commission which eventually led to dishonest acts like using a hidden knife to make a small cut in a fan belt; showing customers a dirty air filter that wasn't even theirs; or squirting oil on shock absorbers to make them appear to be leaking. The degree of dishonesty was only limited by their imagination. The public became very wary about allowing anyone under the hood of their car while traveling on the road and away from their hometown mechanic. This all shows why major oil companies strove to drive a reputation with uniformed attendants and slogans such as "You can trust your car to the man who wears the Star!" It is unfortunate that the dirty, dishonest reputation of a few so heavily reflected on the many fine, honest, educated, highly trained, hard–working service station dealers.

Once a motorist had been taken advantage of, he would naturally approach another gas station with a certain amount of trepidation. For me, it was an almost daily challenge to prove myself as being honest and trustworthy, not so much to my regular customer, with whom we had developed a mutually beneficial relationship, but with the potential new customer. One of my favorite sayings when interviewing a new mechanic was delivered while pointing to all the traffic passing by the station, "If we find it necessary to lie and cheat customers in order to make a living, then I would suggest changing vocations." My technicians made a generous wage, with guaranteed overtime and were not on commission. Often when the mechanic came to me with the question of how to proceed with repairs in any given situation, my response would be "What would you do if it was your mother's car?"

Early on, as an educated young man with a Bachelor's Degree in Marketing, I paid attention to the primary decision maker for automobile repairs, the lady of the house. Studies had shown that the woman had a 70% influence on where the family would go for automobile repairs. This was primarily based on cleanliness of the facility, and how the car was returned to her with both cleanliness and reliability of the repair as her judgment criteria. She wanted to feel that she could communicate with the technicians without fear of repercussions for not knowing the technical terms. I always strove to have the customer speak directly with the mechanic working on their car both before and after the repair which always helped to support a solid understanding and positive working relationship.

On the subject of cleanliness, my station had curtains in the showroom and the lady's restroom windows along with fresh cut flowers. We did not mind the ladies helping themselves to a flower, but eventually we stopped the practice when replacing the vases became expensive. It also never ceased to amaze me as to how many times the restroom curtains would also disappear. Every year, potted geraniums hung under our canopy and the landscape was lush with flowers. Showroom and Service Bay floors were scrubbed daily and no trash or old parts lay around the station. Customers often remarked that they could eat off the floors. When your car was serviced, it was returned cleaner than when dropped off because we would vacuum it and wash all of the windows–inside and out. If the car was around for a prolonged stay, it was often returned to you washed. My wife, Linda, was largely responsible for training the high school kids that would work the evenings and you could see the doubt in their faces that "some woman" was going to train them. That was soon replaced with a new respect for the knowledge she shared.

We received multiple Customer Service awards from both Texaco and Mobil Oil companies which were prominently displayed for new customers to peruse. In the summer of 1989, I had a lady at the pumps ask me if I was the owner. When that was confirmed, she shared her compliments which were especially focused on the well–mannered and trained young people working the unsupervised evening shifts which was when she most frequently visited. I thanked her for the compliment and then she explained that her husband was the District Manager for Phillip 66 and it really irritated him to pay her monthly Mobil credit card bill. I explained that current negotiations for the purchase of the property were pending with Mobil and once I owned the property, I would be free to sign new supply contracts. Within two weeks, and without meeting any representatives, I received a certified letter with a very generous offer from Phillips 66 based on the District Manager's spousal recommendation.

I have already explained why the sale could not go through, but I have always wondered what path my life would have followed if it had. My wife and I continue to take great pride with former customers praise more than 30 years after our closing.

SIXTEEN

SERVICE STATION
EPITAPH

When interviewed prior to the forced closing of my station, I pointed out that while the community was growing, the available sources for purchasing gasoline were shrinking and the restrictive competition would eventually translate to higher prices. The 1970 population of St. Charles was about 13,000, growing by 35% to 17,492 in 1980, and another 29% in 1990 to 22,501. During my tenure in the gas station, there were 13 new traffic lights installed in St. Charles; while at the same time there were 13 fewer service stations available to the consumer. Of the remaining 13 gas stations in 1990, only 4 were still offering full-service. One surely can make the point that only the strong would survive and I won't disagree with that, but keep in mind that there was a not-too-hidden agenda by the oil companies to eliminate dealer-held gas stations in favor of company-owned self-service locations.

I know for a fact that in 1998 the Southland Corporation's 7–Eleven location on Randall Road had one–month sales that were the equivalent of my total 1989 annual volume of $1.3 million. I can also tell you that selling gas is secondary to product sales in the convenience store profit center. The site manager provides very little pricing input for gas as ultimately the price is set by corporate in Dallas, TX. All this was all due to very limited price competition on gasoline. In the 1990's my father owned a Mountain Home, Arkansas gas station convenience store and often commented that the convenience store was more profitable as compared to the five full–service locations he operated earlier in his career.

I also remember a story my father related after a 1961 meeting with Standard Oil executives who shared with him the fact that one penny per gallon equated to $1,000,000/ day profit for the oil company in the Chicagoland market. That was with a population of about 4 million and in what I refer to as the post–war "Donna Reed or Ozzie & Harriet" family structure; one working parent and just one automobile with most everyone living relatively close to work. Standard's market was also shared with more competitors like D–X, Sinclair, Cities Service, Clark, Pure, Sunoco, Purple Martin and so on. That $1 million, if adjusted for inflation, would equal about $8,380,000 per day today. Keep in mind that was for Chicagoland and attempting to extrapolate those numbers to current national volume is mind boggling. Also keep in mind that profits are made every step of the way from the oil well to the pipeline, to the refiner, back to pipeline, and finally to storage facilities before being shipped to the retail market. Every step increases the price prior to the gas making it into your tank.

Our government eventually deregulated the industry and has no desire to kill the "cash cow" that generates more tax dollars, usually based on a percentage, that increase as prices go up. The photo shown on the left below shows just the tip of the iceberg for the taxation of gas in the 1920's when the tax collected exceeded the price of the product and few paved roads existed.

FIGURE 16.1 Courtesy of Pinterest. FIGURE 16.2 Photo by author.

The photo on the right is from the recent display at the St. Charles History Museum. The sign was discovered in the in the attic of my Texaco gas station in 1977 and resided there until the Bentz Family donated it to the St. Charles Museum which was then located in City Hall. Fire–Chief gas was priced at 8.9 cents per gallon plus 4 cents tax at some time during the depression era. It's interesting that this sign from the 1930's reveals that one third of the price is for taxes. Ironically the sign returned to the gas station when the building was remodeled and opened as the new museum location in 2001.

In 1932, the first federal gasoline tax was levied at one cent per gallon to restore declining highway funds during the depression. Between 1934 and 1937, $2.8 billion was allocated and spent on road construction. Adjusted for inflation and not adjusted for either increased volume, or the many new taxes passed since then, that one cent would equal: $52,748,447,761 today, in 2018. My point is that many government taxing bodies, at every level, see fuel taxes as a "cash cow" that feeds on itself as prices rise. As illustrated below, since 1977 there have been only three years (1980–82) in which domestic oil industry profits exceeded government gas tax collections. In the remaining years, gasoline tax collections consistently exceeded oil industry profits, reaching a peak in 1995 when gas tax collections outpaced industry profits by a factor of 7.35 to one.

The following chart reflects Major U.S. Oil Companies' Domestic Profits, Compared to State and Federal Gasoline Taxes 1977–2004 (**figures in billions of dollars**):

Year	Oil Profits	Federal Taxes	State Taxes	Total Taxes
1977	$26.8	$13.7	$29.0	$42.7
1978	$27.5	$13.0	$28.1	$41.1
1979	$34.9	$11.4	$25.2	$36.7
1980	$41.0	$9.4	$22.0	$31.4
1981	$41.4	$8.5	$21.0	$29.5
1982	$35.8	$8.0	$20.6	$28.6
1983	$30.2	$15.0	$22.0	$37.0
1984	$28.7	$16.2	$23.5	$39.6
1985	$29.3	$15.6	$24.6	$40.2
1986	$9.0	$15.9	$25.7	$41.5
1987	$14.0	$15.0	$27.4	$42.4
1988	$16.9	$15.6	$28.1	$43.8
1989	$14.5	$14.5	$28.3	$42.8
1990	$18.6	$14.5	$29.1	$43.5
1991	$11.0	$21.1	$29.7	$50.8
1992	$10.1	$20.9	$30.8	$51.7
1993	$10.6	$20.9	$31.4	$52.3
1994	$10.8	$27.1	$32.1	$59.3
1995	$7.9	$26.3	$31.9	$58.1
1996	$18.9	$26.8	$32.0	$58.9
1997	$18.8	$26.0	$32.6	$58.6
1998	$9.0	$27.1	$33.1	$60.3
1999	$16.8	$26.5	$33.6	$60.1
2000	$34.9	$25.7	$33.3	$59.0
2001	$35.1	$24.9	$33.6	$58.5
2002	$16.2	$24.5	$33.9	$58.4
2003	$31.7	$24.6	$33.4	$58.0
2004	$42.6	$24.2	$34.2	$58.4
Total	**$643.0**	**$533.0**	**$810.1**	**$1,343.1**

Source: Bureau of Economic Analysis, U.S. Energy Information Administration

I am not current on all of the taxes charged by the federal government, states, counties, RTA, and local city tax, but it is obscene. Everyone, especially elected officials, should be asking, "Where does this money go when our infrastructure is in such dire need of repair?" Unfortunately, the trend is to implement another tax instead of investigating the trail of where the money has gone.

When I was in business the city collected a share of the Motor Fuel Tax based on population and one percent of the then seven percent sales tax. Now local municipalities have tacked on even more taxes. For example, effective January 1, 2018, the City of Batavia passed a 1 cent gasoline tax increase that brought the local tax up to 4 cents, a tax that formerly did not exist. I call these the invisible taxes that one does not recognize until traveling out of your market and experiencing the disparity of prices elsewhere.

Even those dealers who were lucky enough to own their facilities found themselves in situations where the supply of gas at a price that would allow them to remain competitive was a diminishing resource. Only some dealers were able to negotiate with another brand of supplier for a more favorable contract. In the entire geographic area discussed in this book I can only name one retail dealer still surviving as a gas station with automotive repair: Stan Oke, Batavia Mobil. Feece Oil has also survived 86 years as a family owned distributorship, which now operates retail facilities. Those former gas dealers surviving as repair-only facilities are: Reber & Foley (Standard); Duke & Lee's (Texaco); Lou's (Pure); Abe & Doc's (Phillips 66); and Kevin's (Texaco). That's a sorry epitaph for the local service station industry that formerly employed over 900 persons in the Tri-Cities alone, not including those involved in Auto Parts Supply and the Automobile Dealerships.

In the early days there was the transition from blacksmith shops to general stores, then to filling stations and repair facilities. Now, in the past few decades we have observed the demise of the local service station dealer as they were replaced by oil company owned facilities or mega pumpers. While some former gas stations are now automotive related repair garages without pumps, most were either razed or repurposed for other applications such as the St. Charles History Museum, professional offices, liquor stores, donut shops and even restaurants. Of all the stations in the Tri-Cities, about six have been repurposed by the oil companies as pumper stations with convenience stores, but many are just simply gone.

The first gas station in St. Charles, built in 1920, has been a restaurant for the past 30 years, but has managed to capture its prior history. As the Filling Station Pub & Grill, the exterior and interior have been appropriately decorated with old gas pumps, signs, and paraphernalia. The neighborhood service station which was once considered too common, has in most cases, disappeared. However, there has been a resurgence of nostalgia, in many cases tied to the collector car industry and service station-themed restaurants.

FIGURES 16.3 & 16.4 Images courtesy Filling Station website

Service Station owners developed a reputation of supporting their communities; they lived here and conducted business here. Being present in the day-to-day operations, they were accessible and most often the first source for solicitation for fundraisers supporting Scouts, 4-H, Little League, Pee Wee Football, High School athletics, Homecoming, yearbook advertisements, Veteran's groups, church programs and so on. Your "Mom 'n Pop" neighborhood gas station owner has been replaced by large corporations with remote, inaccessible ownership. By 1985, the Geneva High School yearbook was down to three neighborhood stations congratulating the graduation of high school seniors in the *Geneva Republican*: Kuchera's Union 76, Duke & Lee's Phillips 66, and Parrillo's Shell; all with children who had attended those very schools. In prior decades there would have been 12-16 service station sponsors and today there are none.

The big corporations do not live and participate in your community. The purpose of this book was let your neighbor's memory live on in the unique architecture and services that we may recall and to perpetuate the proud nostalgic tradition of what full-service meant in the past. It is with great anticipation that I look forward to the future designation of my former service station to being recognized on the National Registry for Historic Landmarks. Although I lament the loss of the former Baker Hotel Garage with its unique Art Deco design, I am proud that we were able to save my former gas station from being razed and that it is now the St. Charles History Museum.

I have found that my research is always a work in progress so please feel free to contact me with additions, corrections, or questions at tricitygas@gmail.com

APPENDIX

A SUMMARY OF TRICITY BLACKSMITHS
The first purveyors of "gasolene" and auto repair

BATAVIA BLACKSMITHS

The locations of Batavia Blacksmiths were primarily concentrated in three areas; North River Street, Island Avenue, and Batavia Avenue with some being located in what we would consider residential neighborhoods.

- **1834: JOHN GREGG–**Batavia's first blacksmith came to town in the spring of 1834
- **1840's: CORNELIUS BOGARDUS (C. B.) CONDE–**North River Street.

Whitely Shaw emigrated from Yorkshire, England in 1844. His Blacksmith business was located on River Street, just north of Wilson. FIGURE A.1 This photo was provided by Great–Great Granddaughter Linda Hoover Garrison.

- **1844–1914: WHITELY SHAW**–As a Geneva blacksmith, Shaw partnered with Julius Alexander, after the Civil War, together they provided steel for the Geneva bridge. He then came to North River Street in Batavia.
- **1850: JACOB GRIMES**–he later changed to dentistry in 1857
- **1870: McGUIRE & GREGG–JOHN McGUIRE**
- **1875–94: JOHN WAGNER**–58 South Batavia Avenue, father to Mrs Carl N. More
- **No Date: DONOVAN**–Wilson & River Streets, later the Shaw building
- **1880's: CHARLES WENBERG & SON**–Charles, Sr started the smithy on Island Avenue in the 1880's and evolved to a carriage factory and was in business for nearly 50 years until the automobile replaced the buggy. **CHARLES WENBERG, JR** started in 1898 and **C.W. PALM** worked here in 1895.
- **1883–1897: GUSTOV PETERSON**–58 South Batavia Avenue, then moved to a shop behind his home at 14 South Jackson Street.
- **1880's? JAMES GLINES**–veteran horseshoer and blacksmith passed in 1917
- **No date: HOWARD O'CONNOR**–blacksmith
- **1894: J. S. R. JONES**–123 Main Street–horse shoeing and repairing specialty

- **1896–1900: A. G. TREMAN & SONS**–horse shoeing a specialty, North Van Buren, then moved out of town.
- **1896: MERIDITH McMASTER**– NE corner of State & River Streets new shop built by William Drake
- **1897–1904: GUSTOF PETERSON**–moved to 14 North Jackson Street His son, **JOHN P. PETERSON**, worked with him and then set up shop in LaFox.
- **1898: CHARLES AND JAMES BIRD**–North River Street
- **1901: CHARLES WENBERG** purchased the shop of M. G. McMASTER and will move his shop from Island Avenue to North River Street. He retired in 1921 and his 1924 obituary said he had been in operation for over 50 years. The building was razed in 1936.
- **1907: CHARLES POMP**–58 South Batavia Avenue, with his son, **OSCAR POMP**.

John Plant, Blacksmith, postcard with 1911 postmark on reverse. Handbill posted on smithy door is for 4th of July Batavia Day Picnic. Should we call this an early open–air SUV with third row seating? FIGURE A.2 Photo from early post card.

- **1911–18: JOHN PLANT**–originally identified as Batavia blacksmith due to Batavia handbill on door, later identified in 1918 Prairie Farmer Directory as North Aurora.
- **1907–1912: GEORGE F. McNAIR**–19 South Island Avenue In 1908 he left to join Ringling Bros Circus and returned at an unknown date, but keep in mind that the Circus traveled a summer route.

- **1913: POMP & PETERSON**–58 South Batavia Avenue **ROBERT PETERSON?**
- **1914: JAMES BIRD**–purchased the smithy of WHITELY SHAW on North River Street
- **1915: W.O. BRIGGS & SON**–have moved to town to take over Island shop.
- **1916–17: PHILS HAWLEY**–123 Main Street (now 315)
- **1917–18: FRED BRIGGS**–19 South Island Avenue, successor to his father, partnered with Pomp.
- **1919–25: CHARLES W. POMP** purchased the interest of his partner, **FRED J. BRIGSS,** in the 19 South Island blacksmith shop. The building was razed in 1931.
- **1925: FRED HANSON**–purchased the **H.A. ERICKSON** blacksmith shop, his former place of employment
- **1932–33: THEODORE E BRANDENBURG**–274 First Street
- **1933: WILLIAM FULTON**–North River Street
- **1931–43: TWIN ELMS SERVICE STATION**– Main & Whipple Street, **ALFRED THRYSELIUS,** Gasolene, blacksmith & welder,
- **1944: BERT HUNT**
- **1960–67: WILLIAM F. MILLER**–328 Hamlet Street (Later relocated to Hart Road)–primarily a farrier, was he possibly related to earlier St. Charles blacksmith?

GENEVA BLACKSMITHS

- **1836: LOGAN ROSS**–Geneva's first blacksmith
- **1837: JULIUS & EDWARD ALEXANDER**–first located north and east of the bridge; second location in 1837 was south and east on what was later to become the site of Mill Race Inn. In 1848 the brothers had sold their shop to the Rystrom Carriage shop in order to pursue the California gold strike, then Julius decided to stay in Geneva and a third location was on built on North River Street. *Source: Geneva Illinois, A History of Its Times and Places*

View from the East Side of Geneva with former Alexander Blacksmith Shop in center by the Fox River, and area which will be populated with dealers, garages, and filling stations in the next 40 years. FIGURE A.3 Courtesy "Souvenir of Cheever Addition to Geneva" J.W. Taylor photographer.

The current remains of the Alexander Bros 1837 Blacksmith Shop that was hidden for decades under the façade of the Mill Race Inn. Thought to be Geneva's oldest existing structure, there are preservationists battling the current demolition plans to facilitate future river–front development and urban growth. FIGURE A.4 Courtesy Geneva History Museum.

- **1853: JOHN RYSTROM**–also noted as first Swedish settlers, settled on east side.
- **1857:** *Fersen's Directory* noted several liveries with wagon repair and smithies.
- **1867:** *Kane County Gazette* noted there were four blacksmiths in Geneva
- **1891: WILLIAM O'BRIEN**–smithy burned down this year.
- **No date: CRANDALL & JONES**
- **No date: JOHN MILAN**
- **1912: JAMES GLINES**–SW corner State & 1st
- **1915: SMITH**– "blacksmith acquitted of murder for striking a man"– *Geneva Republican*
- **1917–18: JOHN NELSON**–SW corner of East State & 1st
- **1928–1940: SIMON H. HENRICKSON**–10 Bennett Street, then 117 E. State, sold to Harz
- **1940–50: FRED HARZ**–rebuilt his shop at the "corner of First and River streets"

ST. CHARLES BLACKSMITHS

- **Earliest: DANIEL MARVIN**–out of town on Norton's creek
- **1837: HORACE BANCROFT**–SW corner East Main Street & 1st Street also operated general store.
- **1843: PROCTOR COOLEY**–West Main Street, later the site of the White Front Hotel
- **WILLIAM ALLISON & JOB KNIGHT**–bought out Cooley
- **1842: JAMES MILLER**–7TH & Oak Street with his son, **CHARLES,** until 1866
- **1844: SETH MARVIN & SYLVESTER WHITE,** later son, **ANDREW JACKSON "JACK" MARVIN** on the west side of Main Street between 3rd and 4th Streets built just to the west of **E. F. WEEKS** blacksmith shop. This site was occupied later by other blacksmiths.
- **1900: JOHN TRUMBULL & O'BRIEN**–West Main and 3rd Street. followed by Poole Bros.
- **1840–53: DAVID BROWNE & WASHINGTON NICHOLS**–3rd Street and Main Street
- **1849: WILLIAM MARSHALL, ROBERT WELTON**–Foundryman
- **1857: SYLVESTER WHITE**–First and Cedar Avenues
- **THOMAS DOYLE**–son Edward
- **1860: EDWARD DOYLE**–116 E Cedar Avenue (Cedar House Art Gallery today)
- **1870: PATRICK DONAHUE**–Main Street west of Irwin block
- 1929 list of blacksmiths as remembered by U. S. Elliott:
- **1881: D. B. MOORE**–West Second Street, north of Main, **JOHN B.**

TRUMBULL, Capt. ALBERT CRANDALL, WILLIAN MONROE, OLLIE HALLOCK, & CHARLES MOORE who shod race horses.

- **1891: FRANK ANDREWS,** two shops on east side; **1901: ANDREWS & ROCK** across from City Hall on First Avenue.
- **1885: C. M. CARLSON & GUSTAVE PETERSON–**in the former Klink wagon building
- **1885: JOHN WATTS**
- **1888–1899: POOLE BROS BLACKSMITHS–FINLEY & CHAS.–**First and Cedar Ave.
- **No date: D. F. SATTERLEE–**shop at his home on 2nd Street, worked at Newton Wagon, son, **LEWIS SATTERLEE** also a blacksmith.
- **1890: DANIEL MULHALL (MUNHALL)**
- **1890: TURNBULL & BEN KAYNER (bought out VICTOR WINQUIST)**
- **1891: DAVID ROBERTS & SON–**Wayne
- **1892: A. C. KAISER–**West 4th Street
- **1896–1942: FRIDOLPH "FRED" SUNDBERG–**21 North 2nd Street & 518 South 2nd Street
- **1912: CARLSON & CRONIN–**SW corner 2nd Street near Cedar
- **1891–26: FRED T. HANSEN–**(107) West Main Street–old street number. Accused of shooting in Bartlett then convicted of 1936 robbery of St. Charles National Bank, sentenced to 20–yrs.
- **1915–40: FRANK HISER–**2nd Street, between Main and Cedar. Per Melvin Peterson (Wasco): "Frank Hiser worked for Col. Baker's Twin Pine Farm. He caught on fire and died from shock in 1940. His sister was my 6th grade teacher."
- **No date: WILLIAM MILLER–**514 1st Avenue
- **1920–30: CARL F. NELSON–**301 East Main Street
- **1928–31 FRED P. HANSEN**
- **1933–36: PAUL LADEWIG–**Case Tractors, 310 West Main Street (the old Fred Hansen shop, later in 1945–60 at 12 Indiana Street)
- **No date: Wm. FULTON–**South Second Street
- **1973: LADD REPAIR–VERN LADEWIG–**725 North 12th Street

RURAL BLACKSMITHS

WASCO. IL
- **1889–1904: WASCO BLACKSMITH SHOP–WILL RUDDOCK**
- **1890–1909: WILLIAM A. HISER–**in Wasco on Route 64

- **1905–08: WASCO BLACKSMITH SHOP–BEN R. KAYNER**
- **1908–48: WASCO BLACKSMITH SHOP–ANDREW ERICKSON**

Wasco Blacksmith Shop–circa late 1950's. FIGURE A.5 Courtesy *Wasco, Illinois: A History.*

- **1948–52: WASCO BLACKSMITH SHOP–DAN REDIGER**
- **1953–1988 WASCO BLACKSMITH SHOP–MELVIN PETERSON and son, TOM**

ELBURN, IL

- **1854: JOSEPH SMITH**
- **1871: H. PAGE**–also a harness maker.
- **1871: McELHOSE & ANDY JOHNSON**
- **J. STEVENSON**
- **1873: A.W. JOHNSON & W.H. TYDEMANS, C.J. ANDERSON, WILL WEIR, McKENZIE, CHARLES HUNT, EMERY ANDERSON J.W. MOWATT**
- **1884: HALE ACERS**
- **1889: GEORGE HOLBROOK** was associated with **STEVENSON**
- **1912–15: GEORGE M. HOLBROOK** in his own shop, Elburn Garage.
- **1920–33: JOHN B. NIX**
- **1934: GEORGE KING**
- **1938: F.L. STORM**–implement dealer and blacksmith

BALDMOUND, IL

- **No date: ANDREW CHALQUIST**–passed in 1943, aged 85 years

LAFOX, IL

- **1936: SIDNEY SHEPARD**
- **1910: JOHN P. PETERSON** set up shop after working with his father in Batavia.
- **1945–1981: RAY COX**

VIRGIL, IL

- **1920: JOHN B. NIX** sold to Reiche and moved to Elburn
- **1920: FRANK REICHE**

KANEVILLE, IL

- **1871–present: NEEDHAM'S SHOP–Blacksmith & Welding–Bart Needham** is a current 5th generation blacksmith. Bart has no knowledge of gasoline sales here but he still repairs cars and trucks.

Needham Blacksmith Shop, Kaneville l–r: William T. Needham, unknown, sons Penn and Charles with arm in sling, and unknown. FIGURE A.6 Courtesy Needham family.

- **NEEDHAM BLACKSMITH SHOP–**Kaneville Road (Main Street), Kaneville, IL Founded by **William T. Needham** in 1871 at the current site. He had multiple sons who carried on the family tradition: **Charles Needham** at this site, and **Independence "Penn" Needham** (born on the 4th of July) who opened his own shop in Maple Park with his brother **Fred Needham** joining him later. **Warren J Needham**, brother to Charles of Kaneville, Fred of Maple Park, and Albert of Batavia, was born in 1881 in Kaneville and passed away January 16, 1948. He lived and worked in Batavia, along with brother **Albert**

Needham, as a blacksmith at the Newton Wagon/Emerson–Brantingham shop/Batavia Body Co.

Third generation in Kaneville were **Gordon and Norris Needham.** Brother, **George H. Needham** worked in the blacksmith shop of Newton Wagon Works, in Batavia. In 1921, George H. Needham, as superintendent of Newton Wagon, was promoted to General Manager. In 1931, George H. Needham also opened a blacksmith shop on South River Street in Aurora.

Back in Kaneville, fourth generation **George N. Needham** was in operation when I was sent to the shop for welding supplies in the early 1960's; and his son, **Bart Needham,** born in 1969, carries on the tradition today. From George N. Needham's obituary: "...he was unequaled when he set torch to steel. Behind the welder's mask, behind his squinting eyes. George was a virtual steel savant. He would stand silent before a mangled machine, then, head cocked, Copenhagen on board and torch in hand, slowly, methodically, he would begin. Simply put, in the words of one who knew him best. "If you brought George a bag of horse manure, he'd bring you back a pony."

One would have to wonder if this shop would qualify nationally as the only blacksmith shop in operation for almost 150 years at the same location and by the same family?

Seated l to r: Charles Needham, Penn Needham, and William T. Needham. *Batavia Herald*, 1899: "The Master Horse Shoers Association of Batavia, Geneva, and St. Charles have raised their prices, effective at once, as follows: new shoes 40 cents; old shoes reset 20 cents; handmade shoes 50 cents and bar shoes $1.00." FIGURE A.7 Courtesy Needham family.

GAS & OIL JOBBERS/WHOLESALERS

- **1890: W.H. Streeter**–Standard Oil products in St. Charles, door–to–door delivery.
- **1892: Benjamin Potter**–Gasoline and oil deliveries based from Tanner & Modine Livery
- **1899–1904: St. Charles Oil Distribution Co.**–Henry Delno–purveyor of kerosene and oil products. Sold to McCornack.
- **1904–35: McCornack Oil**–Charles S. McCornack, 528 S 6th Ave., St. Charles home/office
- **1935–62: McCornack Oil Co**–Martha S. McCornack–Pres, Carl A. Anderson–VP, Elmore McCornack–Sec, Donald C. McCornack–Treas, 112 E Main Street, St. Charles Ph 28
- **1962: Texaco Oil Co/Herb Borman d/b/a McCornack Oil** –refer to chapter 8 for details of about sale of McCornack Oil to Texaco.
- **1964–1965: Kane County Oil**––Herb Borman and Warren Munson. Munson joined Borman in January of 1963 and assumed a leading role in the business at that time. Subsequently, in September of 1964, he incorporated the distributorship under the name "Kane County Oil, Inc." The business continued to operate under the McCornack name until August of 1965 when the distributorship was canceled by Texaco. At that time, Texaco appointed a new distributor, the Collins–Locke Group, conferring upon it the right to use the McCornack name.
- **1965–1985: Texaco Oil Co/Collins–Locke Group d/b/a McCornack Oil Co Division** James H. Collins, Pres; Charles A. Locke, V–Pres; 203 S. 3rd, St. Charles (office in Firestone building); Bob Gerhke Bulk Plant Manager

- **1928–33: St. Charles Oil**– Gerhart N. Rasmussen, with his brother, Igel, as an early partner operated out of their home/office at 1232 South 3rd Street, St. Charles, JU 4–2186. Howard Rasmussen, driver; John Rasmussen, driver. 1930 advertisement: *"Solve Your Oil Heating Problems by using 38–40 Prime White Distillate. Distributors of Frye Drop Gasoline, Penno and Novolene Motor Oils."* Later known as **Rasmussen Oil Co.** (1936–66 Cities Service; then Marathon bulk plant on North First Street until about 1985)

- **1925–29: Geneva Oil Co Service Station–Pure Oil–**Howard Davis, wholesale and retail with outside service pit.
- **1932–33: Geneva Oil Co–**Eric Thorson president, Ehmer Mungerson secretary, Ph 1911. Retail and Wholesale w/bulk storage tank facility.
- **1936–46: Valley Pure Oil** Ph 1911 Retail and Wholesale, above ground tanks removed 1946.

- **1932–1949 Feece Oil Company–**LeRoy "Roy" Feece, agent for Deep Rock, operated Bulk Plant at 35 North Water Street and two service stations in Batavia.
- **1949–Current: Feece Oil–**LeRoy stepped into ownership of the Deep Rock holdings in Batavia. Over the early years, Roy and Dale represented Deep Rock, Cities Service, and Citgo oil companies. It is now operated by Roy's grandchildren, Mike, Troy, and Jill on Hubbard Drive.

- **1941 Standard Oil Agent–**A.G. Perschnick, Sugar Grove Ph 6441

- **1940–56: Johnson Oil–Brilliant Bronze** of Chicago, the company sold to Gaseteria of Indiana in 1956 which branded the gasoline 'Bonded'; then sold to Standard Oil of Oklahoma, the 'OK Oklahoma' brand; followed by Standard of New Jersey in 1957 as ENCO; and then Exxon Mobil.

- **1928–52: Karschnick Standard Oil Jobber–**Otto J. Karschnick had started his career with Standard Oil in 1918, then as an agent from 1928–52.
- **1952–83: Karschnick Standard Oil Jobber–**Otto's son, Darrell Karschnick, as agent, then sold to Parent Petroleum.
- **1983–Current: Parent Petroleum–**Pete Spina, formerly from Kane County Oil.

- **1930's–50's Geneva Standard Oil Jobber–**C.A. "Art" Carlson retired in 1953 with LeRoy W. Lindquist, his former driver, replacing him as agent for the fuel oil dealer.
- **1953–61: Geneva Standard Oil Jobber–**LeRoy W. Lindquist
- **1961: Geneva Standard Oil Jobber–**Clayton Bancroft CE 2–7111

- **1961: LeRoy W. Lindquist Texaco** now associated with McCornack Oil. 1402 West State Street, Geneva CE 2–4829

FIGURE A.8 Courtesy *St. Charles Chronicle*

- **Mar 1966: KANCO,** a division of Kane County Oil, formerly Texaco, now distributors of Sinclair products. Herman Willing Sr, Member. Board of Directors: Warren Munson, Pres; John Richards, Vice Pres; Helen Anderson, Sec–Treas; Pete Spina, General Manager. Office 214 W. Main Street, St. Charles; Bulk plant, Elburn. One gas station directly supplied: Robinson's Hilltop Service, 206 East State Street, Geneva. This is the location as previously discussed in Chapter 5, where in 1981, dealers march against Spina as an Amoco wholesaler wrongly competing in the retail market with decontrolled/unfair price competition.

FIGURES A.9 & A.10 Courtesy 1949 & 1954 *St. Charles Chronicle.*
This business still survives as St. Charles Firestone in 2020.

In the span of fifty years, 1904–1954, the McCornack Oil Company, that once delivered kerosene by horse drawn wagon, has evolved to encompass multiple retail and wholesale locations. It must have been difficult for a man in 1904 to comprehend that eventually one of his locations would become a mega Toyland for children at Christmas and a Garden Center in the spring.

AUTOMOBILE PARTS: T.B.A.

Tires, Batteries, and Automobile Accessory listings found in various advertisements such as the Yellow Pages and Polk City Directories.

1920 AUTOMOBILE ACCESSORIES

- **JOHN DAHLIN TIRES & ACCESSORIES**–51 E. Main Street, St. Charles Ph 144
- **G & H TIRES & VULCANIZING**–119 West Main Street, St. Charles Ph 403 Arthur Grote & Lynn E Hakes

1925 AUTOMOBILE ACCESSORIES

- **EAST SIDE AUTO PARTS**–5 East State Street, Geneva
- **MATL J.A. & CO 125**–127 West State Street, Geneva
- **TRI CITY GARAGE**–11 South Third Street, Geneva
- **UNITY AUTO SUPPLY Co**–first in the Unity building, 300 block of West State Street, Harry Robertson, then 408 W State, Geneva under the ownership of Paul Eberman.

1937 AUTO SUPPLY AND ACCESSORIES

- **WESTERN TIRE AUTO STORE**–323 West State Street, Geneva, (west of theatre). Ralph Rea, closed in 1942 to enlist in Army.

1940–43 AUTOMOBILE ACCESSORIES TIRES ETC.

- **BILL'S LION AUTO SUPPLY**–Bill and Mary Silverman 302 (202) West Main Street, St. Charles, Ph 2943
- **PRICE'S ECONOMY AUTO SUPPLY**–116 East Main Street, St. Charles Ph 435

1947 AUTOMOBILE SUPPLIES AND PARTS–RETAIL

- **BEAL OMER MOTOR CO**–415 West State Street, Geneva Ph 719
- **BILL'S AUTO PARTS**–302 (202) West Main Street, St. Charles Ph 2943
- **VALLEY AUTO PARTS CO**–15 South 3rd Street, Geneva Ph 617
- **PRICE'S ECONOMY AUTO SUPPLY**–116 East Main Street, St. Charles Ph 435

1947–56 AUTOMOBILE SUPPLIES AND PARTS–RETAIL

- **McCORNACK AUTO SUPPLY–FIRESTONE**–116 East Main Street, St. Charles
- **VALLEY MOTOR SUPPLY** 9–11 West State Street, Geneva

1956 AUTOMOBILE ACCESSORIES AND PARTS–RETAIL

- **BILL'S AUTO PARTS**–202 West Main Street, St. Charles Ph 2943
- **McCORNACK AUTO SUPPLY–FIRESTONE** 201 South 3rd Street, St. Charles
- **VALLEY MOTOR SUPPLY** 9–11 West State Street, Geneva

1958-60 WHOLESALE AUTO PARTS

- **PRESTIGE PARTS CO**–919 West Wilson, Batavia
- **TASCO PRODUCTS INC**–630 West State Street, Geneva
- **VALLEY AUTO PARTS**–13 South 3rd Street, Geneva

1960 AUTOMOBILE ACCESSORIES AND PARTS–RETAIL

- **BILL'S AUTO PARTS**–202 West Main Street, St. Charles Ph 2943
- **McCORNACK AUTO SUPPLY–FIRESTONE** 201 South 3rd Street, St. Charles
- **VALLEY MOTOR SUPPLY** 9–11 West State Street, Geneva
- **WESTERN TIRE & AUTO SUPPLY** 1433 West Main Street, St. Charles
- **WESTERN TIRE AUTO STORE–**115 West State Street, Geneva

1962-64 AUTOMOBILE ACCESSORIES AND PARTS–RETAIL

- **BATAVIA AUTO PARTS**–143 First Street, Batavia 1962–66
- **BILL'S AUTO PARTS**–202 West Main Street, St. Charles Ph 2943
- **McCORNACK AUTO SUPPLY–FIRESTONE**–201 South 3rd, St. Charles
- **GENEVA TIRE & AUTO SUPPLY**–129 West State Street, Geneva
- **VALLEY MOTOR SUPPLY** 9–11 West State Street, Geneva
- **WESTERN AUTO ASSOCIATE STORE**–112 East Main Street, St. Charles
- **HEARLEY'S WESTERN TIRE & AUTO SUPPLY** 1433 W. Main, St. Charles

1968-69 AUTOMOBILE ACCESSORIES AND PARTS

- **BILL'S AUTO PARTS**–202 West Main Street, St. Charles Ph 2943
- **GENEVA TIRE & AUTO SUPPLY**–129 West State Street, Geneva
- **PRESTIGE PARTS CO**–919 West Wilson, Batavia
- **RYAN AUTOMOTIVE**–Jack Ryan 18 South 8th Street, Geneva 1966–1980
- **VALLEY MOTOR SUPPLY** 9–11 West State Street, Geneva
- **VALLEY AUTO PARTS**–23 South 3rd Street, Geneva
- **THOMPSON AUTO**–Jim Walsh, 830 West Main Street, St. Charles 1968–1974

1970'S AUTOMOBILE ACCESSORIES AND PARTS

- **VALLEY MOTOR SUPPLY** 9–11 West State Street, Geneva
- **BILL'S AUTO PARTS**–202 West Main Street, St. Charles, Ph 2943. After Bill's passing, his wife, Mary, continued to own the business with Jenny & Kathy handling the operation.
- **RYAN AUTOMOTIVE** 18 South 8th Street, Geneva
- **ROTHECKER AUTO PARTS**, Jon Rothecker Jr, North Bennett Street, Geneva
- **THOMPSON AUTO SUPPLY**–Bill Ryan Sr, 830 West Main Street, St. Charles. No relation to Jack Ryan of Ryan Automotive. In 1974, Walsh sold to Bill Ryan and sons, Bill and Dan and they kept the Thompson name to avoid confusion with Ryan Automotive.

Tom Ryan, Dan Ryan, Bill Ryan Jr, Bill Ryan Sr, Chuck Kelly, and Dave Stuttard–c. 1980.
FIGURE A.11 Courtesy Dan Ryan and Family.

- **THOMPSON AUTO SUPPLY**– The family participation grew as Bill's son, Tom, graduates and joins the firm. In 1978, they purchase a commercial building at 6 North Ninth Street, St. Charles and an adjoining home on properties almost directly behind their old location. Over the years, as an independent supplier, they have been associated with companies such as Car Quest and Bumper to Bumper. Bill Ryan Sr retired about 1982, leaving sons Bill Jr, Dan, and Tom in charge. A son–in–law, Dave Stuttard, also joins the family run operation. They have had a second location on East Main, St. Charles and then construct a new facility on West Wilson Street, Batavia to better serve the Tri–Cities.
- **NAPA**–South 3rd Street, St. Charles (former McCornack Firestone building). Branch of Aurora Automotive, Elden Madden early Manager.